Sustainability Assessments

This book looks at how multinational enterprises address sustainability within their business activities. Contextualised within a rapidly developing country in Asia, it explores how management practices, tools and techniques are implemented by foreign multinational enterprises (MNEs) operating in the Philippines. The book introduces a useful three-stage and six-step sustainability assessment framework for company practices. The three stages are framed around impact identification, impact assessment and impact monitoring, with the six steps associated with these stages, including the initiation step, scoping, impact analysis, alternative selection, monitoring and evaluation, and feedback and follow-up.

The book also highlights how voluntary guidelines and global sustainability platforms play an instrumental role in directing the practices of organisations when implementing corporate sustainability.

Hermann Lion is a Research Associate at Swinburne Business School, Swinburne University of Technology, Australia.

Jerome D. Donovan is a Senior Lecturer in Entrepreneurship and Innovation at Swinburne University of Technology.

Cheree Topple is a Senior Lecturer in Management at Swinburne University of Technology.

Rowan Bedggood is a Senior Lecturer in Marketing at Swinburne University of Technology.

Eryadi K. Masli is a Lecturer in Entrepreneurship and Innovation at Swinburne University of Technology.

Routledge Advances in Management and Business Studies

Collaborative Research in the United States
Policies and Institutions for Cooperation among Firms
Albert N. Link

Green Human Resource Management in Chinese Enterprises
Jie Shen, Jenny Dumont and Xin Deng

Developing the Workforce in an Emerging Economy
The Case of Indonesia
Edited by Kantha Dayaram, Linda Lambey, John Burgess and Tri Wulida Afrianty

Cross-Cultural Leadership
Being Effective in an Era of Globalization, Digital Transformation and Disruptive Innovation
Ahmad Muhamad Salih

The Global Pharmaceutical Industry
The Demise and the Path to Recovery
Daniel Hoffman and Allan Bowditch

Public Management and Vulnerability
Contextualising Change
Edited by Gareth David Addidle and Joyce Liddle

Sustainability Assessments
Insights from Multinational Enterprises Operating in the Philippines
Hermann Lion, Jerome D. Donovan, Cheree Topple, Rowan Bedggood and Eryadi K. Masli

For more information about this series, please visit www.routledge.com/Routledge-Advances-in-Management-and-Business-Studies/book-series/SE0305

Sustainability Assessments

Insights from Multinational Enterprises Operating in the Philippines

Hermann Lion, Jerome D. Donovan, Cheree Topple, Rowan Bedggood and Eryadi K. Masli

Routledge
Taylor & Francis Group
LONDON AND NEW YORK

First published 2021
by Routledge
2 Park Square, Milton Park, Abingdon, Oxon OX14 4RN

and by Routledge
52 Vanderbilt Avenue, New York, NY 10017

Routledge is an imprint of the Taylor & Francis Group, an informa business

British Library Cataloguing-in-Publication Data
A catalogue record for this book is available from the British Library

Library of Congress Cataloging-in-Publication Data
A catalog record has been requested for this book

ISBN: 978-0-367-86322-7 (hbk)
ISBN: 978-1-003-01838-4 (ebk)

Typeset in Galliard
by codeMantra

Contents

Figures

Tables

Preface

This research investigates how organisations address sustainability within their business activities. Contextualised within a rapidly developing country, the research explores how management practices, tools and techniques are implemented by foreign multinational enterprises (MNEs) operating in the Philippines. Foreign MNEs have been identified as not only a key source of economic development and progress but also a basis for increasing the standards and practices being implemented within the Philippines by the private sector.

Framing this investigation is the development of a consolidated sustainability assessment framework, which provides the basis for examining the practices of these foreign MNEs. Despite being identified as a key basis in supporting the implementation of more systematic practices to address sustainability, there is scant empirical literature on how this is adopted by the private sector. This is particularly the case in developing countries, where sustainability assessments may have the greatest impact on connecting the private sector with sustainability.

A three-stage and six-step sustainability assessment framework is developed to guide this investigation. The three stages are framed around impact identification, impact assessment and impact monitoring, with the six steps associated with these stages, including the initiation step, scoping, impact analysis, alternative selection, monitoring and evaluation, and feedback and follow-up.

In empirically testing this framework, this research utilises a constructivist paradigm and qualitative research approach. A case study design is utilised to examine the practices of 24 organisations across the manufacturing, utilities and mining sectors, with 92 personnel involved in interviews across these organisations. This primary data was triangulated against secondary data sources, including sustainability reports, and analysed through thematic analysis linked to the sustainability assessment framework. A Computer Assisted Qualitative Data Analysis software (NVivo) was utilised to assist the data analysis.

Based on the thematic analysis of interviews and secondary data across these 24 organisations, empirical support has been provided for the broader sustainability assessment framework that has been developed. The findings indicate that while the framework is not reflective of a linear process within actual practice, it does cover the main management practices being implemented by foreign MNEs operating in the Philippines. Building on this, the data also provides key insights into the main tools and techniques being utilised by organisations across the process, which presents a unique contribution to the literature.

The findings and implications of this research suggest that while regulation provides a basis for triggering some practices of organisations, it is only a starting point. It is clear from the analysis of the organisations within the sample that voluntary guidelines and global sustainability platforms play an instrumental role in directing the practices of organisations when implementing a sustainability assessment.

Abbreviations

AEC	ASEAN Economic Community
ASEAN	Association of South East Asian Nations
BAT	Best Available Technology
BOI	Board of Investment (Philippines)
CAQDAS	Computer Assisted Qualitative Data Analysis software
CBA	Cost-Benefit Analysis
CDP	Carbon Disclosure Project
CMR	Compliance Monitoring Report
CNC	Certificate of Non-Coverage
CO_2	Carbon Dioxide
DENR	Department of Environment and Natural Resources (Philippines)
ECC	Environmental Compliance Certificate
EHS	Environment Health and Safety
EIA	Environmental Impact Assessment
EIARC	Environmental Impact Assessment Review Committee (Philippines)
EIS	Environmental Impact Statement
EMB-DENR	Environmental Management Bureau – Department of Environment and Natural Resources (Philippines)
EPRMP	Environmental Performance Report and Management Plan
FDI	Foreign Direct Investment
FPIC	Free and Prior Informed Consent
GDP	Gross Domestic Product
GHG	Greenhouse gas(es)
GRI	Global Reporting Initiative
HIA	Health Impact Assessment
IAIA	International Association for Impact Assessment
IEE	Initial Environmental Examination
IFC	International Finance Corporation
ISA	Integrated Sustainability Assessment
ISO	International Standards Organization
KPI	Key Performance Indicators

LCA	Life Cycle Assessment
LCSA	Life Cycle Sustainability Assessment
LGU	Local Government Unit
MCA	Multi-Criteria Analysis
MCDA	Multi-Criteria Decision Analysis
MEPEO	Mining Environment Protection and Enhancement Officer
MGB	Mines and Geosciences Bureau (Philippines)
MMT	Multipartite Monitoring Team
MNE	Multinational enterprise
NFT	North Field Test
NOX	Nitrogen oxides
OECD	Organisation for Economic Co-operation and Development
PCO	Pollution Control Officer
PEISS	Philippines Environmental Impact Statement System
SDG	Sustainable Development Goals
SDMP	Social Development Management Plan
SEA	Strategic Environmental Assessment
SIA	Social Impact Assessment
TEMSIM	Tasmanian Electric Market Simulation Model
TNC	Transnational Corporation
UNCTAD	United Nations Conference on Trade and Development
UNGC	United Nations Global Compact

1 Introduction

Introduction

Despite the importance of private sector activities to support sustainable development, remarkably little is known about private sector practices of how they bring this about. This book details the findings of a research project that directly engages with this topic. It will illustrate and critique how the private sector, specifically foreign multinational enterprises (MNEs), is implementing specific processes, tools and techniques to address sustainable development within their business activities.

This chapter will present an overview of the current context in which this study is anchored. The first section of this chapter will outline the importance of sustainable development in the global agenda and the contribution of the private sector towards achieving this. Within this context, sustainability assessments are identified as a key process in enabling the private sector to address sustainable development in a systematic way. The next section will explore the unique country context that underpins this research, looking specifically at the Philippines. Following this, the significance of this research will be presented, including the two major research questions directing the research. Following this, the research approach will be briefly examined before concluding with an overview of the chapters in this book.

Setting the context: sustainable development and the role of the private sector

Global efforts to address sustainable development have proliferated over the past two decades with governments, civil society and the private sector increasingly coordinating activities to achieve this pursuit (Borgert et al. 2018a; Topple et al. 2017). This has most recently been punctuated by the introduction of the Sustainable Development Goals (SDGs) in 2015, which were established through the 2030 Agenda for Sustainable Development (UNDP 2015). As Adams (2017:5) reflects, with the adoption of this global agenda, businesses are being looked upon to contribute more actively towards the SDGs and, in fact, the "long-term success and survival of some industries and businesses depends on the achievement of one or more of the SDGs".

Global efforts, such as those through the 2030 Agenda, have signalled a shift in the recognition that businesses must now contribute and be accountable for their activities' impacts and broader sustainability outcomes. While the goal of achieving sustainable development through the SGDs has been internationally recognised, it appears also evident that businesses will be a key player in achieving these goals (Topple et al. 2017). In engaging with sustainable development, corporate sustainability is the field of research that is focussed on how business translate this into their activities. Within this research domain, it has been recognised that businesses still face key hurdles when integrating sustainability consideration into their business activities. As recently noted by Hacking (2019:2), the "key challenges remaining are [...] how to connect the SDGs, set at a global level, to the local-level".

Moldavska and Welo (2018) underline the importance of integrating sustainable development and the SDGs into the business activities, but also recognise that the current research into how to do this is in its infancy. Recent work by Ike et al. (2019) has tried to consolidate the previous work in the field, providing further clarity in how businesses are aiming to better integrate sustainability into their management practices. Their analysis of the current literature calls for a shift from the "why" and "what" into "how" business can implement more sustainable practices into their business activities. When looking at how organisation can better integrate sustainable development into their business practices, a range of methodologies have emerged (Ike et al. 2019), with no clear consensus. While no consensus appears to be found when looking at how to integrate sustainability considerations, one of the leading decision-making processes that has emerged in the last decade is the sustainability assessment (Hacking 2019).

Sustainability assessments can be broadly described as a process that enables decision-makers to assess, adjust and monitor project (including business) activities across environmental, social and economic dimensions (Donovan et al. 2017). The historical evolution of sustainability assessments shows that they have emerged from the broader field of impact assessments, as a process helping decision-makers to better integrate sustainability considerations. While they have proven to be a prominent process among policy makers, their use has also been theorised and explored at project level (Borgert et al. 2018a; Donovan et al. 2017). Sustainability assessments are perceived to be a pragmatic process to assist the private sector with the achievement of sustainability (Moldavska & Wela 2018).

Over the last decade, the sustainability assessment domain has witnessed a proliferation of research, and with that, an emergence of multiple terms to describe it. Across the literature, sustainability assessment has been commonly described as an EIA-driven integrated assessment; an objectives-led integrated assessment or assessment for sustainability (Pope, Annandale & Morrison-Saunders 2004); a sustainability impact assessment (Lee 2006); an integrated assessment (de Ridder et al. 2007); an integrated sustainability assessment (Shields, Blengini & Šolar 2011); an internal sustainability assessment (Morrison-Saunders & Pope 2013); and, more recently, a corporate sustainability assessment (Donovan et al. 2017).

As can be inferred from these multiple descriptions, the literature on theoretical perspectives and contexts to understand sustainability assessment (Borgert et al. 2018b) is voluminous, to say the least.

For the purposes of this book, we draw on Borgert et al. (2018a) who identify the main features common to the multiple constructions of a sustainability assessment. In broadly classifying these features, Borgert et al. (2018a) describes that the sustainability assessment is first and foremost a process (i.e., Hacking & Guthrie 2008; Pope et al. 2017). Beyond this, they emphasise the outcome focus of this process, with the objective of informing decision-making when considering environmental, social and economic issues and impacts (for example see Dalal-Clayton & Sadler 2004; Dizdaroglu 2015; Morrison-Saunders et al. 2014a). It has also been identified that it can occur at any point throughout the entire life cycle of projects, plans or policies (Borgert et al. 2018a; Donovan et al. 2017). This may be driven by different types of actors within the process, including the private sector, public sector and consultants.

Given the focus of this book on how the businesses utilise sustainability assessments, we adopt Borgert et al.'s (2018a) definition of sustainability assessment. Here, sustainability assessment is defined as *"a process aimed at informing decision-making of different actors when considering sustainability dimensions across policy, plan, programme or project contexts"* (100). In taking this definition, we not attempt to delineate between the many and varied definitions that have sought to offer a unique perspective on defining sustainability assessment. This includes avoiding the differentiation of a sustainability assessment according to a temporal dimension for application, including ex-ante, ongoing or ex-post assessments.

With this context of sustainability assessment providing a process by which the private sector can better integrate sustainability development into their business activities, we now move onto to exploring the unique context of this study – the Philippines.

The Philippines: a unique example of a developing country engaging with sustainable development

One of the first major global efforts towards addressing sustainability emerged in the 1960s and 1970s, with the introduction of the EIA. This is seen as the predecessor of all impact assessments and is where the sustainability assessment emerged from – and has since grown from. The EIA was, as the name suggests, particularly focussed on environmental aspects of sustainability, although, it nevertheless covered aspects of social and economic sustainability.

EIAs quickly saw global uptake and acceptance, and are now mandated in over 191 nations, with an increasing number of nations also regulating social, health or cultural impact assessments (Morgan 2012; Pope et al. 2013). While developing country are often perceived to lag behind the introduction of environmental regulation and compliance actions, the Philippines was actually an early adopter of EIAs, with environmental laws enforcing the EIA in 1978 (Presidential Decree 1151).

Indeed, the Philippines has demonstrated a pro-active nature to the adoption of sustainability-related policies and laws. It has most recently implemented requirements for the largest companies in the Philippines, listed on the stock exchange, to report on their sustainability performance through annual reporting requirements. This move by the Philippines has recently been praised by UNCTAD (Hacking 2019) and depicts a turning point into how sustainability considerations are managed in the Philippines, and makes this context particularly novel for this study.

This points to a strengthening domestic legal system and regulatory guidance for the private sector in dealing with sustainability, with increased transparency requirements by large listed companies in the Philippines. While this is a positive move forward, the requirements for foreign multinationals operating within the country remain linked with existing national regulations – with the majority of these companies not listed on the Philippines stock exchange.

Given the importance of – and controversy surrounding – the role of foreign multinationals in supporting sustainable development globally, the study of their practices presents a further novel aspect of this study. The positive link that is often depicted between foreign multinationals and sustainable development is not necessarily straightforward. Manifested benefits are largely based on the economic growth caused by foreign investment, which relies on different investment policies, regulations and local characteristics from which the receiving country then sets the ground for economic and sustainable development to be achieved (Cadeddu, Donovan & Masli 2013; Kosack & Tobin 2006; Ranis, Stewart & Ramirez 2000).

Therefore, without a supportive investment climate and aligned policies, foreign investment can also have substantial negative impacts. These include: the 'crowding-out' of local businesses, outflows of financial resources through profit repatriation, increased imports for production, limited skills transfer due to the type of employment generated and tax avoidance (Kosack & Tobin 2006; Ranis, Stewart & Ramirez 2000). Determining the impact of foreign investment and the operation of multinationals and their contribution towards sustainable development is extremely difficult, inhibiting the ability to establish the necessary investment policies to fully capture the development.

However, recent political decisions have shown an orientation towards easing requirements and restrictions on foreign investment and multinationals operating in the Philippines. This includes the most recently introduced Bill 300 (2019) that amends the provisions to the Foreign Investment Act, and the Corporate Income Tax and Incentives Rationalization Act. Both these actions have sought to not only reduce the list of excluded industries from foreign investment but also reduce the barriers and costs of operating in the Philippines (including requirements around foreign expertise and local labour employment).

With this easing of regulations for foreign multinationals, the significant growth that has been experienced in foreign investment and the changing regulatory context for listed companies, the study of how foreign multinationals are addressing sustainability will reveal insights into the broader progress of the private sector in contributing towards the Philippine's sustainable development. Beyond this, looking at existing studies on the Philippines, there remains a distinct paucity of research that has been conducted on sustainability and business.

Only three key studies were identified that specifically look at how sustainability or impact assessments are conducted. The first two studies (Bravante & Holden 2009; Ingelson, Holden & Bravante 2009) specifically looked at the EIAs within the mining sector exploring how EIAs are conducted. While they provide further clarity into the current environmental legislation and planning requirements of mining organisations, the studies do not provide clear insights into how organisation put the environmental regulation into practice. These studies also did not address other sustainability considerations, such as social and economic.

More recently, Escamilla, Habert and Wohlmuth (2016) conducted a sustainability study of the housing sector specifically looking at CO_2 emissions. While this technical paper provided insights into the assessment of the housing sector, it only provided an industry analysis failing to address the business practices and impact. No further research in the Philippines has been found to date, further solidifying the contribution this study can have to exploring this unique context.

Contribution to knowledge

Building from this brief overview into sustainability assessments and the Philippines as a key context for this book, three major contributions to knowledge can be identified and will be explored in more depth through later chapters. Specifically, this book presents a consolidation of extant knowledge in this field of research through the development of a procedural framework for sustainability assessment (Chapter 2), examining and arranging tools and techniques that have been identified to be used by business. The second contribution will, by the empirical testing of this entire framework, provide empirical evidence to support the framework. And finally, as noted earlier, this book will contribute to the dearth of studies that have been conducted in the Philippines, despite its unique context.

A procedural framework for sustainability assessments

A range of perspectives within the extant literature for examining sustainability assessments includes a features or dimensions perspective (Binder, Feola & Steinberger 2010; Hacking & Guthrie 2008; Pope et al. 2017); or an indicator or methods perspective (Li et al. 2017; Schöggl, Fritz & Baumgartner 2016). The process (or procedures to follow) of a sustainability assessment guides practitioners in how they consider different sustainability issues, particularly from a private sector perspective (Donovan et al. 2017). Despite this emphasis, there remains a lack of commonly accepted procedures for how the private sector should undertake a sustainability assessment (Pope et al. 2017).

A large number of studies have proposed conceptualisations of single stages or steps within the sustainability assessment process (see, for example, Borgert et al. 2018a, 2018b; Morrison-Saunders et al. 2014a). However, no study has yet proposed a consolidated framework, specifically adapted to the project level and private sector perspective (Donovan et al. 2017). Efforts focussing on a procedural perspective have been limited, with Borgert et al. (2018a) lamenting that "limited research has engaged with this perspective, particularly research that provides empirical insights" (100). This is particularly the case from the perspective of studies that have not only attempted to show a larger perspective on sustainability assessment framework but also consider the distinct tools and techniques that are used across the different steps within this framework.

The current research will thus contribute towards filling a significant gap in the literature by using extant theoretical and empirical evidence to inform the development of a procedural framework for sustainability assessment (Chapter 2), particularly attending to the private sector perspective.

Empirical testing of the procedural framework in a business context

A second key contribution of this book is to empirically test this procedural framework, providing evidence on actual business practices. As highlighted earlier (and to be demonstrated in Chapter 2), there is a clear gap of knowledge with scant empirical evidence within this field of study.

Very few studies have been conducted within the field of sustainability assessment from the perspective of the private sector (see Binder, Feola & Steinberger 2010; Coteur et al. 2016; Donovan et al. 2017; Morrison-Saunders & Pope 2013). Of value here is the study's focus on providing specific details relating to each step of the framework and the sustainability considerations of business. The empirical findings from this study will provide insights on the decision-making process when business utilise sustainability assessment, including the tools and techniques they utilise.

This study seeks to investigate the use of sustainability assessments by the private sector and more specifically, by large foreign multinationals operating in the Philippines. This is particularly important in the context of developing countries, where business is a critical and undisputable element in achieving sustainable development.

Empirically validate the entire framework through a unique context

As noted earlier, the Philippines context provides a unique context as the current legislative context calls for the further transparency in requiring submission of sustainability reporting. While this is currently required for public listed organisations, it depicts a change in the current approach towards how organisations engage with sustainability in the context of the SDGs. The paucity of research on the Philippines means that this study will provide a distinct contribution to extending knowledge on business practice in the Philippines.

Building from these contributions, theoretical, empirical and country context, these gaps in knowledge have led to the following research questions that will guide this study:

- How are sustainability assessments used by businesses in the Philippines?
- How are tools and techniques utilised across the different stages and steps of the sustainability assessment?

The next section briefly discusses the research context for this study before providing an overview of the book's chapters.

Research context

This study follows a constructivist paradigm, which is appropriate given the focus of this research on the processes implemented to conduct a sustainability assessment from the perspective of the decision-makers involved in the process. This directs this inquiry to focus on the unique perspectives offered by the respondents and contextualising these phenomena within their understanding.

This study adopts a qualitative research methodology, with a case study design using semi-structured interviews. Twenty-four organisations were involved conducting interviews with 92 personnel at both the subsidiary (in the Philippines) and headquarter operations. Secondary data was also used to provide additional insights into the decision-making process and as a basis for triangulating the data collected.

Building upon this approach, this study also adopted a cross-sectional perspective, with eight organisations within the mining sector, nine with the manufacturing sector and seven from the utilities sector. This study is thus the largest one conducted spreading across the entire sustainability assessment process and across three key industries. The outcome is expected to be useful for informing not only the practices of the private sector across the ASEAN region, but also for policymakers when considering the necessary direction needed to maximise the contribution of foreign multinationals towards sustainable development.

Structure of this book

This introductory chapter has provided an overview of the research context and its aims. This study is framed around the following five chapters:

Chapter 2 presents the existing research related to procedural frameworks for sustainability assessments. This will provide the platform for the development of a conceptual framework on a procedural sustainability assessment from the private sector perspective. The main tools and techniques used within each stage and step of the framework are described. This review bridges the gap between theoretical knowledge and practice by providing key empirical cases for each step of the sustainability assessment. It concludes with the methodology design and decisions which informed this research.

Chapter 3 is the first chapter focussed on the data analysis and results, and provides the findings for the first stage of the sustainability assessment: the Issue Identification and Prioritisation Stage. This stage is comprised of two key steps, the initiation and scoping step. This chapter is structured around the management practices, tools and techniques that are used by organisations undertaking these steps, providing insights into all three sectors within this study.

Chapter 4 presents the findings for the second stage of the sustainability assessment: the Impact Assessment Stage. It specifically explores how organisations are conducting impact analysis and alternative selection, and how this translates into selecting the best mitigation/enhancement solutions to address these impacts. This chapter follows a similar structure to the previous chapter, looking across the management practices, tools and techniques, with analysis of each of the three sectors within the sample.

Chapter 5 presents the findings of the last stage of the sustainability assessment: the Impact Monitoring and Follow-up Stage. It explores how organisations monitor and evaluate their sustainability performance and implement changes in response to their performance outcomes. Monitoring processes represent an important part of the assessment process as they are central to measuring the impact of the applied mitigation strategies. A variety of tools and techniques used by organisations will be presented in this chapter.

Chapter 6 concludes this research, presenting the key outcomes from examining the two research questions underpinning this study. This includes presenting an updated framework detailing the key tools and techniques across the entire process. The final section of this chapter presents the practical implications, detailing the significance of the research, the key limitations of the study and next steps for future endeavours.

2 Sustainability assessment research

Introduction

This chapter presents a detailed analysis of current knowledge of a procedural-based framework for sustainability assessment. Of particular interest here is a procedural framework from the perspective of the proponent or private sector (Binder, Feola & Steinberger 2010; Donovan et al. 2017; Morrison-Saunders & Pope 2013; Shields, Blengini & Šolar 2011) – a discrete approach or theoretical context within the voluminous literature on sustainability assessment.

The chapter first discusses the contextual literature that underpins the procedural framework used for this study. It then presents three main stages identified in the current literature: (i) issue and impact identification and prioritisation, (ii) impact assessment and (iii) impact monitoring and follow-up. Key empirical studies from a project level, proponent-led perspective will be used to shed light on the management practices that typically occur during each stage in private sector organisations. This will assist to bridge the gap between theoretical and practical knowledge.

These cases will also make note, where possible, of the different tools and techniques that were implemented at each stage within the sustainability assessment. The chapter concludes by explaining the methodological approach adopted for this study. This includes an overview of the organisations involved in the study and the characteristics of these organisations.

Understanding the context for a procedural framework of sustainability assessment

A significant amount of literature within the sustainability assessment research domain has focussed on providing different theoretical positions and contexts to help understand sustainability assessments. These have provided significant utility in positioning the literature where a sustainability assessment could be described as either:

1 Features, elements, dimensions and categories (*e.g.*, Arodudu et al. 2017; Binder, Feola & Steinberger 2010; Bond & Morrison-Saunders 2011; Hacking & Guthrie 2008; Lee 2006; Pope et al. 2017)

2 Tools, methods or indicators (*e.g.*, Li et al. 2017; Schöggl, Fritz & Baumgartner 2016)
3 Procedures (*e.g.*, Sala, Ciuffo & Nijkamp 2015; Shields, Blengini & Šolar 2011)

Uncovering the theoretical positions reflected amongst these terms reveals a diverse yet challenging literature to navigate where some of the terms are arguably used interchangeably or in parallel to describe the same or similar approach being adopted. Although not exhaustive in its coverage of all approaches to the sustainability literature, the diverse approaches captured here reflect the absence of an over-arching framework to understand sustainability assessments.

Of specific interest to this research, with its focus on key management practices and the tools and techniques used across the sustainability assessment, is the procedural approach. Whilst a clear definition of a procedural framework remains elusive there are multiple constructions within the literature that shed light on the concept of a procedural framework of sustainability assessment. This study will now turn its attention to these key literature sources for framing the procedural framework.

Two seminal sources of sustainability assessment that underpin the procedural approach are offered from Lee (2006) and Hacking and Guthrie (2008). These two frameworks present a broader contextualisation of the literature that is pertinent to this focus of study. Lee (2006) presents a common framework constructed around the context of the assessment, the process and the methods. He argues that since every assessment is different, it should consider the type of case and context involved, including the characteristics, regulation/institutional context and resources available. The process relates to the main stages or steps of the assessment, and the methods relate to how the impacts associated with the proposal are assessed (technical or participatory).

On the other hand, Hacking and Guthrie (2008) focus on the categories of context, process and features within the sustainability assessment. Here, they identify that the *context* category relates to the importance of different features embedded within the context of the planning or decision-making and its relationship with the assessment. The *process* category – which is of great interest to this study – concerns how, when and who undertakes the assessment. And finally, *features* relate to the types of analysis and output from the assessment. Hacking and Guthrie (2008) focus, in particular, on looking at the features in which to characterise different types of assessments:

- Comprehensiveness (the degree of sustainable development themes covered)
- Extent of integration (the techniques used and/or the themes covered/aligned/connected/combined/compared)
- Strategically focussed (the focus or perspective, and the degree to which it is broad and forward-looking)

Whilst both of these frameworks are unique in their conceptualisation of sustainability assessment they are common, with the emphasis on the ‘process’-related elements of sustainability assessment. Within the context of understanding a procedural framework perspective, these articles justify a focus on the 'how' (Hacking & Guthrie 2008) or more specifically, the 'main stages or steps of the assessment' (Lee 2006) without specifically detailing these for the context of the private sector. The development of a procedural framework for sustainability assessment will be discussed next.

The development of a procedural framework of sustainability assessment

There are multiple perspectives for developing a procedural framework of sustainability assessment. Borgert et al. (2018a) were instrumental in identifying these perspectives which spanned a life cycle assessment (LCA) perspective (Arushanyan, Ekener & Moberg 2017); a strategic or policy perspective (de Ridder et al. 2007; Gibson, Hassan & Tansey 2013; Lee 2006) and a proponent or private sector perspective (Binder, Feola & Steinberger 2010; Coteur et al. 2016; Donovan et al. 2017; Morrison-Saunders & Pope 2013; Shields, Blengini & Šolar 2011). Clearly, the latter perspective is most relevant to this study, with its focus on the private sector, and, therefore, renders the other perspectives redundant.

The most pertinent studies to inform a procedural framework from a project-based, private sector perspective include Binder, Feola and Steinberger (2010), Shields, Blengini and Šolar (2011), Morrison-Saunders and Pope (2013) and Donovan et al. (2017). These studies have been drawn upon significantly throughout the development of this procedural framework in relation to the stages and steps of the sustainability assessment. For this reason, they will be discussed at a high-level here with detailed analysis occurring throughout the conceptual framework within the relevant steps.

Binder, Feola and Steinberger (2010) examine the development of an indicator-based sustainability assessment that extends across normative, systemic and procedural dimensions. The normative dimension relates to the question on "how to assess whether the studied system is sustainable" (Binder, Feola & Steinberger 2010:73) and requires consideration of the sustainability concept, goal setting and assessment types. The systemic dimension relates to how the system is represented and includes the indicators and parameters for how to describe the social, environmental and economic aspects of this system. Finally, the procedural dimension relates to the design of the assessment and can be represented into a set of 'ideal sub-phases' that comprises a preparatory phase and five main steps including indicator selection, indicator measurement, assessment, applicability and follow-up.

Shields, Blengini and Šolar (2011) also developed a procedural framework that is comprehensive in its coverage of the project-level, private sector perspective. Their framework focusses on integrating and evaluating different potential tools to achieve sustainability. The process commences with the identification of the project's key stakeholders and capturing their value sets and objectives, plus the potential impacts of the project on "land, communities and people" (1216). Following this is the *scoping* step which considers all sustainability aspects of the project, including the environmental, social, economic and technical aspects. Alternatives are then considered and evaluated according to what is socially and environmentally sustainable, and economically and technically feasible. Implemented alternatives are then monitored and evaluated over the course of the project's life cycle.

Prolific publishers in the sustainability assessment literature, Morrison-Saunders and Pope (2013) have studied 'internal sustainability assessments'. According to their research, there are a set of common steps that include identifying the sustainability issues that are relevant for the context. From this, another step is to examine the proposal or the associated options through assessing these different issues that have been identified. Within this process, there should be some level of stakeholder engagement or community participation. As a final aspect, a decision should be made on the proposal by a relevant decision-maker that has been nominated to do so.

A more recent procedural framework is offered by Donovan et al. (2017) who developed a four-stage framework that captures a sequence of sustainability practices across seven steps. This framework is comprehensive and is one of the largest studies of its kind to examine the sustainability assessment practices of 23 multinational organisations across Thailand. These organisations were largely from the services and manufacturing sectors with a smaller sample from mining.

While these studies have provided various insights into potential approaches to mapping and developing the procedural framework, they are characterised by a number of limitations that will be addressed through our approach. First, the majority of these studies have not focussed solely on the development of a procedural framework with often only very brief details on the actual steps or their relevance for management decision-making. Another major limitation in all these studies is the lack of tools and techniques detailed across the different steps and stages, not only inhibiting the ability of businesses to implement the sustainability assessment effectively but also failing to address the continued contentious nature of what tools are purely theoretical and what are actually used in practice by business.

We build beyond these limitations, first and foremost, looking for detailed and relevant insights into each of the steps and stages within the context of a business approach. Moreover, we have sought to find detailed empirical insights into these steps and stages, including in detailing what possible tools and techniques could actually be used to facilitate the sustainability assessment. The procedural framework here is built around four key stages, building from the approach of Donovan et al. (2017), including: (1) issue identification and prioritisation; (2) impact analysis, monitoring and evaluation; (3) alternative selection; and (4) feedback and follow-up.

This form of procedural framework is iterative and, consistent with Shields, Blengini and Šolar (2011), reflects a recurring decision-making process across the framework. These studies have been critical for informing the development

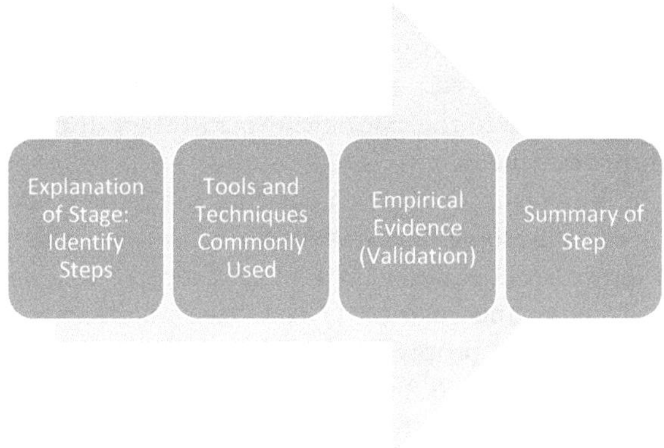

Figure 2.1 Structure for each stage of the sustainability framework literature review.

of a procedural framework of a sustainability assessment from the private sector perspective. The key stages and steps will be discussed in the next section. The format that will be followed in each stage is depicted in the following diagram (see Figure 2.1).

Issue and impact identification and prioritisation stage

Issue and impact identification and prioritisation, the initial stage of the sustainability assessment, enables decision-makers to identify and select sustainability issues and impacts that are relevant to the scope of a planned development activity and the context which surrounds it. While it is evident within the literature that there is ambiguity about a common process for conducting the two steps within this section (initiation and scoping), the overall purpose of this stage is clear. Within issue and impact identification and prioritisation, the processes and activities generally centre on how to initiate and undertake the sustainability assessment.

This section will present the first stage of a sustainability assessment and discuss the main theoretical foundations underpinning the *issue and impact identification and prioritisation stage,* which includes the initiation and scoping steps. It will then present the various tools and methods typically adopted by organisations within this stage of the sustainability assessment followed by empirical cases that demonstrate the processes within these steps.

The initiation step of a procedural framework for sustainability assessment

Across the sustainability assessment literature, a definition and common process for the *initiation* step is difficult to locate. While it is well recognised that initiation activities, more broadly, are found across a range of impact assessment literatures, including Health Impact Assessments (HIAs), Environmental Impact Assessments (EIAs) and Social Impact Assessments (SIAs), the conflicting theoretical and empirical insights present a raft of challenges for researchers and practitioners in the field (Borgert et al. 2018a). Despite these conflicts, there is no doubt that the first step in the assessment is critical for directing a process to conduct the entire assessment.

With the focus of the current study on developing a procedural framework for sustainability assessment, some clarity about the processes of this step is needed. This has been drawn from three main studies. Binder, Feola and Steinberger (2010), Shields, Blengini and Šolar (2011) and Sala, Ciuffo and Nijkamp (2015) shed light on the common processes within *initiation* and help highlight the important aspects of this step. Subsequently, these theoretical works have been paramount to the development of further research in this field, notably Donovan et al. (2017) and Borgert et al. (2018a).

Starting chronologically, Binder, Feola and Steinberger's (2010) sustainability assessment process consists of three dimensions: the normative, procedural and systemic. Of interest to this research is the procedural dimension which is about how the assessment is conducted. This then relates to how the system is assessed as being sustainable (normative dimension) and what indicators are used to describe the system (the systemic dimension) (Binder, Feola & Steinberger 2010).

A preparatory or set-up phase begins the assessment process and within this first step basic elements of the assessment are defined: "The system under consideration, the scale of analysis, and the user groups of the assessment itself, as well as the stakeholders to be involved and the type of their involvement" (Binder, Feola & Steinberger 2010:74). At this point, stakeholder involvement could be either participatory, transdisciplinary or expert in nature. Within this type of indicator-based sustainability assessment, the authors emphasise the role of stakeholder involvement to comprehensively capture a full suite of social, environmental and economic issues that relate to the system that is being evaluated. With these basic elements of the assessment defined, attention then turns to the next three steps they propose, which includes: (1) selection of indicators, (2) indicator measurement and (3) assessment.

Moving beyond the indicator-based assessment of Binder, Feola and Steinberger (2010), Shields, Blengini and Šolar (2011) reiterate the importance of stakeholders to the assessment process within their integrated, iterative framework. In their study of ex-ante sustainability assessments in the minerals industry, they identify a range of tools to be used in an Integrated Sustainability Assessment (ISA) framework. This framework is procedural in nature and connects the multiple aspects of a decision-making framework with various analytical tools to help facilitate the process of sustainable resource management.

Building from an earlier model proposed by Shields and Šolar (2004), the framework begins with identifying the "stakeholders, their value sets and objectives related to the project under consideration and the land, communities and people it has the potential to impact" (Shields, Blengini & Šolar 2011:1216). The authors note that this first step overlaps with the scope of the project or investment which they propose should reflect a multi-stakeholder approach. These initial steps occur before alternatives are developed.

The third study by Sala, Ciuffo and Nijkamp (2015:318) presents key procedural steps based on the organisation's (or stakeholder's) approach to sustainability, the sustainability targets, the decision context and the methodological choices for the assessment. Of interest to this study is the approach to sustainability which consists of the values and sustainability principles of the organisation.

As highlighted across the literature, 'sustainability' tends to be viewed as a value-laden concept and therefore the achievement of sustainable development through a sustainability assessment tool can also be targeted for critique. This is due to the context-specific nature of defining sustainability. Within this initiation step, organisations are strongly encouraged to provide details about the values of the stakeholders involved in the project/plan or policy. By providing multiple stakeholder interpretations of the goal of sustainable development, it not only provides a more holistic picture of what sustainability means for the organisation and its stakeholders, but it also helps ensure the credibility of the sustainability assessment methods.

From here, values are translated into sustainability principles which guide what is to be achieved more broadly, with sustainability targets to be defined. These principles may be informed from different perspectives or have different sources, which will depend on the organisation's geographic position or the nature of the principles, such as those espoused in the report "Resilient People, Resilient Planet: A Future Worth Choosing" (UN 2012) or more recently, the Sustainable Development Goals (SDGs). This initiation process ultimately captures the activities that internal and external stakeholders want to achieve with regards to evaluating the sustainability of an implemented project/plan or policy.

These three frameworks clearly show the importance of stakeholder involvement in the initiation step of sustainability assessments. They explain the importance of building a broad understanding of the context in which the project is, or will be, operating, and the sustainability values and principles of the organisation for informing decision-making and evaluation. Whilst much can be derived from the common elements in these theoretical frameworks of initiation to inform the development of an ISA framework for the private sector, there is currently no private-sector, project-specific framework available. This has motivated the current study.

In saying this, Donovan et al. (2017:69), who provide one of the more recent and comprehensive studies from the private sector perspective, proposed a definition within the sustainability assessment framework where the step of 'screening' (an equivalent step to initiation in the context of their study), "identif[ies] the appropriate issues that emerge for a new or continuing project". Building on this work, Borgert et al. (2018a) envision initiation being 'framed' by "the contextualisation of the project, including stakeholder selection, system and scale for the assessment and identification of relevant sustainability issues or criteria for the assessment" (103).

The main tools and techniques which can be used to facilitate the initiation step are presented next.

Tools and techniques for the initiation step

Across the sustainability assessment literature there is considerable research that considers various sustainability assessment tools. However, two areas are contentious. First, a proportion of literature has explored various tools transposed from other impact assessment contexts and adapted for sustainability assessment (see Morrison-Saunders et al. 2014a; Sala, Ciuffo & Nijkamp 2015). This can be problematic for practitioners and academics alike if they have strong views about integrating the impact assessment literature (see Morrison-Saunders et al. 2014a; Tajima & Fisher 2013). Second, there are differences among scholars as to whether the tool should be used across different times and levels. For example, whether a tool should vary depending on whether it is being applied for a policy, plan or project. Or whether the tools used for ex-ante points in time should be also used for ongoing projects. Lastly, there is some debate as to whether sustainability assessment tools are equally suitable for the private sector.

This section will next provide an understanding of the main tools applicable at the project level for private sector organisations for conducting a sustainability assessment: checklists, established lists and corporate plans and policies. We note that it is common for one tool or technique to be used for multiple steps of the framework. Where this occurs, details of the tool will be featured when it is first applicable within the sustainability assessment, and when it is applicable to subsequent steps, only brief details will be provided.

Sustainability checklists

Checklists are a key tool for decision-making and are found across multiple steps in the sustainability assessment process (Eales et al. 2005; Lee 2006; Milner et al. 2005). Initially borrowed from the UK policy context, checklists were first popular in the EIA field and have been more recently adopted for sustainability assessment. Eales et al. (2005) define the checklist as "… a list of questions or criteria organised around a series of impact categories that address economic, social and environmental concerns" (114). Devuyst (1999) explains that early implementation of the checklist provides value as it enables assessors and decision-makers to:

> […] think creatively and come up with innovative measures to steer initiatives in a more sustainable direction. The questions are designed to prompt consideration of the potential impact associated with the options or proposal under scrutiny.
>
> (Devuyst 1999:471–472)

At the organisational level, these questions or criteria should reflect the sustainability goals of the project, which can be useful for triggering an internal reflection process whereby decision-makers reflect on the possible impacts of their project (Eales et al. 2005). Additionally, the checklists can be shared across various project stakeholder groups, enabling further knowledge sharing and broadening of the sustainability factors to be considered (Devuyst 1999).

Donovan et al.'s (2017) study of manufacturing and service MNEs in Thailand reinforces that checklists can be shared. They found that various stakeholders (often local community groups) contributed their own perspectives by adding new points to the checklist regarding sustainability issues and possible impacts that were deemed important. In addition, the recent study by Borgert et al. (2018a) of Indonesian multinationals clearly highlighted the use of checklists for compliance purposes.

Established regulatory lists

Checklists tend to be an internally driven method to identify a broad range sustainability factors that need to be considered to achieve the overall sustainability goals of the project and consequently, the organisation (Donovan et al. 2017). Established lists, on the other hand, tend to be enforced through regulations and can therefore look very different depending on the country of operation. Within the private sector, organisations face a raft of regulatory constraints that need to be addressed prior to the implementation of a project (see Borgert et al. 2018a, 2018b; Donovan et al. 2017). Regulations directly inform the decision-maker about what factors must be considered in their project. These can differ based on a range of criteria, such as the size of the project, its location and the type of activity the project involves. Furthermore, the list may vary depending on the industry in which the project is operating (Borgert et al. 2018a; Donovan et al. 2017).

Within the context of established lists, regulations set by local, regional or national levels tend to focus more on EIAs or SIAs rather than an integrated sustainability assessment (see Borgert et al. 2018a; Donovan et al. 2017). Hence, these established lists tend to be 'silo' representations of environmental or social indicators rather than a holistic sustainability focus.

Established lists offer the advantage of providing decision-makers with a pre-defined set of criteria to follow. However, this could also hinder internal reflections on the sustainability aspects of the project, as the list is determined by regulations and usually cannot be amended (Donovan et al. 2017). This suggests that the robustness of the established list will be dependent on the value of sustainability to the authorising agent and the parameters they establish within their 'sustainability' regulations.

Corporate plans and policies

The use of corporate plans and policies as a tool for driving the initiation step of sustainability assessment has received little attention in the scholarly literature. However, some inroads have been made by two recent studies which show that the policies and standards of multinationals influence organisational decision-making during the sustainability assessment initiation step (Borgert et al. 2018a; Donovan et al. 2017). The values and principles of the organisation filter into the formulation of the corporate plans and policies, which informs organisational practice at all levels. In terms of sustainability practices, it could be seen in both the Borgert et al. (2018a) and Donovan et al. (2017) studies that the extent to which the MNE is committed to global sustainability platforms, such as the Global Reporting Initiative (GRI) or the United Nations Global Compact (UNGC), informs their plans and policies. This subsequently influences their decision-making capacity relating to sustainability. This was particularly evident when looking at the relationship between headquarters and subsidiary operations (Donovan et al. 2017) and will be discussed in various relevant sections throughout this chapter.

International organisations and standards

Scholars have studied the use of international organisations and standards (such as GRI and UNGC), but little is known about how organisations are using and implementing the associated standards or initiatives espoused by these organisations within the sustainability assessment process.

According to Schneider and Meins (2012), some limited insights are provided by the two main international guidelines or standards – the UNGC and the GRI. For organisations that prescribe to the UNGC initiative, they must comply with ten responsibilities across the areas of human rights, labour rights, environmental dimensions and anti-corruption. Organisations must report on their efforts to implement the intentions of the UNGC initiative. Organisations face de-listing from the initiative if they do not comply with the responsibility contained within the list. GRI standards are a little different from those of the UNGC initiative. The GRI recommends the use of a materiality assessment methodology within the initial stages of implementing a project. This is linked to established and industry-specific categories. However, the use of the materiality assessment is not explained in the GRI standards. Other than Donovan et al. (2017), the research to date provides limited detail into how organisations should use those standards to inform their decisions through sustainability assessments. In addition, Borgert et al. (2018a) explore the use of materiality analysis for Indonesian multinationals committed to the GRI sustainability standards. Both of these studies highlight the use of materiality analysis in the initiation and scoping steps of the sustainability assessment.

Sustainability criteria and indices

Beyond the standards or guidelines established by large international organisations, there are a multitude of sustainability criteria or indices options. These tend to be simple measures – often quantitative in nature – that represent the three dimensions of sustainability: economic, social and environmental (Ness et al. 2007). Ideally, these sets of sustainability criteria or indices would be simple to use, wide in their scope, quantifiable and enable determination of trends and tools sensitive to change (Ness et al. 2007). These characteristics are desirable for their ability to allow tracking over time, which can be useful for informing future decision-making. One study involving 127 Finnish companies across mining, hospitality, construction and energy sectors found that the most prevalent tool or approach used was sustainability criteria and indices, with over 50% of companies using these (Myllyviita, Antikainen & Leskinen 2017).

Sustainability criteria and indices could be viewed as similar to Established Lists although the nature of the latter is set by regulatory bodies which can be more restrictive that what organisations might set for themselves, or in compliance with international standards.

Participatory approach

The participatory approach to sustainability assessment has been traditionally used to assist with policymaking but more recently has been evident in use with private sector projects (see Borgert et al. 2018b; Donovan et al. 2017). It involves the participation or consultation with stakeholders (de Ridder et al. 2007). Van Asselt Marjolein and Rijkens-Klomp (2002) define these as "methods to structure group processes in which non-experts play an active role in order to articulate their knowledge, values and preferences" (168). There are many forums in which views can be proffered including conventional or electronic focus groups and consensus conferences (de Ridder et al. 2007) or brainstorming and workshops (Borgert et al. 2018a, 2018b; Donovan et al. 2017). The participatory approach and its specific tools are common across the steps of the sustainability assessment as is evident when reading the empirical cases in this chapter.

Expert knowledge or judgement

Expert knowledge or judgement is critical to adequately inform decision-making within organisations. Lee (2006) discusses expert judgement and the impact of different researchers and technical specialists to create simple (or complex) methods for assessment throughout a procedural sustainability framework. Orenstein et al. (2010) explain that the use of expert knowledge early in the sustainability assessment process helps with the identification of sustainability issues relevant to the project, and which might be overlooked by non-expert stakeholders. In their study, the issues determined by the expert panel were then used to generate engagement with external stakeholders of the project. As a tool, drawing upon expert judgement or knowledge is fairly common in the impact analysis stage of the framework (stage 2) where assessment actually occurs (Lee 2006).

Empirical studies

This section will now explore research conducted on how the initiation step occurs in practice. These cases are a mix of ex-ante and ongoing examples from the private sector at the project level. They include:

Ex-ante projects:

i Scarborough Field (Bond, Morrison-Saunders & Howitt 2013)
ii North Field Test (NFT) (Orenstein et al. 2010)
iii Gorgon Gas Project (Pope, Annandale & Morrison-Saunders 2004; Pope, Morrison-Saunders & Annandale 2005)

Recent ongoing projects:

i Multinationals in Thailand (Donovan et al. 2017)
ii Manufacturing Multinationals in Indonesia (Borgert et al. 2018a)

Scarborough field

Scarborough Field is a large gas field located offshore on the coast of Western Australia (Bond, Morrison-Saunders & Howitt 2013). In 2005, BHP Billiton conducted an internal sustainability assessment to select a new site for a large liquefied natural gas (LNG) facility. Decision-makers had the task to screen and identify a potential site in a 400 km radius within the Scarborough field and assess it against a list of specific ecological, socio-economic and safety requirements. These were all embedded within the BHP Billiton Corporate Charter (Bond, Morrison-Saunders & Howitt 2013). Stakeholders were engaged at this initial stage to ensure the transparency of the decision-making process.

Although specific details are somewhat difficult to obtain, the implications from this case are useful for the practice of the initiation step in ex-ante projects. When the preferred location was identified, BHP Billiton decided to complete an engineering cost-benefit analysis (CBA) of eight potential sites, including their preferred site. Interestingly, Bond, Morrison-Saunders and Howitt (2013) suggest that the initially preferred location presented the most efficient cost-benefit solution. Once approved by the various project stakeholders, the organisation decided to continue and use the mandatory EIA process. This vignette emphasises the importance of engaging stakeholders early in the initiation step to help generate a diverse set of sustainability issues and impacts for a list. Furthermore, it highlights the transparency of the process and the benefits of adopting an inclusive method to produce a more optimal outcome supported by multiple stakeholders.

North Field Test

Orenstein et al. (2010) provide insights into how setting clear goals has helped to achieve positive results in the ex-ante impact assessment undertaken by Shell. The NFT is a large 'heavy' oil field, located in north-central Alberta in Canada. The North Test Field had a twofold mission; the first was to assess the technical feasibility of a new extraction technique for 'heavy' oil and the second was to assess its economic viability for full-scale development (Orenstein et al. 2010). In order to study the impacts of the NFT, Shell carried out a state-of-the-art impact assessment across ecological, social, health and economic dimensions.

To achieve this, a multidisciplinary team of external consultants was put together, each leading different aspects of the assessment. The initiation step started with an exploratory discussion among the team leaders who screened the main sustainability factors to consider and potential impacts of the project from their expert knowledge. Orenstein et al. (2010) demonstrate that this integrative approach, thinking through mapping the potential impact across ecological, social and health dimensions, led to the identification of an exhaustive list of sustainability factors that were considered for this project. For example, the NFT emissions had a direct impact on the surface water quality, which led to poorer fish health and diversity, resulting in negative impacts towards the traditional livelihoods and health of Indigenous communities. Figure 2.2 below visually captures how this process was executed.

An additional finding of this study at the initiation step involved the specifics of internal stakeholder engagement. Orenstein et al. (2010) suggest that the level of stakeholder engagement at the project level is guided by "project size, potential for significant impact, overall development plans for an area, and stakeholder concerns" (148). Stakeholders' inputs are key to the success of a project and to accurately determining the most significant issues that might arise. In the NFT case, to engage internal stakeholders, a specific team from within the organisation was gathered, whose task was to address "non-technical" issues. The role of this team was to frame the broader sustainability goals and values that would underpin the project. The team was internal to Shell, and contained experts in "environment, social performance, regulatory affairs and communication" (Orenstein et al. 2010:151). External stakeholders were not directly engaged at the initiation step, but the internal task-force facilitated external stakeholder engagement at the next step of *Scoping*. This empirical example highlights the use of expert knowledge across an internal interdisciplinary team and early stakeholder engagement in the identification of potential sustainability issues and impacts.

Gorgon gas development

Pope, Morrison-Saunders and Annandale (2005) focus on the Gorgon Gas Development, one of the largest gas reservoirs discovered to date in Australia. The development of the Gorgon Gas field was undertaken by Chevron-Texaco. Before the launch of the extraction operation, Chevron-Texaco needed to complete a mandatory EIA, as required by the state laws of Western Australia; yet what is of most interest to this case is Chevron-Texaco's completion of an 'internal sustainability assessment' to guide their decision-making process. Completing an internal sustainability assessment in parallel with the regulatory requirements is usually rare. This case provides unique insights into how organisations are addressing sustainability concerns voluntarily.

Of particular interest in this case was the discrepancy in Chevron-Texaco's sustainability principles/criteria and that of the State Government of Western Australia. For example, the organisation's principle of 'Economic Benefit Delivery'

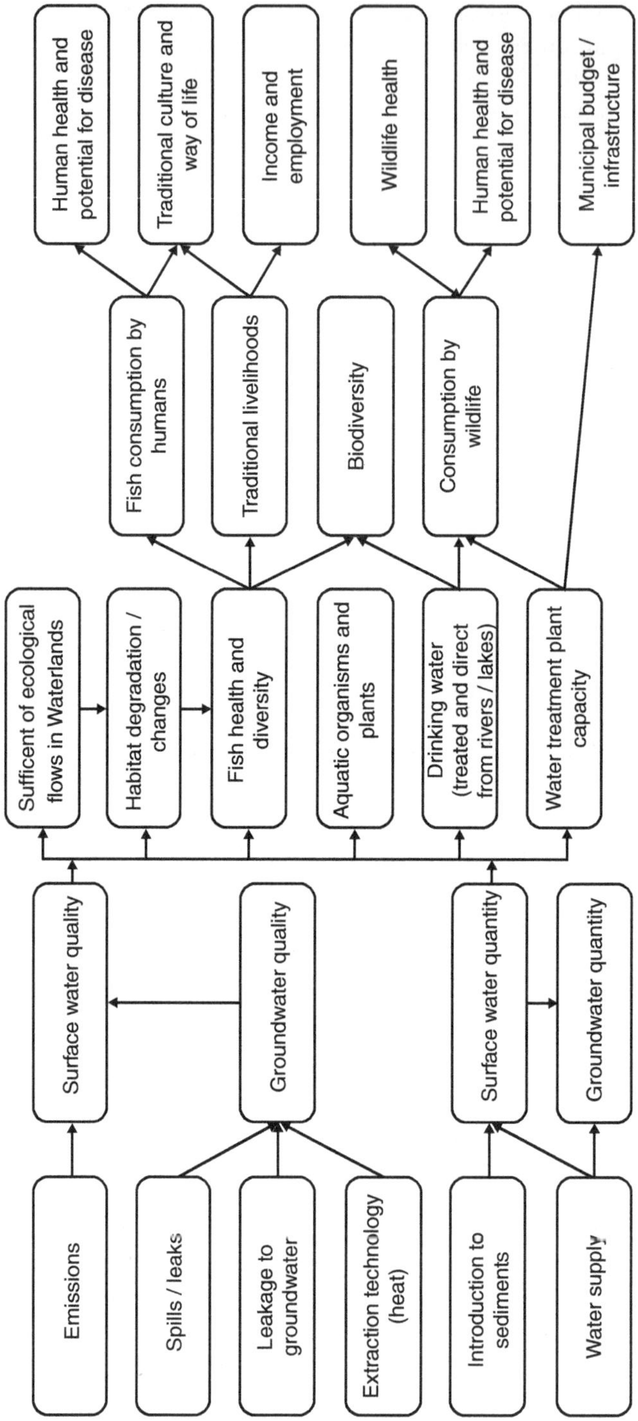

Figure 2.2 North Field Test by Shell: simplified integrated environmental, social and health concerns (Orenstein et al. 2010).

meant that the economic return of 'profitability' was an important criterion for Chevron-Texaco. They viewed the Gordon Gas Development as a profitable investment revealed by the following quote from the organisation: "the Gorgon gas development will create profitable investment opportunities for the Gorgon Venture and for other industrial gas projects in Australia that depend on gas as a feedstock" (Pope, Morrison-Saunders & Annandale 2005:300–301). By comparison, the State Government's principle was for 'long-term economic health'. This example demonstrates the potential differences in sustainability interpretations that different entities might adopt and, as evidenced in this case, that the sustainability criteria proposed in an organisation's corporate document could be considerably different to those outlined in a government decision-making tool (Pope, Morrison-Saunders & Annandale 2005). Furthermore, it highlights the limitations of corporate plans and policies with the potential for 'questionable' sustainability goals and considerations to emerge.

These next two cases shift from an ex-ante practice of initiation within the sustainability assessment to examination from an ongoing practice lens.

Multinationals in Thailand

In their study of sustainability assessment practices of multinational enterprises in Thailand, Donovan et al. (2017) highlight the importance of international standards and global sustainability platforms in directing organisations to consider a broad set of sustainability issues and impacts. Each global initiative highlights issue categories of importance, which is used by the organisation to identify potential issues around these issue categories. Donovan et al. (2017) found that approximately 22% of MNEs within their sample were using a range of different global sustainability platforms and international standards, such as GRI, UNGC, CDP and ISOs to inform their sustainability impacts and issues.

Previous research had neglected to show how organisations were using these standards and platforms at the strategic and managerial level within their sustainability assessment process. However, Donovan et al.'s (2017) study provides some insight into how these standards and platforms are being implemented. For one organisation in their sample, an extensive stakeholder engagement process, with both internal and external stakeholders, generated many sustainability issues that needed to be considered for the project. These were then aligned with the company's corporate sustainability plan and the global initiatives to which the corporation prescribed. Together, they determined the sustainability issues that the corporation would focus on for the project.

Furthermore, Donovan et al. (2017) found that some MNEs implementing GRI standards were using materiality assessments whereby stakeholder sustainability issues of importance are plotted on a matrix alongside the organisation's sustainability issues of importance. The inference here is that the organisation will choose to prioritise issues that are selected by both the organisation and its stakeholders. Whilst there was evidence of materiality assessments being used in the initiation step, they were more frequently used in the scoping step of sustainability assessments.

Manufacturing multinationals in Indonesia

Borgert et al. (2018a) also provides an ongoing account of the initiation step in practice, specifically from a procedural framework perspective. Focussed on nine MNEs operating in the manufacturing sector of Indonesia, their study sheds light on both the regulatory context and the voluntary processes of initiating sustainability assessments. At first, the initiation step was found to be driven predominantly by a regulatory compliance environment related to the host country in which the MNE operated. This context directed the initiation activities of the organisation and led to the use of checklists where the organisation identified mandatory and relevant sustainability issues to inform their plans and operational activities (Borgert et al. 2018a).

The majority of MNEs extended their consideration of sustainability issues beyond local regulatory requirements which was largely directed by their headquarters. As described by Borgert et al. (2018a), the sustainability commitments at the level of headquarters cascaded down to the subsidiary level and subsequently framed the latter's initiation activities. For many of the MNEs in the sample, their global commitments were influenced by international standards or sustainability platforms like the GRI and CDP. The adoption of some industry-specific sustainability issues and/or sustainability standards or principles were aligned with corporate plans and policies and translated into sustainability commitments and actionable processes for the organisation.

There was also evidence to suggest that MNEs were using established lists to identify key sustainability issues to guide their sustainability focus. In about half of the sample, MNEs were also making use of a materiality analysis to augment the use of established lists in the initiation step of their sustainability assessments (Borgert et al. 2018a). It is clear that many of the practices of MNEs in Thailand and Indonesia, as evidenced in these two cases, are similar.

Initiation step summary

Initiation is the first step in a sustainability assessment and is critical for determining the sustainability issues that will be considered throughout the project. The examination conducted in this section of key procedural framework studies, as well as several case studies, suggests that the initiation step is likely to commence with:

- Determining the organisation's approach to sustainability through understanding its values and sustainability principles
- Identifying its internal and external stakeholders
- Anticipating the projects broad impacts
- Understanding the context surrounding the project

As part of the process, it was found that during the initiation step, organisations can be highly influenced by the use of international standards and global sustainability platforms to direct their sustainability commitments. Furthermore, these standards and platforms can also influence the use of tools such as checklists, established lists, corporate plans and policies, and a materiality analysis. Some of the techniques that were adopted in this step included expert judgement and participatory forms of engagement.

Scoping step

The scoping step follows initiation within sustainability assessments although some experts argue that the two steps overlap (Shields, Blengini & Šolar 2011). We suggest that there are some key differences. While initiation is broadly about how to initiate the assessment, scoping is generally about determining which sustainability issues merit further investigation. Scoping should also provide a refinement of the methods to be employed in the subsequent stages of the sustainability assessment. This section will present the main details of the scoping step, including a focus on tools and techniques used in this step followed by empirical studies.

The scoping step of a procedural framework for sustainability assessment

While Shields, Blengini and Šolar (2011) identify an overlap between the initiation and scoping steps, they also offer a thorough conceptualisation of *scoping* with the inclusion of LCAs, among other tools, to assist with measures of preference. These authors suggest that scoping "sets the boundaries of the system under study, the sources of the data and the functional unit to which the achieved results refer. It is analogous to scoping in the ISA [Integrated Sustainability Assessment]" (1219).

Some scholars call for more research on the importance of the scoping step in the sustainability assessment, arguing for more effective integration across the impact assessment domains (Canter & Ross 2014; Morrison-Saunders et al. 2014a). Morrison-Saunders et al. (2014a) suggest that an integrated approach to scoping is required "to determine which of the plethora of sustainability issues could be considered" (5).

As emphasised by Canter and Ross (2014), gathering the important sustainability issues for possible consideration is key during the first step of initiation. However, during the scoping step, decision-makers must contextualise and finalise the sustainability objectives "derived from overarching sustainability principles which are highly integrated" (Morrison-Saunders & Pope 2013:56). Cautiously, the authors warn that consolidation at the scoping step might cause trade-offs between the key sustainability dimensions – economic, social and environmental – as the scoping process requires decision-makers to select a limited range of issues that will be considered for the remainder of the project.

One of the key challenges is determining what sustainability issues of a project should be included in the scoping step and how to bring together discipline-specific expertise (Canter & Ross 2014). Creating a structure that gives equal consideration to sustainability issues from across the economic, social and environmental domains "poses a considerable challenge for integrated assessments to achieve the necessary 'win-win-win' outcomes envisaged to derive from sustainability development and sustainability" (Duncan & Hay 2007:293).

In the current study, we define scoping as the refinement and prioritisation of sustainability issues for analysis of potential impacts, which is consistent with how others have defined it (*e.g.*, Donovan et al. 2017; Morrison-Saunders et al. 2014a). There are various tools and techniques that are commonly employed during scoping. These are presented in the next section.

Tools and techniques for scoping

This section will detail a range of tools and techniques that appear to be the most suitable for a project during the scoping step of a sustainability assessment.

Sustainability indicators

Sustainability indicators or indices have long been a tool of interest in the impact assessment literature. These indicators are an attempt to "simplify, quantify, analyse and communicate complicated information to support policymaking and public communication" (Myllyviita, Antikainen & Leskinen 2017:239).

Indicators are commonly measured, calculated and tracked over time. Bond, Morrison-Saunders and Howitt (2013) call for the use of sustainability indicators at the scoping stage when integrating the three dimensions of sustainability. The use of indicators allows decision-makers to better understand each dimension of sustainability and therefore make better decisions, especially when having to make trade-offs. Sustainability indicators are often found embedded in various methodologies. One of the most prominent methodologies to use sustainability indicators is Multi-Criteria Analysis (MCA) and has been extensively studied at the policy and project level.

Multi-Criteria Analysis

MCA has been extensively used at a policy level (Ness et al. 2007). According to de Ridder et al. (2007), MCAs support comparisons between options based on set criteria. MCA can accommodate both qualitative and quantitative data to identify the advantages and challenges of each alternative and, therefore, is often described as an umbrella methodology (Ness et al. 2007). MCA provides a transparent method to analyse complex issues with the view of selecting a preferred alternative (see Table 2.1). Interestingly, MCA appears to be particularly suited for the scoping step as it can handle a large number of diverse sustainability criteria and options (Ness et al. 2007).

Table 2.1 Example of an MCA matrix

Criteria	*Weight 1*	*Weight 2*	*Alternative 1*	*Alternative 2*	*Alternative 3*	*Alternative 4*	*Alternative 5*	*Alternative 6*
aaaa			Score	Score	Score	Score	Score	Score
bbbb			Score	Score	Score	Score	Score	Score
cccc			Score	Score	Score	Score	Score	Score
dddd			Score	Score	Score	Score	Score	Score
eeee			Score	Score	Score	Score	Score	Score

MCA is not only useful at the scoping step but can be implemented throughout the sustainability assessment.

Materiality analysis

As discussed earlier, Donovan et al. (2017) show how GRI and its materiality analysis offers a useful tool for understanding the issues of importance amongst a project's multiple stakeholders, leading to the refinement of issues within the scoping step. Building on details gathered in the initiation step, the two axes of the materiality assessment (importance of sustainability issue to stakeholder vs. importance of sustainability issue to the organisation) allow decision-makers to not only identify the importance of each issue for each stakeholder, but to also rank each issue according to a specific set of criteria. Suggested criteria vary from environmental considerations (*e.g.*, water quality) to social considerations (*e.g.*, access to education). Other than what is documented in Donovan et al. (2017), the emergence of such new techniques within the sustainability assessment is not detailed in the broader literature.

Life Cycle Assessment

LCA is one of the most well-developed tools in the impact assessment field (Ness et al. 2007). When considering a traditional LCAs, it aims to:

> capture and describe the environmental effects associated with a product, process or activity over its whole life cycle by calculating the material and energy requirements as well as emissions to air, water and soil by assessing the related environmental consequences.
>
> (Shields, Blengini & Šolar 2011:1219)

There are four major stages to conducting an LCA, including goal and scope definition, life cycle inventory, life cycle impact assessment and interpretation of the results (Shields & Shelleman 2017).

Guidelines to conducting LCAs have been established by the International Standards Organisation (ISO) (Ness et al. 2007; Shields & Shelleman 2017).

More recently, this tool has been extended to incorporate the three dimensions of sustainability – environmental, economic and social aspects – and is known as a Life Cycle Sustainability Assessment (LCSA). However, the LCSA remains at a conceptual level (Myllyviita, Antikainen & Leskinen 2017).

Participatory approach

As discussed earlier, in relation to the initiation step, participatory approaches are also common at the scoping step. These can be seen in the Orenstein et al. (2010) case where they conducted workshop style consultations with a range of their local, project stakeholders. Orenstein et al. (2010) provides interesting insights into how stakeholders are able to efficiently scope a range of sustainability factors and add specific, detailed knowledge to this selection and refinement process. Not only does stakeholder engagement help decision-makers to carry out procedural trade-offs (Morrison-Saunders & Pope 2013) but it also ensures a further layer of integrity towards the project (Orenstein et al. 2010). Further details of the participatory approach in action follow this section.

International organisations and standards

Similar to the initiation step, global sustainability platforms and the use of their standards influence scoping practices. In addition to the materiality analysis which is supported by the GRI standards, Donovan et al. (2017) and Borgert et al. (2018b) discuss the establishment of broad sustainability issues and their influence on corporate plans and policies. Borgert et al. (2018b) research more specifically centres on the role of management and team structures to help drive these scoping practices within headquarters and for the subsidiary.

Empirical studies

This section will present the selected empirical investigations that explore the scoping step at a project level. First, Orenstein et al.'s (2010) in-depth case on the NFT is re-visited and illustrates a dual scoping process adopted for an ex-ante project. The Basslink project (Duncan & Hay 2007) draws upon an external perspective that is enforced by regulation. Two cases from Borgert et al. (2018b) and Donovan et al. (2017) are re-visited and provide key details of scoping and the use of tools for ongoing projects.

North Field Test

As mentioned previously, Orenstein et al. (2010) explored the integrated impact assessment for Shell's NFT. Within the first phase, Shell assembled an external team of consultants with expertise from each of the three dimensions of sustainability – environment, economic and social. The consultants conducted a technical scoping activity using documentation Shell had collected about stakeholder issues and concerns related to the company and developed a preliminary list of technical (expert-based) issues. The external consultant team then conducted workshop-style consultations with a range of local, project stakeholders, with the aim of collecting their views on issues that were important to them in the event that the project went ahead. From here, these issues were refined for impact analysis. This example is useful for identifying the different lens that expert consultants and community members use to view issues, and highlights the value of a dual scoping process that adopts both a technical and a participatory approach to refining the most significant issues for consideration.

Basslink project

Similar to the Scarborough Field project in Western Australia, the Basslink project is another example of how MCA is used to scope issues. Duncan and Hay (2007) examined the project viability of Basslink, a major energy infrastructure development within the World Heritage area of the Gordon River in central Tasmania, Australia. During the scoping step of the Basslink project, environmental experts were quick to highlight the implications of water level changes downstream from the water hydro electrical installation. Experts questioned the minimum and maximum water levels to be maintained by the project proponent.

Throughout an extensive MCA process, it quickly became apparent that there was a clear link between water flow restrictions and financial costs (for example, less water stored or released produces less electricity sold to the main grid, which has negative implications for revenue). Despite the recommendations put forward by the proponent's environmental researchers about issues relating to volume of water discharge and impact on the surrounding ecosystems, the proponent prioritised the cost implications associated with the issue over the environmental concerns. This case is illustrative of the concerns articulated in the literature elsewhere, relating to the lack of integration between the domains of sustainability where socio-economic issues take precedence over the environmental concerns of the project (see, for example, Morrison-Saunders & Fischer 2006; Therivel & Fischer 2012).

Multinationals in Thailand

Donovan et al.'s (2017) study of 23 multinationals in Thailand is a more recent investigation and which drew upon one of the largest sample sizes in the sustainability assessment domain. Whilst their study has a specific focus on procedural frameworks for the entire sustainability assessment, it does provide some useful insights of how the private sector engage with scoping in a sustainability assessment.

A key finding from their study centred on the commitment that MNEs in Thailand have made to adopting international standards and global sustainability platforms and how it shapes the MNE's scoping practices. These commitments lead to the establishment of a broad set of sustainability issues and indicators for the MNE to focus upon, with refinement and prioritisation occurring through the use of a materiality analysis where the sustainability issues of most importance were measured for both internal and external stakeholders. This resulted in a prioritisation of sustainability issues that reflected the preferences for both the organisation and its key stakeholders.

Multinationals in Indonesia

The most recent case of interest is Borgert et al.'s (2018b) study of nine manufacturing multinationals operating in Indonesia. Their findings focussed on the scoping step of the sustainability assessment and examined the rationale for undertaking the assessment and the team composition and management structures of the scoping step.

They found that both regulations and the internal policies of the parent company were instrumental in influencing the scoping practices of MNEs. Businesses were first motivated to comply with regulations and the sustainability requirements of the host government, which could exist at multiple levels, including municipality, regionally/provincially and nationally. Beyond the compliance context, MNEs invariably adopted external, voluntary guidelines or standards. These were found to frame the boundaries of the organisation's scoping practices. In some cases, the parent company may have adopted other guidelines or standards, which could then have considerable impact on the affiliate's internal policies.

In many cases, the findings revealed collaboration of teams and personnel across parent and affiliate organisations, and also across management levels, with the development of internal policies and operations in a top-down fashion. In saying this, there was evidence of affiliate organisations taking up authority in on-the-ground activities when collaborating with local third-parties and in translating the parent company's commitments to global standards and guidelines into workable strategies and practices to suit the local context.

Scoping step summary

In this procedural framework of a sustainability assessment, scoping is defined as a refined appraisal of sustainability issues to be assessed for the next stage of impact analysis. Within this step it becomes evident that both technical and participatory approaches are critical to ensure win-win-win outcomes, as highlighted by Canter and Ross (2014). The works of Orenstein et al. (2010) and Donovan et al. (2017) show the importance of engaging with stakeholder groups through the use of technical and participatory approaches within the scoping step to capture a multi-perspective view of sustainability issues of significance and to help determine the most important factors to be considered for assessment. The Basslink case shows how an MCA can be used to scope issues where Borgert et al.'s (2018b) research shows the influence of global sustainability platforms on corporate plans and policies, and organisational practices.

Impact assessment stage

From the initiation and scoping of key sustainability issues in the first stage of the sustainability assessment, decision-makers must then determine the potential impacts of the proposed project and make adjustments where necessary. This occurs within the Impact Assessment stage which is comprised of two key steps: *impact analysis* and *alternative selection*. These two steps are inherently linked, although the step of alternative selection tends to be recurring across the sustainability assessment. From the analysis of sustainability issues related to the business activity, the decision-maker determines how the organisation will proceed based on the possible impacts of each issue. The alternative selection step examines the various possibilities to not only minimising/eliminating negative sustainability impacts but also includes possible enhancements of sustainability outcomes.

This section will detail the theoretical foundations for each step and then present the main tools and techniques deployed within impact analysis and alternative selection. The section will then conclude with empirical cases that demonstrate the processes of each step.

Impact analysis step

The impact analysis step tends to be recognised as one of the more technical or complex steps of a sustainability assessment (Bond, Morrison-Saunders & Pope 2012; Bond, Morrison-Saunders & Howitt 2013; Pope, Annandale & Morrison-Saunders 2004). Within impact analysis, the refined sustainability issues of the assessment are analysed to understand the effects and/or implications it will have for the business, the environment and its broader stakeholders. It is at this stage of the sustainability assessment that the types of tools and techniques used will likely differ for ex-ante and ongoing projects as the former tends to relate to predictions and the latter tend to be 'live'. Adding further complexity is the limited number of cases that detail the impact assessment stage for ongoing projects (see Donovan et al. 2017).

This section will describe the impact analysis literature that has been identified at the project level and will then focus on the various tools and techniques available to project proponents to conduct the analysis. It will present a small number of cases with an emphasis on the impact analysis step.

The impact analysis step of a procedural framework for sustainability assessment

Although difficult to identify a single most important step in the sustainability assessment, impact analysis is arguably the most defining step of impact assessment. As outlined by the International Association for Impact Assessment (IAIA), impact analysis ultimately identifies "the future consequences of a current or proposed action" (for ex-ante projects). Lion, Topple and Donovan (2017) elaborate further by describing impact analysis within the sustainability assessment as the "process of determining the potential or actual impacts of the planned activity/activities" (40). While these definitions provide clarity and succinctness, it tends to have a limited depth in the sustainability assessment literature.

For example, Binder, Feola and Steinberger (2010) emphasise measurement and assessment within this step. Measurement refers to the quantification of indicators and processes, while assessment relates to both the aggregation and integration of indicators plus the specific assessment procedure. Although the article fails to elaborate on the assessment procedure itself, it provides detail about comparing different assessment approaches according to: "(i) a scoring system; (ii) reference values and thresholds; (iii) stakeholder assessment; (iv) linear programming; and (v) indicator ranges and sustainability solution space" (Binder, Feola & Steinberger 2010:76).

Alternatively, the procedural model offered by Shields, Blengini and Šolar (2011) offers a different lens for viewing sustainability assessment where impact analysis occurs *after* alternative selection. This is not an uncommon conceptualisation with others, most notably Morrison-Saunders and Pope (2013) and Gibson, Hassan and Tansey (2013) who suggest that a range of options are assessed against sustainability issues and indicators. Within Shields, Blengini and Šolar (2011) model, the prediction of social and environmental impacts is loosely inferred as impact analysis where baseline system data is collected and analysed. This model of sustainability assessment is discussed in greater detail for the next step of alternative selection and is likely to shed greater clarity about the step of impact analysis.

For ex-ante assessment, impact analysis requires very precise knowledge and increases in complexity when trying to predict future impact in an uncertain environment. Previous environmental and social assessment processes have suffered from poor assessment methodologies and have been often criticised for being closer to 'art' than a 'science' (Gibson, Hassan & Tansey 2013).

Tools and techniques

Many of the methods and tools relevant to the impact analysis step have been discussed already within the first stage of the sustainability assessment. However, they do cross over and have further use in subsequent steps of the procedural framework. While international organisations and standards, and their influence on corporate policies and plans, have been mentioned in earlier steps, baseline studies and predictive modelling are introduced for the impact analysis step.

Baseline studies

Baseline studies emerged in 1970 with the implementation of the US National Environmental Protection Act (NEPA) and have been extensively developed from an EIA perspective. As Duinker and Beanlands explain,

> from a very general level, it implies, (a) *measurement* to test for change, (b) an adequate *quantitative* knowledge of conditions both *before* (the baseline)

and *after* (the so-called monitoring project initiation, and (c) the use of acceptable statistical procedures for data analysis.

(5)

Bond, Morrison-Saunders and Pope (2012) argued that sustainability assessments mimic EIAs and therefore it is essential that such baselines are also conducted in sustainability assessments. When establishing the baseline, decision-makers should focus on establishing the most appropriate indicators in order to properly assess the baseline of the environmental, social and economic dimensions (Therivel 2004). Appropriate indicator selection will ensure the accuracy of the analysis and possible mitigation measures. Standards and international guidelines might provide the necessary guidance for decision-makers to select an appropriate set of indicators.

Once the baseline study is completed, decision-makers should then focus on identifying the highly significant impacts. Initially, the impacts were grouped into five main categories: high, major, moderate and low/negotiable (Duinker & Beanlands 1986). Later, Sippe (1990) introduced the concept of "negotiable" vs. "non-negotiable" impacts, classifying their social and environmental acceptability. This concept was later reinforced by Sadler (1996), who suggested the use of critical vs. non-critical resource losses. While such concepts have been primarily explored from an environmental point of view, Morrison-Saunders and Pope (2013) suggest that "the notion of demarcating acceptable from unacceptable impacts is core to sustainability assessment and to the effective management of trade-offs" (57). We concur with this view. In order to accurately analyse and evaluate potential impacts, decision-makers should use specific methodologies, providing the necessary guidance in this complex process.

Predictive modelling

De Ridder et al. (2007) define modelling tools as one of seven major categories within integrated assessments for sustainable development. These models typically come from the natural and economic sciences and attempt to simulate real-world processes based on empirical data (de Ridder et al. 2007).

Empirical studies

There are very few cases that provide detailed coverage of tools and techniques typically adopted in the impact analysis step of a sustainability assessment, and fewer still that focus on the private sector. Two notable exceptions, the Basslink project and MNEs in Thailand, are presented in this section.

Basslink project

The Basslink Project mentioned earlier provides useful insights through its use of quantitative modelling to inform the impact analysis step within a sustainability assessment.

A predictive model, known as the Tasmanian Electric Market Simulation Model (TEMSIM), was used to undertake analyses of simulated operations at the three power stations – the Gordon, Poatina and John Butters – in a range of different conditions. Each power station was found to have considerably different patterns of operation with Basslink. The analyses of the TEMSIM illustrated the potential impacts to water quality and fluvial geomorphology (these were found to be rather minor when compared with broad, environmental issues common to mining practices). While metal plumes from the mining site and mine tailing in the river bed were identified as being more likely to occur from using the John Butters power station (Locher 2001), the significance of these issues did not warrant the development of key mitigation strategies (Donovan et al. 2017).

Multinationals in Thailand

Beyond ex-ante projects, Donovan et al.'s (2017) project is one of the few that have examined the step of impact analysis for ongoing or post projects in the private sector. Overall, this study found that when looking at service and manufacturing MNEs combined, there was considerable dependence on headquarters or the corporate strategy to influence the methods and systems put in place for impact analysis. Similarly, there was a trend for international standards and various global sustainability platforms to influence activities within impact analysis. These included GRI, UNGC, CDP and ISOs requirements, amongst others.

A key example of impact analysis practices was evident in one service multinational based in North America. This multinational was committed to GRI standards for sustainability reporting plus other international guidelines including the Sustainability Trade Initiative and CDP. These multiple standards and guidelines provided measurable areas the organisation must assess and report on. Looking specifically at one of the organisation's broad sustainability issue categories of diverse workforce engagement (as identified within the previous step of scoping) shows a narrowing down to specific gender and racial areas and indicators. Here, both qualitative and quantitative data are captured for each indicator and used to inform various strategies, initiatives and practices. Outcomes and case studies are provided often using descriptive qualitative data to provide more depth and context to the quantitative data collected.

Impact analysis step summary

Impact analysis is where each issue identified and prioritised in the first stage is analysed to understand the effects and/or implications it will have for the business, the environment and the local community in which the activity is located. Little is documented in the literature about the tools and techniques used to effectively manage the analysis of the potential issues and impacts that inform organisational decision-making which could look quite different for ex-ante and ongoing projects. Quantitative modelling was evident in ex-ante projects where predictive assessment is required. For ongoing projects, there was some evidence to suggest that tools and techniques used in earlier steps would continue to have utility in impact analysis. These included the early adoption of international standards and global sustainability platforms which informed sustainability issue categories and the influence of corporate strategies and policies which provide measurable areas for organisations to assess and report on. While analysis of empirical findings to date inform this summary, more research is needed to gain greater insight to current business practices.

Alternative selection step

From the analysis of sustainability issues related to the business activity, the decision-maker determines how the organisation will proceed based on the possible impacts of each issue. The alternative selection step examines the various possibilities to minimise/eliminate negative sustainability impacts, as well as identifying ways to enhance possible sustainability outcomes. At the extreme end, the proposed activity might be abandoned and replaced with an alternative that minimises any negative sustainability impacts. A less extreme option might be to develop a mitigation strategy to address the impact, should it be negative. If the impact is likely to be positive, the organisation might provide a level of enhancement.

This section will provide an overview of the current knowledge on mitigation and enhancement at the project level, and will conclude with the few identified empirical studies which demonstrate the use of mitigation strategies in sustainability assessments and identify some of the tools and techniques used in this step.

Alternative selection step of a procedural framework for sustainability assessment

The alternative selection process is well established in the EIA and other impact assessment literatures. However, few sustainability assessment studies have investigated its main characteristics at the project level from a private sector perspective (Bond, Morrison-Saunders & Howitt 2013).

The work by Shields, Blengini and Šolar (2011) on ex-ante integrated sustainability assessments make reference to management alternatives following the initiation and scoping steps. Within the alternative selection step, alternative approaches for managing a project situation or investment decision are proposed "which address the objectives of the firm, the expectations of the financiers and shareholders, legal requirements and the desires and needs of stakeholders to varying degrees" (Shields, Blengini & Šolar 2011:1216). In the ex-ante process, once alternatives have been established, predictions are made about the social and environmental impacts for each one. Then, baseline data is collected and analysed so that it can be later compared with measures taken during or after the project. While focussed on the social and environmental sustainability of each potential impact, the technical and economic feasibility is also considered, which results in either a revision or a rejection of each alternative. A separate process of trade-off analysis takes place with the feasible alternatives, which might involve sharing of results with key stakeholders. Once the alternatives have been mutually accepted, they are move to a process of implement. As the project continues, these are monitored and changes made where needed (this occurs within the final stage of a sustainability assessment followed by final stage of impact monitoring and follow-up).

Whilst this explanation of alternative selection might suggest it follows a linear process, when applied in real contexts, the cyclical nature of sustainability assessment becomes evident. This is because this step can sequentially follow on from impact analysis or be the result of a mitigation or enhancement strategy proposed from the impact monitoring and follow-up stage.

As discussed earlier, it appears that the objectives of the selected alternative/s should be aligned with the sustainability objectives established in the earlier stages of the assessment. Therivel (2004:168) identifies different types of mitigation strategies that can be applied at the project level. These include:

- Avoid impacts altogether
- Reduce the magnitude and/or severity of impacts
- 'Repair' impacts after they have occurred
- Compensate for impacts (try to balance out negative impacts with other positive ones, but not necessarily in a like-for-like manner)
- Enhance already positive impacts

Morrison-Saunders and Pope (2013), in considering the prediction of impacts for alternatives in ex-ante projects, describe how the use of multi-criteria decision analysis (MCDA) can be useful for highlighting potential trade-offs in the selection of the most preferred option. As they state: "this in turn facilitates the mitigation of residual negative impacts to ensure acceptability, and the enhancement of positive benefits from the preferred alternative" (58). It is thus evident that the alternative selection step relies heavily on mitigation or enhancement strategies. "[i]t is about how to deal with different types of impact – be it negative (through mitigation) or positive (through enhancement strategies)" (Donovan et al. 2017:64).

Tools and techniques for alternative assessment

The selection of alternatives and implementation of the most appropriate mitigation solutions can be a challenging task for decision-makers and requires the careful selection of appropriate tools and techniques. MCDA can be particularly appropriate at this step (Morrison-Saunders & Pope 2013; Pope, Annandale & Morrison-Saunders 2004), as can MCAs, which were discussed in earlier steps. In addition, there is evidence in the literature of organisations adopting participatory approaches and of international organisations and standards influencing their practices during this step.

Multi-Criteria Decision Analysis

MCDA offers interesting characteristics that allow stakeholder engagement and trade-off management. Some of these features have been presented in earlier steps of this process, but in this section, additional information will be provided on the specific application of MCDA in the context of alternative selection and the implementation of mitigation strategies.

MCDA allows decision-makers to assess the proposed activity against each sustainability criteria. This allows them to identify the least favourable options, and to either discard, mitigate or replace the activity, thus producing an acceptable sustainability outcome. MCDA also provides additional insights into how each project activity, and the alternatives, score against the sustainability criteria. For example, the best overall sustainability options might need the implementation of additional mitigation strategies when assessed against specific sustainability criteria.

MCDA offers both the necessary flexibility and structure to provide clear guidance for the determination of the most suitable activities/strategies that optimise sustainability outcomes. Additionally, MCDA also allows decision-makers to incorporate stakeholders into the choice of mitigation strategy. The decision matrix produced by the MCDA tool allows for the input of stakeholder knowledge through the weighting of each option as it relates to the context, which is heavily influenced by internal and external stakeholders (Labuschagne, Brent & Van Erck 2005).

MCDA bridges the gap between the qualitative and quantitative tools, such as CBA, or net present value, which might be better equipped to capture the challenges and complexity of social and environmental issues. MCDA provides a strong qualitative tool, allowing decision-makers and stakeholders to grasp the specifics of the possible impacts and proposed mitigation strategies for each project activity (Labuschagne, Brent & Van Erck 2005). The current consensus argues for a mixed methods approach in which both quantitative and qualitative methods should be implemented.

The current literature has not explored the organisational perspective for this step, and few studies have explored the methodologies used by organisations within sustainability planning.

Multi-Criteria Analysis

MCA has been extensively used within internal sustainability assessments (Bond, Morrison-Saunders & Howitt 2013). As discussed in the previous section, MCA is presented through a matrix, with options on one side, and the possible project impacts on the other side. MCA provides decision-makers with an overview of 'weak' and 'strong' sustainability mitigation solutions by assigning a score to each mitigation strategy and 'testing' it against the of sustainability objectives. The mitigation strategy selected for implementation should arise from a consensus between the various parties involved in the project. Stakeholders should validate the selected mitigation strategy and suggest additional changes (or options) if necessary.

International organisations and standards

As with previous steps, organisation is influenced by international standards and guidelines when conducting sustainability assessments (Schneider & Meins 2012), and do so during this step as well. When exploring the specific sustainability standards and guidelines, organisations currently incorporate a range of measures to help decision-makers select appropriate mitigation strategies.

For example, GRI proposes a specific framework which can help organisations to select and implement appropriate mitigation solutions to maintain sustainability targets and preferences, whilst ensuring appropriate stakeholder engagement. The implementation of such methodologies has not been examined in considerable depth at the project level, and not at all within the private sector, with the notable exception of the work by Donovan et al. (2017), which will be discussed in the next section.

Empirical studies

This section will present three empirical cases which demonstrate the alignment of specific mitigation strategies with the sustainability objectives of the project. These include Orenstein et al.'s (2010) NFT, the City of South Perth (Pope & Klass 2010) and Donovan et al.'s (2017) MNEs in Thailand.

North Field Test

The NFT has been consistently used as a relevant case for presenting the empirical findings of earlier steps of a sustainability assessment. As discussed previously within the initiation and scoping steps, expert consultants used participatory approaches to engage with their key stakeholder groups. The assessment team repeatedly engaged with community stakeholder groups testing possible alternative strategies to reduce any negative impacts, and to ensure these strategies met the needs of the community (Orenstein et al. 2010). This formed an approach to alternative selection though it did not reveal the use of specific tools, such as MCDA or MCA.

City of South Perth

An example of a project drawing upon the MCDA tool was found in a small-scale sustainability assessment conducted by the City of South Perth in Australia (Pope & Klass 2010). MCDA offers a clear pathway for identifying acceptable mitigation strategies (Morrison-Saunders & Pope 2013). Interestingly, this sustainability assessment was conducted internally and its main goal was to determine the sustainability aspects of planting new trees in the Sir James Mitchell Park.

From their case study, Morrison-Saunders and Pope (2013) explain that stakeholders were clearly engaged at the beginning of the process with a key sustainability consideration being the "enhancement of ecological integrity, maintenance of views, public safety and maintenance costs" (58), amongst others. During the impact assessment and alternative selection steps, five tree planting options were proposed and assessed against sustainability criteria that was co-developed with stakeholders.

This created a scoring system where decision-makers could identify the highest scoring option which translated to being the most sustainable option. However, it became evident that the highest scoring option overall also had a low score in the criterion of "provision of suitable habitat for birds and other fauna" (58). As a result, decision-makers implemented a key strategy to mitigate this impact associated with the preferred option, by adding a number of specific tree species which enhanced the overall sustainability outcome of the project, without compromising other sustainability criteria (Morrison-Saunders & Pope 2013).

Multinationals in Thailand

In Donovan et al.'s (2017) study of MNEs in Thailand, 50% of manufacturing companies were classified at a World Class level for addressing the impacts they are creating. Around three-quarters of these organisations were using both the GRI standards and the UNGC principles to address their impacts and inform alternative strategies for implementation.

One MNE in this sample – a company with more than 10,000 employees in their Thai operation – utilised a range of ISOs and also aligned their sustainability activities to the GRI 3.1 standards. The home country headquarters and the board of directors were largely responsible for operational decisions relating to their sustainability activities of the subsidiary in Thailand. This informed the identification of broad sustainability issue categories, then issue areas within each issue category and then indicators to measure the impact of their development activities in Thailand. Key alternatives were also proposed to address the sustainability performance of specific indicators which were lower than desired. In this way, corporate policies and values guided decision-making and processes undertaken during the alternative selection step (among others).

With a specific focus on the environmental dimension, the organisation adopted a LCA (tool) to evaluate waste water mitigation strategies within their production processes. The implementation of one solution to mitigate all waste water pollutants was successful in addressing a multiple of water pollutant indicators that had been identified within the issue areas and sustainability issue categories established at the project's inception. This case provides sound evidence of what might be considered 'best practice' by an MNE during this step. This work needs expanding to determine the extent of similar practices being adopted by others, a key ingredient driving the current study.

Alternative selection step summary

Alternative selection is an iterative process, where any newly proposed mitigation or enhancement strategy is examined for its ability to align with the sustainability objectives of the project. This helps ensure that proponents are fulfilling the sustainability outcomes set at the beginning of the assessment. Decision-makers should re-visit the impact analysis step with new mitigation strategies that reduce negative – or enhance positive – sustainability outcomes and thus more effectively meet the sustainability objectives of the project. Details of the empirical cases within alternative selection indicated use of participatory approaches to engage with stakeholders as evidenced with the NFT case. The City of South Perth case showed how adoption of the MCDA's a scoring system can help determine a preferred mitigation strategy to ensure more sustainable outcomes. Similarly, Donovan et al.'s (2017) project in Thailand demonstrated the influence of the GRI's sustainability indicators and how they led to the use of LCA to address waste water pollutants.

Impact monitoring and follow-up stage

Impact Monitoring and Follow-up is the final stage of the sustainability assessment framework. This phase is generally comprised of two main steps:

i Monitoring and Evaluation – the actual impacts of the implemented activity/ project
ii Feedback and Follow-up – involves re-visiting decision-making practices and addressing impacts through new mitigation or enhancement strategies to achieve the sustainability goals of the organisation

This section will provide an overview of the impact monitoring and follow-up stage and discuss the key literature that informs a procedural framework for a sustainability assessment. A similar process will be followed as for the previous stage, where each step contained within this stage will be covered in detail, before identifying the tools and techniques used and discussing the findings of relevant empirical case studies.

While the two processes of *monitoring* and *evaluation* are inherently different (Bond, Morrison-Saunders & Howitt 2013), it is often challenging to delineate between the two (Donovan et al. 2017), so we merge them into a single step in this section. From a project perspective, there are few studies that have examined this step in an in-depth manner (Morrison-Saunders & Pope 2013; Morrison-Saunders et al. 2014b) and fewer still that have investigated this stage from an ex-post or ongoing project perspective. The majority of impact assessment studies tend to investigate monitoring and evaluation protocols from an EIA perspective (Marshall, Arts & Morrison-Saunders 2005; Morrison-Saunders et al. 2014b; Wessels 2013) or from a strategic environmental assessment (SEA) perspective (Gachechiladze-Bozhesku & Fischer 2012; Therivel 2004). Only extrapolations to the sustainability assessment literature have been made.

Monitoring and evaluation step of a procedural framework for sustainability assessment

Within the step of monitoring and evaluation, the performance or outcome of the project across the sustainability dimensions is determined. During this step, the impacts of the implemented activities are captured (Lion, Topple & Donovan 2017) and performance against the organisation's sustainability objectives is evaluated (Morrison-Saunders et al. 2014b). Mishra and Saxena (2009) describe this step succinctly, suggesting that it is through monitoring that the impacts of the implemented strategies can be properly evaluated.

Binder, Feola and Steinberger (2010) assert that the final phase of their procedural model is where "the results are reported, management advice developed, and the indicators monitored over time" (74). Lion, Topple and Donovan (2017) provide a more streamlined understanding of monitoring and evaluation despite having organised these as separate steps in their earlier research. Within previous conceptual frameworks, Lion, Topple and Donovan (2017) demonstrated how organisations identify and prioritise their sustainability issues within the monitoring and evaluation step, and that tools and techniques are aligned against the former to capture data through a longitudinal approach evaluating these against benchmarks (or baseline data) and future performance goals (Donovan et al. 2017). Of significance here is that benchmarking occurs where strategies can be evaluated through benchmarked performance (Coteur et al. 2016) and a longitudinal record of performance is captured to inform future decision-making (Mishra & Saxena 2009).

Within their procedural framework of sustainability assessment, Shields, Blengini and Šolar (2011) detail a monitoring and evaluation step that ideally involves an ongoing role for public participation. As part of this iterative process, they suggest that the assessment is an ongoing process where "adaptation and revision" is required (Shields, Blengini & Šolar 2011).

The Sala, Ciuffo and Nijkamp (2015) procedural framework of sustainability assessment shares similar characteristics with that proposed by Shields, Blengini and Šolar (2011). Sala, Ciuffo and Nijkamp's (2015) sustainability assessment is based on a conceptual framework that identifies indicators and a range of data sources to assist with measurement. Furthermore, targets are established, and comparisons occur between the indicator performance data and the organisation's targets, with benchmarking taking place, where possible. This process emphasises continuity and capacity where the sustainability assessment is facilitated by continuous monitoring, where repeated measurements are taken, and a high level of responsiveness is provided, allowing for adjustments to be made, if required. Sala, Ciuffo and Nijkamp (2015) also support the transparency of the majority of factors in the process, like data, data sources, models and results. In addition, they support ongoing engagement with stakeholders and encourage the publication of results.

Tools and techniques

Therivel (2004) suggests that the monitoring and evaluation step should 'test' the implemented mitigation strategies against the predicted impacts in the previous stage – these relate to ex-ante projects but also translate to the ongoing context. When testing the implemented strategies, decision-makers should use the same indicators and sustainability objectives that were established in the baseline studies at the impact analysis step. These are discussed next.

Baseline data

Monitoring through quantitative techniques has been extensively developed in various fields of impact assessments. Quantitative measurements have been described within the EIA literature (Glasson 2005) and used at project and planning levels. Morrison-Saunders et al. (2014b) suggest that methods should be in line with methodologies used in the baseline studies that were conducted in the impact assessment stage. From this line of thinking, it is implied that baseline studies should be used as points of reference, setting the acceptable limits on all sustainability dimensions, as reflected by Morrison-Saunders et al. (2014b):

> When such limits are exceeded (or at risk of being exceeded), appropriate adaptive management action should be initiated, the results communicated and the new actions subject to ongoing follow-up.
>
> (Morrison-Saunders et al. 2014b:40)

Additionally, these authors emphasise that the project proponent carries out the monitoring of impacts through the form of compliance reports, which, in some cases, are approved by regulatory agencies. Their study suggests that such monitoring and evaluation reports should be available to the public to further increase transparency. Increased transparency is supported by others (Marshall, Arts & Morrison-Saunders 2005) and is partly captured in international standards, such as the GRI, discussed next.

International organisations and standards

As stated previously, the development of standards and guidelines frequently used for sustainability reporting are also being used within the sustainability assessment context. These offer additional methods for business organisations to monitor and report on the impact of their activities. The GRI allows for a standardised reporting system for organisations to monitor and report upon their activities and impact on environment, social and economic dimensions. Through this standardisation process, organisations are guided in their monitoring and subsequent evaluation processes.

The GRI standards offer decision-makers a clear overview on what has to be monitored and how each specific issue and impact should be monitored. Additionally the GRI encourages the disclosure of monitoring information. This allows organisations from the same industry to share information, which may inform better mitigation strategies and greater scrutiny of their activities. Thus, the GRI allows for cross-industry examination, as well as enabling decision-makers to easily communicate project impact results with regulatory agencies and stakeholders.

The application of such international standards and guidelines within sustainability assessment will be discussed in the next section by examining the empirical work conducted.

Empirical studies

Empirical studies that have specifically focussed on the monitoring and evaluation of sustainability assessments as part of a full procedural framework are difficult to locate at the project level. This is confirmed by Morrison-Saunders and Pope (2013) who explain that there is a paucity of cases at the project level that investigated this step, although extrapolations can be drawn from the broader impact assessment fields including EIAs, HIAs and SEAs, and from the insights observed in Donovan et al.'s (2017) study of MNEs in Thailand.

Multinationals in Thailand

More recently, Donovan et al. (2017) provide key insights into the organisational practices undertaken during this step for the private sector. For one large service MNE in Thailand, Donovan et al. (2017) detailed the monitoring and evaluation activities relating to their supply chain engagement. The organisation had introduced clear measures to monitor the sustainability activities of their Tier 1 suppliers using a longitudinal approach. These measures were compared with baseline data and performance targets.

Of further significance to this case study was the commitment of the headquarter organisation to sustainable outcomes of their project in Thailand. The organisation had adopted GRI standards, and as a result, required their Tier 1 suppliers to undertake GRI reporting which revealed the direct sustainability activities across their product life cycle and additional positive impacts for their value chain.

Additional instances of MNEs in Thailand evaluating their sustainability performance against different targets and baseline measures were also evident in Donovan et al.'s (2017) study. They found that the majority of MNEs that operated at the highest level of performance, at World Class standards, provided baseline indicators, annual progress reviews and targeted outcomes linked with performance expectations across time horizons. Similar to the large service MNE, they also found that the headquarter operations of these 'world class' MNEs were critical drivers of monitoring and evaluation practices within the sustainability Assessment. These practices were usually anchored against multiple international sustainability standards or guidelines, including the use of the GRI and the UNGC.

Summary of the monitoring and evaluation step

For ongoing and completed projects, the monitoring and evaluation step comes into play after project implementation. It is within this step that the impacts of the implemented activities are captured on an ongoing basis, which are measured against the organisation's sustainability objectives. Mixed methods are often encouraged at this step to cover the full gamut of sustainability issues. The limited empirical research that has been conducted at the project level reveals the use of GRI standards by MNEs to help monitor and evaluate the sustainability performance of the project.

Feedback and follow-up step

Feedback and follow-up is the final step of the impact monitoring and follow-up stage and for the whole (procedural) sustainability assessment. Other than the work of Donovan et al. (2017) and Lion, Topple and Donovan (2017), there is little in the literature addressing this step at the project level for the private sector. Leading authors such as Morrison-Saunders and Pope (2013) and Morrison-Saunders et al. (2014b) provide some details about follow-up from a broader planning and policy perspective. However, the bulk of the research on 'follow-up' comes from the EIA literature (*e.g.*, Marshall, Arts & Morrison-Saunders 2005; Sadler 1996). This section will present the main details currently known about the feedback and follow-up step, including a focus on the tools and techniques used and reference to empirical studies.

The feedback and follow-up step of a procedural framework for sustainability assessment

During this final step, feedback and follow-up on the project's activities and impacts forms a loop "where decision-makers reanalyse, re-mitigate and re-enhance the project impacts" (Lion, Topple & Donovan 2017:56). This, in effect, brings the assessment process full-circle. Due to this step, it is important to note that the project implementation does not mark the finality of the sustainability assessment nor the activities that may be required. For this step, decision-makers need to have a process for re-assessing the project's impacts against the sustainability goals and objectives initially established earlier in the assessment process.

Consistent with previous steps of the sustainability assessment, clear definitions of the feedback and follow-up step are limited, other than what is borrowed from other impact assessment literature, mainly EIAs. Early, preliminary work on conceptualising this step for sustainability assessment by Morrison-Saunders and Arts (2004) describe follow-up as "the monitoring and evaluation of the impacts of a project or plan (that has been subject to EIA) for management of, and communication about, the environmental performance of that project or plan" (4). In more recent research by Morrison-Saunders et al. (2014b) this definition has evolved with reference to the IAIA where follow-up is seen as a step "comprising monitoring, analysis/interpretation, management and communication of post-approval decision development activity" (39). Binder, Feola and Steinberger (2010:74) share similar sentiments with regards to this definition and view follow-up as being where "results are reported, management advice developed, and the indicators monitored over time".

Although feedback and follow-up are considered to be an essential step of a sustainability assessment (Morrison-Saunders & Pope 2013; Morrison-Saunders et al. 2014b), the inference is that this final step in the process is perhaps overlooked or forgotten. Parallel to the paucity of literature in this space, Donovan et al.'s (2017) research found that MNEs in Thailand invariably overlooked this step even when they adopted a full cyclical process of sustainability Assessment. Generally, their study shows that feedback and follow-up is not done well by MNEs. Using their classification of 'World Class practices', the few MNEs that executed the feedback and follow-up step well were "actively implementing new mitigation and enhancement strategies to address different issues and impacts as they emerge[d], and adjust[ed] existing strategies based on their performance outcomes from evaluation" (Donovan et al. 2017:85). This finding supports the importance of looking to not only international standards but also the practices of large MNEs who are leaders in their field.

Building from the procedural model of sustainability assessment developed by Shields, Blengini and Šolar (2011), the iterative nature of their model suggests that the final steps within ex-ante and ongoing assessments could utilise identical methods. They emphasise that where the goal of follow-up in an ex-ante project is to "evaluate the accuracy of the ex-ante forecasts … quality and responses [are evaluated in] ongoing assessments … to determine if different actions could have led to better outcomes" (1217).

Tools and techniques

There is limited knowledge of the specific tools and techniques that organisations use, or should use, in the feedback and follow-up step of sustainability assessments. Conceptual developments suggest that decision-makers use the same tools and techniques as those used in baseline studies to ensures that the project's issues and impacts are re-assessed and re-analysed in the same context.

Given the proliferation of literature on follow-up in EIAs (Marshall, Arts & Morrison-Saunders 2005; Morrison-Saunders & Pope 2013; Sadler 1996), one method that could translate across from EIAs to sustainability assessments is feedback loops. Lion, Donovan and Bedggood (2013) suggest that such loops should exist when organisations apply EIAs at the project level. To be effective, they suggest that follow-up loops are used so that the project proponent constantly re-analyses and where necessary, re-mitigates current and arising issues and impacts. It was suggested that organisations are able to learn and integrate previous project experiences into their decision-making process. In addition, Morrison-Saunders et al. (2014b) suggest that where feedback loops include the mitigation strategy implemented, should also involve stakeholder groups to aid with effectiveness. In particular, stakeholders who are directly impacted by the decision-maker's mitigation strategy should be a key part of the process. The current literature calls for further investigation regarding such feedback loops and the specifics of stakeholder engagement.

Empirical studies

There are very few empirical studies that investigate feedback and follow-up within sustainability assessments. Rarer still are studies that have investigated practices from the project proponent perspective. Once again, the most comprehensive work on this step in the sustainability assessment literature is Donovan et al.'s (2017) study of service and manufacturing MNEs in Thailand.

Multinationals in Thailand

Donovan et al. (2017) provide a suite of case study vignettes that shed light on practices undertaken by MNEs during the feedback and follow-up step, across varying performance levels. For one service-based MNE that was conducting this step (at what was deemed by the authors to be a World Class level), it was evident that they adopted a range of international standards and guidelines, like GRI. Focussing on one of its main sustainability issues of women in the workforce and gender equality, the MNE collected data on a range of measures such as women in leadership groups and the number of women in management positions. With these measures, they set organisational targets, monitored and evaluated their performance outcomes against baseline measures and targets, and then refined their enhancement or mitigation strategies based on their performance. The case study provided a clear example of the organisation's proactive engagement with their priority sustainability areas extending across the life cycle of the sustainability assessment process.

Summary of feedback and follow-up step

Feedback and follow-up is the final step in the last stage of a sustainability assessment. It provides the necessary guidance for decision-makers to implement further mitigation or enhancement strategies where (and if) needed, which helps to ensure the overall sustainability outcome of the project. Bond, Morrison-Saunders and Howitt (2013) emphasise that the sustainability considerations in which the project unfolds is dynamic and constantly evolving. Therefore, this step is critical to providing a full-circle commitment to the organisation's sustainability goals. Decision-makers can incorporate these changes through the implementation of monitoring systems and follow-up methods. Additionally, the use of feedback 'loops' borrowed from EIAs and the continuous improvement focus of the sustainability assessment have been briefly conceptualised (Morrison-Saunders et al. 2014b; Lion, Donovan & Bedggood 2013), with Donovan et al.'s (2017) study of MNEs in Thailand demonstrating insights from corporate practice about the feedback and follow-up step of the sustainability assessment process.

Table 2.2 Research design areas and key decisions

Theoretical perspective	Constructivist
Methodologies	Exploratory Qualitative
Approach	Case study • Semi-structured interviews • Reports and standards
Time horizon	Cross-sectional
Context	MNEs in the Philippines
Method of analysis	Thematic

Methodology for the current research

The current research project seeks to gain greater understanding of the decision-making process and mechanics of sustainability assessments for projects undertaken by the private (business) sector. To ensure a rigorous study is conducted, and thus robust data obtained, numerous research decisions were made as part of the overall research design. For any research investigation, decisions for six key areas need to be made (informed by Green 2002). These are presented in Table 2.2.

Each of these areas and decisions will be discussed in further detail in the following sections.

Research design

Due to the complexity of ecological, social and economic interactions, conducting sustainability assessments is an evolving and largely informal process (Bond, Morrison-Saunders & Howitt 2013; Bond, Morrison-Saunders & Pope 2012). This implies that research on this process should be of an exploratory nature. Moreover, Saunders, Lewis and Thornhill (2015) argue that "[n]ot only are business situations complex, they are also unique" (116). Therefore, an understanding of the different interactions and the people involved in this process was essential to gain an understanding of the fundamental process undertaken by organisations when conducting a sustainability assessment.

Theoretical perspective

The current study was embedded in a constructivist paradigm, as it aimed to understand the process of sustainability assessments and the multiple perspectives on the way they are conducted within organisations, as 'constructed' via the perceptions and opinions of key decision-makers. The seminal work of Guba and Lincoln (1989) informed our choice of paradigm for this research. They explain the key assumptions that underpin the constructivist theoretical perspective which include, for example, that 'truth' is constructed by consensus or consistency among participants, that 'facts' are interpretations, that 'phenomena' can be explored only within a context and that 'cause and effect' is highly interpretive.

Given that sustainability assessments are in their infancy, and, as yet, little empirical work has been conducted in the field, we have assumed that the view and opinions of people conducting them are valid and constructed from their lived experiences. In this sense, the constructivist paradigm assumes a relativist ontology that acknowledges multiple constructions of reality, which are informed by the multiple meanings and values individuals hold about sustainability and its outcomes, whether held individually or shared amongst a group (Guba & Lincoln 1994).

The aim of this research is not to find 'facts' or 'causes'. Rather, it aims to capture the 'emerging' constructions about sustainability assessments as practiced by corporations, so that a more informed construction can be developed, beyond what is currently 'known'. This will enable us to develop a more sophisticated framework that reflects the sustainability assessment processes undertaken by the private sector, which may help guide future decision-making.

Methodologies

EXPLORATORY

The limited research on sustainability assessments (Donovan et al. 2017) implies that the field is still being developed and thus is considered to still be in its infancy. This situation lends itself to conducting exploratory work. As stated by Brown (2006), an exploratory investigation "tends to tackle new problems on which little or no previous research has been done" (43). It helps uncover the general nature of 'the problem' (in this case, how organisations conduct sustainability assessments) and considers the various decision alternatives and variables for inclusion (Aaker et al. 2007). Once this foundation is built, then descriptive or causal investigations can follow. Therefore, an exploratory research design is appropriate to better comprehend how sustainability assessments are conducted within organisational decision-making processes, which enables the researcher to adopt a deeper, interpretive lens (Aaker et al. 2007).

QUALITATIVE

Adopting a qualitative methodology is consistent with conducting exploratory research. Qualitative research enables the phenomena investigated to be understood, with deep insights obtained (Zikmund et al. 2011). This approach is consistent with the views of Patton (2002) who suggests that where "little work has been done, few definitive hypotheses exist and little is known about the nature of the phenomenon, qualitative inquiry is a reasonable beginning point for research" (193).

We believe that qualitative methods are well suited to exploring the use of sustainability assessments. The outcome of this investigation will inform the development of a more comprehensive theoretical framework for sustainability assessments for the private sector.

Approach

CASE STUDY

Robson (2002) defines a case study as "a strategy for doing research which involves an empirical investigation of a particular contemporary phenomenon within its real life context using multiple sources of evidence" (178). As explained by Saunders, Lewis and Thornhill (2015), case studies are often used in exploratory studies involving businesses due to their ability to investigate a specific decision or decision-making process. Within business research, case studies have been frequently utilised to answer 'how' and 'why' type questions (Yin 2003).

Yin (2003) identifies two main types of case study designs: single or multiple case studies. He emphasises that both case study designs have the potential to create a successful outcome, but that a multiple case study design is preferred where the availability of resources allows it. This ability to access multiple organisations was possible, hence, this study chose to adopt a multiple case study approach. Accordingly, numerous organisations engaged in a new development, and are required to conduct a sustainability assessment, were targeted. More details on participants will be described shortly in the 'context' section.

Primary data collection: semi-structured interviews

Interviews are considered to be one of the most important sources of information when adopting a case-study approach, particularly when they adopt a semi-structured form (Yin 2003). In addition, semi-structured interviews are well suited to exploratory investigations (Saunders, Lewis & Thornhill 2015). They enable a variety, and even disparity, of views to be collected, thus informing the depth and breadth of the phenomenon being explored. This method was thus ideally suited to the current research project.

To better understand how organisations implement sustainability assessments, it is critical that the insights of experienced decision-makers in the respective organisations are obtained. By conducting semi-structured interviews with senior managers involved in decision-making, a level of fluidity and flexibility in responses is both possible and desirable (Yin 2003), as it enables participants to share their ideas and thoughts freely. In this environment, it is more likely that unforeseen results and new insights into the specific decision-making processes will emerge (Saunders, Lewis & Thornhill 2015).

By interviewing these people, as well as key stakeholders, the current study captured their views and opinions on their organisational processes as to how they assess and address the environmental, social and economic impacts of their project's operations.

Interview protocol

This section presents the interview protocol adopted in this research study. Strong interview protocols are essential to guarantee the rigour of the study.

- Interview guide

  To conduct semi-structured interviews in a robust manner, two main points were considered. First, the researchers followed an interview guide to ensure no deviations from the original enquiry took place during the interview process. Hence, while the semi-structured approach allowed for flexibility which enables participants to introduce, in detail, aspects they considered important, some level of consistency also guided the overall interview to ensured they stayed 'on track'. Second, the questions that comprised the interview guide were formed. These were informed by the earlier analysis of the literature, which captured key findings to date, and which revealed the areas that are key to investigate. An additional criterion was to ensure that each question was general enough to generate sufficient discussion whilst enabling respondents to delve deeper in key areas. The interview guide contained ten key questions and was validated by three experienced researchers prior to the study commencing.
- Informed consent

  When obtaining data directly from people, it is vital that ethics protocols are followed. In particular, when gathering sensitive and/or personal information, participant privacy and confidentiality must be observed (Saunders, Lewis & Thornhill 2015). This provides them with the freedom to be honest and protects the integrity of the information provided. Furthermore, participants should not be pressured to participate. To address these two ethical domains, research must obtain informed consent.

  This means that participants are *informed* about the purpose of the study, what information it seeks, who will be invited, and what will be done with the data (which includes protecting their privacy and ensuring confidentiality). It also means that participants *consent* to be involved in the study, being aware of all that is entailed, and that they do so freely and without pressure. Accordingly, an 'informed consent form' was developed so that participants could read what was being asked of them, and what would be done with the information they provided, prior to them providing any information. All those invited signed the informed consent form.

  As part of the informed consent process, participants were also asked to agree to having their interviews audio-recorded. These recordings were later transcribed so that researchers could properly analyse the interview data. However, participants were first provided a copy of their interview transcription, and invited to make adjustments to any inaccuracies it reflected. Only the adjusted, or approved, transcriptions were used in the analysis for this project.

- Duration of interviews

  Interviews ranged from 45 to 120 minutes in duration. The first ten minutes of the interview were allocated to providing participants with basic information about the background of the study and offering the option to withdraw from the study, if they wished to. The remaining time was allocated to gathering the insights and views of the interviewees on the specific research questions in the interview schedule. Interviews were arranged at the most convenient time for participants, in an appropriate location where electronic recording was permitted. These were usually held in a private office on the site of the organisation's project, or via the telephone if the participant was from the headquarters of the organisation.

Secondary data collection: reports and publications

It is important to determine the efficacy of interview data, which reveals the accuracy and validity of the key points identified in the transcriptions. This was achieved by triangulating the insights gained from participants interviewed with secondary data sources obtained from organisational reports (*e.g.*, annual report, sustainability report), government documents and archival material (*e.g.*, newspaper articles). The importance of triangulating results is further explained in the' rigour of the study' section towards the end of this chapter.

These secondary 'grey' sources included:

1. *Annual reports and internal organisational reports*: these were obtained from participants from each organisation involved in the study.
2. *Publicly available governmental documents*: these were obtained from various government websites which provide extensive information about environmental impact mitigation and publicly discloses a range of monitoring reports. This information was used during the analysis of the compliance level of organisational practices, as well as for substantiating or verifying content from interviews.

To ensure the anonymity of participating organisations and decision-makers interviewed, all identifiable material was removed from the data sources, and pseudonyms, symbols or general titles (*e.g.*, 'decision-maker') were used to replace identifiable information, names or people.

Time horizon

CROSS-SECTIONAL

Cross-sectional studies collect and identify data at a specific point in time (Saunders, Lewis & Thornhill 2015; Zikmund et al. 2011). In the context of this study, choosing a cross-sectional time horizon allowed the research team to interview a large number of organisations and to understand how sustainability issues were being integrated into the decision-making process. This study also had a secondary objective; to assess the regulatory compliance level of each participating organisation. Given that compliance levels typically evolve over time (as a result of changes in regulations or experiential learnings), to capture the current state-of-play effectively, variation in government regulations had to be neutralised as a variable. Hence, the 'changes over time' element would have confounded the data. Hence, a cross-sectional study was adopted to capture the sustainability assessment process of businesses and not, for example, the changing legislation or evolving practices.

Context

MNES IN THE PHILIPPINES

This project was supported by the Philippines Board of Investments (BOI), who manage an extensive list of foreign multinationals operating in the Philippines. Accordingly, large, multinational enterprises (MNEs) with a large-scale development operation in that country were considered as the broad sample set. It was then a matter of determining other defining characteristics of those organisations who would be well-placed to provide the information this study sought. These aspects are outlined below.

Sampling strategy

Sampling strategies within qualitative studies need to follow the concept of ***purposeful sampling***. While there are many sampling strategies, the most suitable for the current investigation was criterion sampling (a purposeful sampling method). This method involves selecting cases that meet certain criterion (Patton 2002). In this case, it meant that prospective participants were selected to be involved in the study if it was deemed they could provide information-rich data on specific development projects, and by so doing, illuminate the enquiry (Patton 2002). Two major criteria were used to select appropriate cases:

1 Recent FDI: the selected participant needed to have been recently engaged in a major foreign direct investment (FDI) located in the Philippines.
2 Size of investment: the likelihood of using comprehensive assessment tools is higher in larger investments, and so a minimum level of investment of US$10 million was set as the threshold. The FDI volumes were triangulated with publicly available documents internal to the organisation (*e.g.*, annual reports) as well as the BOI records. With this threshold in mind, the size of organisations was defined as follows:
   - Small: organisations with an investment between US$10–20 million.
   - Medium: organisations with an investment between US$20–50 million.
   - Large: organisation with an investment exceeding US$ 50 million.

Sampling framework

With assistance from the Board of Investment (BOI) in the Philippines, organisations with significant recent foreign investment were considered for inclusion. In order to capture the decision-making process, it was essential to identify investments that occurred recently, and in which key decision-makers of the investment would be likely still working at the organisation. A decision was made to put a 15-year cap on such operations. Hence, 'recent' investment was defined as operations that occurred within the past 15 years.

The BOI list also contained significant background information, such as size, date of approval and country of origin of the investment. In some cases, the researchers were able to access further investment information, such as monitoring reports and financial statements. Organisations with small investments (<US$15 million) were excluded from the list.

The next decision to scope the project was informed by the industry in which the organisations operated. Three main industries in the Philippines were identified as likely to contain suitable organisations (large enough foreign direct investment and began operations within the past 15 years). Therefore, the organisations were selected on the basis that they operated in one of the three main industrial sectors of the Philippines: manufacturing, mining and utilities organisations. These organisations were initially invited through 'cold' invitation letters and phone calls. Once the candidates agreed to participate, interviews were scheduled and conducted.

A minimum of two interviews per organisation were conducted. First, managers and sustainability officers of the established subsidiary were interviewed. This allowed the gathering of valuable information about the local operations. Second, a key decision-maker involved in the investment process from the organisation's headquarters was interviewed. This permitted the collection of additional data, which enabled the data to be triangulated, thus validating the information provided by the subsidiary and headquarters.

Sample description

The practices of MNEs in the Philippines were evaluated over the life cycle of the investment, capturing both pre-entry decisions as well as operational activities and, in particular, industries (*e.g.*, mining), the rehabilitation phase.

Throughout the data collection, there was a significant tendency for respondents to focus on the operational side when evaluating development decisions and strategies. Feasibility studies, together with regulatory requirements around EIAs/SIAs, clearly set a context for the broader operational aspects of organisations in the Philippines.

While the pre-entry decisions formed an important aspect of determining MNE performance, the operational aspect of their business activities provided a better context for understanding the breadth and scope of sustainable development considerations within the daily operations of organisations and the likely impact of their activities on local development.

Table 2.3 Investment size and HQ location of interviewed organisations

Identifier	*Sector*	*Size*	*HQ Region*	*Subsidiary Interview*	*HQ Interview*
PH01	Mining	Large	Australia	Yes	Yes
PH02	Mining	Large	North East Asia	Yes	Yes
PH03	Mining	Large	North America	Yes	Yes
PH04	Mining	Medium	North East Asia	Yes	Yes
PH05	Mining	Small	Africa	Yes	Yes
PH06	Mining	Small	Europe	Yes	Yes
PH07	Mining	Medium	ASEAN	Yes	Yes
PH09	Mining	Medium	North East Asia	Yes	Yes
PH10	Manufacturing	Medium	North America	Yes	Yes
PH11	Manufacturing	Large	ASEAN	Yes	Yes
PH12	Manufacturing	Medium	ASEAN	Yes	Yes
PH13	Manufacturing	Medium	North America	Yes	Yes
PH16	Manufacturing	Large	North East Asia	Yes	Yes
PH17	Manufacturing	Large	India	Yes	Yes
PH18	Manufacturing	Large	North East Asia	Yes	Yes
PH19	Manufacturing	Medium	Australia	Yes	Yes
PH31	Manufacturing	Large	Europe	Yes	Yes
PH20	Utility	Large	North East Asia	Yes	Yes
PH22	Utility	Large	North America	Yes	Yes
PH23	Utility	Large	Europe	Yes	Yes
PH25	Utility	Small	ASEAN	Yes	Yes
PH26	Utility	Medium	North East Asia	Yes	Yes
PH28	Utility	Small	Europe	Yes	Yes
PH29	Utility	Small	ASEAN	Yes	Yes

Table 2.3 provides a short description of the participating organisations and their respective industries, including the headquarter location and investment size. A total of 92 personnel were interviewed from these organisations (with a minimum of two from any single organisation).

Sample characteristics

Figure 2.3 depicts the location of headquarter operations. The majority are located in Europe, North America and the ASEAN region. Collecting such a diverse range of organisations allowed for the development of an accurate picture of organisation practices across the world, and thus beyond the Philippines, for some aspects. This broad range of organisations means the transferability of the findings of this study to other organisations is high.

Figures 2.4–2.6 provide an overview of the participating organisations per investment size (small, medium and large). Investment size appears to be equally distributed across all industries and thus provides a fairly representative picture of the assessment practices.

The investment size of organisations in the selected industries present some variations. These variations will not allow a cross-industry comparison. Further studies will be required to provide additional insights into the divergence of practices across the selected industries in the application of sustainability assessments.

With the addition of secondary data (reports), together with transcriptions of interviews, more than 9000 pages of information on organisational practices was gathered, synthesised and analysed. This amount of information reinforced the credibility and transferability of the research findings. The secondary sources were used at various time for triangulation. These points are made clear in the results chapters.

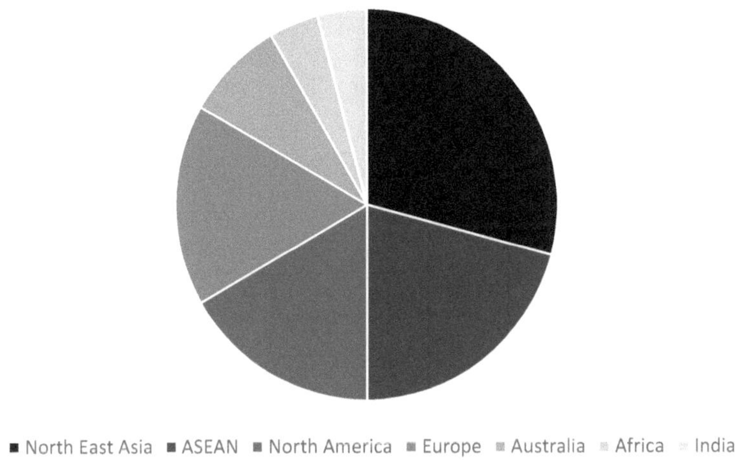

Figure 2.3 Geographic location of the data sample.

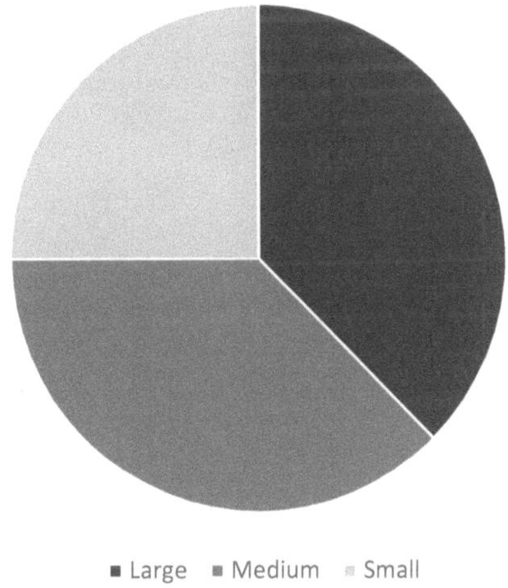

Figure 2.4 Investment size distribution in the mining industry.

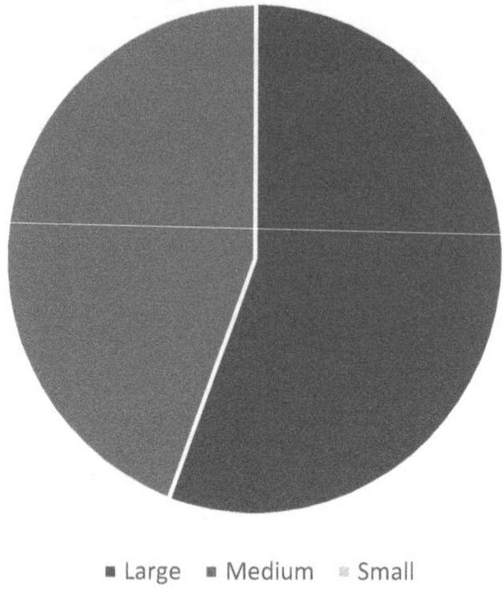

Figure 2.5 Investment size distribution in the manufacturing industry.

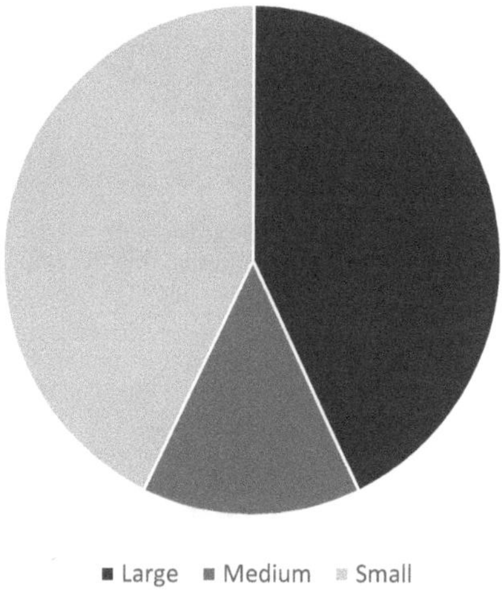

Figure 2.6 Investment size distribution in the utility industry.

Method of analysis

THEMATIC

Also known as 'classic content analysis', *thematic analysis* inductively analyses qualitative data which may involve multiple analytic techniques. However, it typically moves beyond a content level analysis of words or phrases to "focus on identifying and describing both implicit and explicit ideas within the data"

(Guest, MacQueen & Namey 2012:10). To assist with conducting thematic analysis, and to manage the large volume of data systematically, NVivo Software was used to code data into a category (thematic) system.

Data interpretation

The sustainability assessment framework detailed earlier provided the key structure for how the qualitative data would be categorised and coded. The views and opinions of the decision-makers on each of the sustainability assessment stages were grouped together to provide a better understanding of their decision-making process. Across the data, as new and unforeseen categories emerged, the qualitative date was grouped together and categorisation completed, with specific words or sentences applied to the different categories (*e.g.*, 'stakeholder engagement'). In this way, key 'themes' emerged as to common practices and decisions throughout the sustainability assessment process.

Coding the data

Codes are defined as specific elements within the data that relate to specific characteristics (Ezzy 2002; Strauss 1987). The process of assigning specific codes to certain texts was informed by the data itself (data-driven coding) as well as what should be expected given the stage of sustainability assessment (theory-driven coding). Data-driven coding allows codes to arise from the data pool, minimising theoretical interference. On the other hand, a theory-driven approach means the researcher must keep the project's research questions and known theoretical frameworks in mind when coding the data (Patton 2002).

The data first coded related to each research question. This allowed essential information about the investment and organisational characteristics (size, number of employees, headquarter location, use of specific standards and guidelines) to be captured. The rigour of the coding process was further increased through the use of specific software and tools, which involve conducting word-frequency analysis and thematic pattern recognition. Such tools provided further insight of the responses from the 92 personnel and ensured that multiple themes were identified through the assistance of NVivo. The coding process, which has been described in the literature as non-linear and "often confusing, frustrating and somewhat chaotic" (Ezzy 2002:90), was computer-analysed to reduce the risk of code duplication (Strauss & Corbin 1990). This was achieved through constant tracking and comparison. The main themes and sub-themes (code names) that emerged from the data categorisation process are presented in Figure 2.7.

A study on coding saturation by Guest, Bunce and Johnson (2006) noted that a large majority of codes can be identified after a relatively small number of interviews (12). In the context of this study, with 92 personnel involved in interviews, suggesting that all content would have been thoroughly captured by these codes.

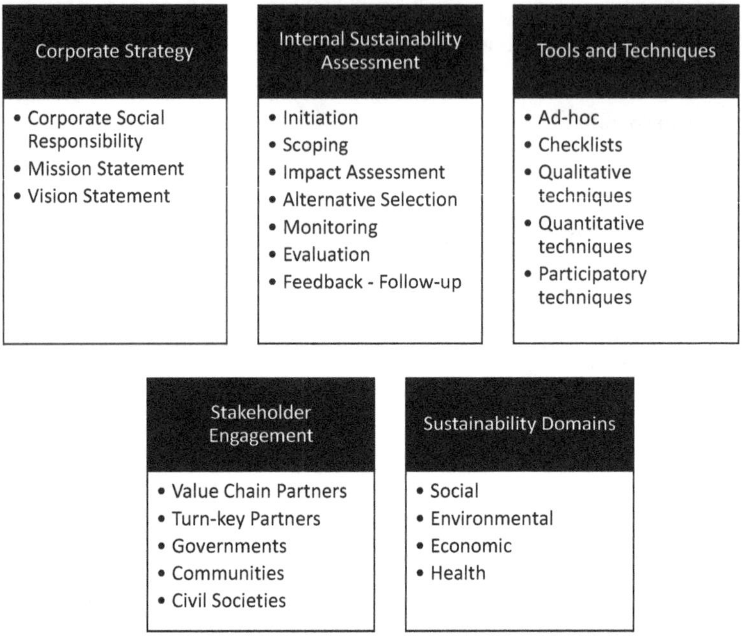

Figure 2.7 Themes and sub-themes (codes) from data categorisation.

Computer-assisted qualitative data analysis

CAQDAS was beneficial in managing the volume of data (*i.e.,* 9000 pages of text). One of the key advantages of CAQDAS is the standardisation and formalisation of processes. Sinkovics and Alfoldi (2012) claim that CAQDAS relies on the same principles as classic qualitative analysis but offers further scalability. Coding and unitising the data still requires the effort of the researcher, but CAQDAS offers researchers new capabilities through overview matrices and visual models to identify relationships between the main identified themes. Some researchers have argued that CAQDAS creates the risk of the fragmentation of qualitative material, which could mislead the interpretation of the qualitative data (Bryman & Bell 2015, Fielding, Lee & Lee 1998). However, this risk is small in comparison with the advantages of CAQDAS, and the "formalisation of processes which contribute to more reliable research findings" (Sinkovics, Penz & Ghauri 2008:695).

Additionally, the digitalisation process, which occurs at the very beginning of the CAQDAS procedure, provides additional support for data interpretation (Huberman & Miles 2002). Sinkovics, Penz and Ghauri (2008) argue that "computer software helps to support researchers in the analytical process of coding and analysing textual data, makes data easily accessible to collaborators and thus strengthens credibility, replicability and substance of research results" (709). The use of a platform such as CAQDAS is also supported by the call from Yin (2003) for strong protocols and tracking processes to validate qualitative research and improve the rigour of qualitative studies.

Summary

This chapter provided a conceptual sustainability assessment framework that underpins this research study, useful for guiding the examination of sustainability practices of MNEs in the Philippines. From the existing empirical evidence available, this conceptual framework is based on three distinct stages including: (i) Issue Identification and Prioritisation, (ii) Impact Assessment and (iii) Impact Monitoring and Follow-up. The six steps across these stages comprise: Initiation, Scoping, Impact Analysis, Alternative Selection, Monitoring and Evaluation, and Feedback and Follow-up.

The literature review identified key gaps that have motivated the current study, which is guided by addressing the following research questions:

Research Question One:

- How are sustainability assessments used by businesses in the Philippines?

Research Question Two:

- How are tools and techniques utilised across the different stages and steps of the sustainability assessment?

The methodological framework used to underpin this study was explained including the strategies and data collection methods utilised in this research. Essentially, this study adopted a case study approach to investigate answers to these questions and conducted a substantive qualitative investigation using primary and secondary data to determine current organisational practices on conducting sustainability assessments.

3 Issue identification and prioritisation stage

Introduction

This chapter presents the findings of our investigation as they pertain to stage one of a sustainability assessment: Issue Identification and Prioritisation. The discussion in Chapter 2 revealed that this stage allows decision-makers to identify and select the most important sustainability issues to be addressed in the project. Comprising two steps of initiation and scoping, the practices of MNEs in the Philippines were revealed during interviews with key decision-makers. The key areas revealed from analysing this data are presented. This forms the first main result of the study, which will be followed by our findings as they relate to the next two steps of Impact Assessment and Monitoring and Follow-up (see Figure 3.1).

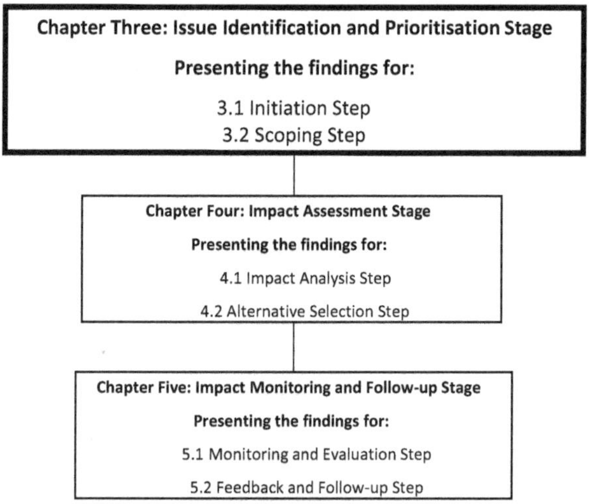

Figure 3.1 The three stages of sustainability assessments: findings of the current study per step.

Initiation step

To recap, this step involves initiating the sustainability assessment and begins the process by identifying the breadth of sustainability issues to be considered by organisations. This is particularly oriented around the identification and articulation of the broad sustainability goals for organisations. This is generally informed by each project's specific context, including the size of the project, location and industry.

The analysis of organisational activities of MNEs in the Philippines that are undertaken during this step are presented. This is drawn from both interview data and relevant secondary data sources. Two main sections will capture the findings: first, MNEs were classified as being either 'World Class', adopting 'International Standards' or as being 'Compliance Driven'. These classifications provide high-level insights into the general practices of these organisations from the different levels of activity and their industry-specific context. Second, the key management practices and sustainability considerations of decision-makers for MNEs, as revealed from analysing interview data, are presented. This includes the main areas identified by participants across social, environmental and economic dimensions, as well as the key tools and techniques adopted. The chapter will conclude with a summary of the key results from the data analysis undertaken.

Practice classification of MNEs – initiation

In reviewing the practices of MNEs in the Philippines, at a Broad level, it was found that approximately 38% (n = 9/24) of organisations fall within the 'World Class' category, 25% (n = 6/24) fall within the International Standards category and 38% (n = 9/24) of organisations can be classified as being 'Compliance Driven' (see Figure 3.2). Organisations were classified based on the analysis of the interviews with participating decision-makers, internal annual reports and publicly available documents. This finding reveals that participating organisations were equally split across the different classifications which has several implications. First, from a research lens, the data obtained for this study will likely capture the broad activities occurring in the field beyond the sample taken and thus findings will have both breadth and depth, increasing their relevance.

Second, two-thirds of organisations are operating beyond minimum compliance requirements suggesting that host regulations are not generally keeping pace with practice. Third, over one-third of organisations are only complying with the minimum standards set by regulations or their practices are not holistically engaging with international standards. The latter was deemed to be occurring if organisations were adopting ad hoc international standards that did not comprehensively funnel down to informing their identification of sustainability factors, which is a critical component of the initiation step.

Participating organisations were drawn from three industries (mining, manufacturing and utilities) and so, of interest, was to determine whether this influenced the extent to which organisations undertook sustainability assessment

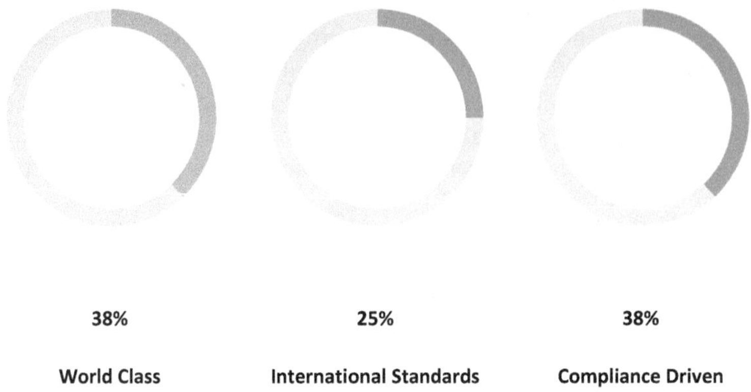

Figure 3.2 Practice classification – initiation.

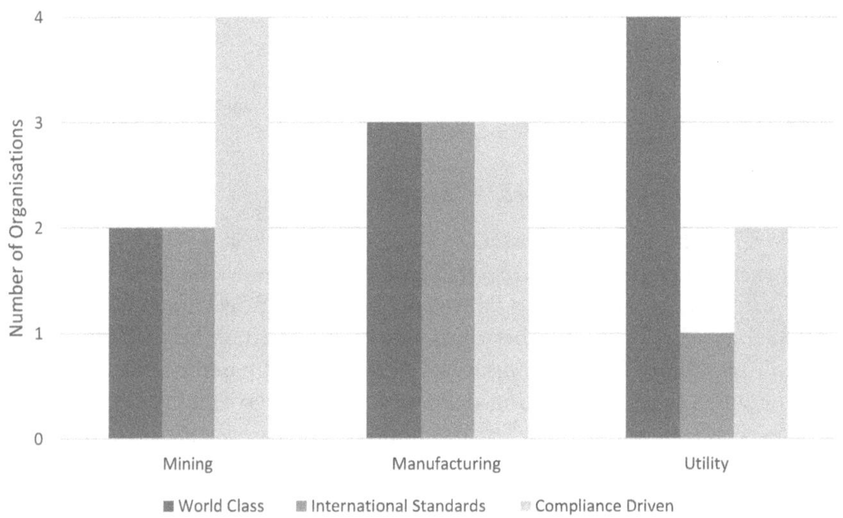

Figure 3.3 Number of organisations within each industry per practice classification – initiation.

activities during the initiation step. The following bar chart captures the breakdown of organisations per industry and 'practice' classification (see Figure 3.3). It is evident that, across industries, a variety of practices are implemented to varying standards. However, it is also evident that the utility sector has the greatest number of organisations embracing World Class sustainability practices for 'initiation', with 57% (n = 4/7) of organisations classified into this group. These organisations tend to adopt global sustainability guidelines or, at the very least, meet a range of international standards when undertaking their initiation process. The higher level of regulatory adherence evident within the utility sector can be explained by the large investment size of projects required in this sector. This was often linked to the requirement to leverage external funding and/or greater local scrutiny of their activities.

For the mining sector, a higher proportion of organisations were found to be using only the regulatory requirements as a basis for identifying key issues to consider in their sustainability assessments, with 50% (n = 4/8) falling into this category. Thus, being Compliance Driven clearly dominates the practices of mining organisations. This focus on regulations for mining organisations primarily reflected the pressure they experienced in meeting environmental certification requirements (embedded within the Environmental Compliance Certificate (ECC) processes) and the requirement to develop Social Development Management Plans (SDMP). Hence, organisations being 'compliance driven' in the mining industry reflects, at least in part, the more comprehensive regulatory requirements in the Philippines for this sector.

With regards to the manufacturing sector, three organisations were assigned into each 'practice category'. The organisations within the World Class category were observed to have the most significant global footprint when it comes to sustainability with a focus on adopting global processes and practices for their operations. This was reflected in their general business practices as well as in their sustainability approaches. All manufacturing organisations were focussed on meeting, at a minimum, the requirements of the government around the environmental compliance certification and some sub-sector regulatory requirements specific to manufacturing processes, and two-thirds went beyond these requirements.

With this broad overview established, the following section explores how these findings translate into actual practices within the initiation step. In particular, the findings will present the key sustainability issues identified by these organisations, and how this differs across different classification categories, through an analysis of exemplar cases.

Management practices during initiation

This section will outline the specific practices and sustainability issues considered by organisations across each classification category. This will include an examination of the role of the corporate headquarters (in the MNE's home country); sustainability commitments, frameworks and policies; and the role of regulation in directing their practices. In each of the following sub-sections, a broad overview of the general practices of organisations in each category is provided before moving to a more in-depth analysis of an exemplar case from each category.

Practices of World Class organisations during initiation

A key component of organisations within the World Class category was the comprehensive way in which decision-makers identified key sustainability issues that should be considered within their operations. This included drawing from broad issue areas associated with global sustainability platforms, comprehensive sustainability-related policies and significant previous project experience that informed the decision-making processes. Stakeholder engagement was regularly conducted by organisations within this category which helped to shed light on the local context regarding important sustainability issues.

WORLD CLASS MINING

One of the most comprehensive, and complex, examples of an organisation within the World Class category was PH01, a major mining company which was in the process of initiating its operations within the Philippines. Two key executives involved in the project planning were interviewed, as well as a range of key subsidiary representatives including the CEO, COO and Community Relations Manager. This, along with extensive secondary data and reporting on their operations, provided detailed insights into their sustainability practices during the initiation step.

The project planning executives identified their own previous experience as being a critical component in the early stages of the mining development. Both executives were based in the headquarter operations and were veterans of the industry (with over two decades of experience each). They had previously conducted similar developments across Australasia and South America. This breadth of experience informed how both executives went about establishing a comprehensive and systematic process of examining sustainability issues. This is also reflected in how they managed the complexities of the project. Not only was this mining venture a very large investment, but it also involved a range of joint venture partners, local stakeholders and international partners who were involved in financing the operations.

Beyond the regulatory requirements of the government, the organisation had to consider International Finance Corporation (IFC) social and environmental standards, GRI standards, the UNGC and a range of other international standards. Moreover, the organisation also needed to conform to all of the corporate sustainability goals and objectives of its joint venture partners. This led to a process of broadly screening potential issues within the local context utilising a range of global sustainability platforms, but also adapting this to ensure a range of different sustainability issues were considered to account for different corporate perspectives. The breadth of organisations involved, their goals and their adoption of international standards generated complexities in how the decision-making team went about identifying issues for the project. As one of the executives reflected:

> [This] gives us an interesting problem: do you do your studies and your applications to be granted legal permission to proceed; or do you do your applications and your studies to international standards; or both? And the real answer is 'both' because on the one hand you don't want to overwhelm the regulators with information that they're not expecting to see or have no

> context from which to process it. At the same time, you will not finance your project if you haven't achieved international standards.

In practice, it was revealed that different partners to the joint venture split the formal requirements for undertaking different parts of the assessment (*i.e.*, EIA, SIA, HIA, FPIC, etc.), although it was clear that this all came together to inform how the team mapped the sustainability-related issues they were going to consider. This was also influenced by the fact that the organisation was utilising international financing for the project (which is a common practice for the joint venture partners involved). Drawing on international financing reinforced the importance of identifying the full breadth of sustainability issues and meeting globally accepted standards. One of the respondents further reflected upon this, saying:

> When you go to get some financing for something such as this, it doesn't matter which type of financing you're going for. People from the investment community and the banking community are going to want to understand the standards under which you will operate are globally acceptable. Because the last thing you'd want is the Human Rights Watch in Montreal having a crack at you during the construction period with delaying or causing the cessation of your development because you haven't crossed of the T's. So it's a difficult project because you've got so many different and often conflicted standards that you have to comply with. But the way to manage that is you have smart people who have done it before.

In terms of process, there was a strong emphasis on first considering the broadest issues held by the value chain, from the national economic impact of the construction and operation of the mine to local issues and concerns. This was reflected in the sustainability issues that were considered beyond the mine, where it was clear that they considered issues from both upstream and downstream connections which elucidated how their operations would affect local communities. They also prioritised utilising Filipino companies to provide the major components of their value chain. As one executive reflected:

> We've already outsourced that so in terms of a theme for development of this project... you have other Filipino corporates building, owning and operating projects supporting infrastructure and facilities. But there's a great deal of potential here to bring more Filipino money and interest into this project than just us.

Incorporating local businesses was considered at all levels, from major components of their value chain, such as power generation and infrastructure development, down to local communities that could be integrated into the actual production requirements. For example, providing local produce to feed workers, as articulated by one participant, included: "*Drivers, cleaners, cooks, chefs, growers of chickens, vegetable growers, suppliers of other hardware and equipment, suppliers of clothing, airline providers, taxi drivers, hoteliers, restaurateur"*. The importance of local sourcing across the value chain of their operations was evident throughout the initiation step. Though here, many sustainability issues revolved around the socio-economic empowerment of local communities.

Decision-makers revealed that this broad identification process was central to the success of the entire assessment, as the initiation step laid the foundation for subsequent steps. This was evident in a mind-mapping session conducted with the executives, in which they detailed the intricate links between all the sustainability issue categories they incorporated into their planning. They then linked these back to a range of government regulations and international standards. Figure 3.4 below depicts the mind map utilised by the team in PH01.

Within each 'box', the organisation explored various issues further. For example, within the 'environmental' category, the organisation considered issues such as those related to: mine water management, potential impacts on water resources, rehabilitation and closure of the site and the distribution of economic benefits. Stakeholders were also involved during this process, identifying issues such as the potential impacts on communities, biodiversity, visual amenity and air quality. In addition to a stakeholder engagement programme, a range of processes and Impact Assessments were integrated into their planning, including:

- Resettlement planning with residents currently within the proposed mine site
- Seeking Free and Prior Informed Consent (FPIC) from Indigenous communities

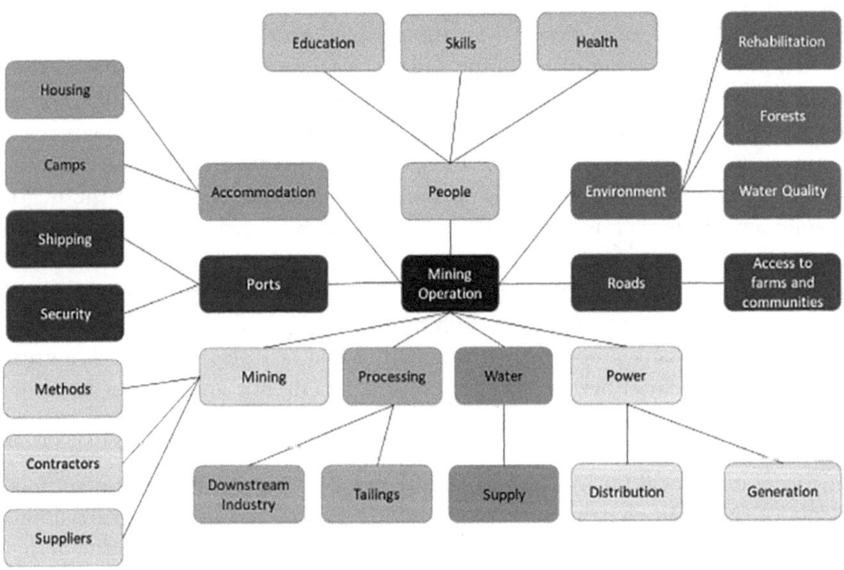

Figure 3.4 Initiation mind map. Adapted from a participating organisation.

- Undertaking a Health Impact Assessment (HIA) with the relevant health agencies and local community stakeholders
- Environmental and Social Impact Assessments
- Initiatives relating to community development programmes

Stakeholder engagement activities played a key role in identifying further issues that required consideration within their operational planning. It also highlighted the influence that globally accepted sustainability standards, local regulations and experience had in bringing together a holistic view of the sustainability issues to be addressed. This was most broadly characterised by a technical mapping of sustainability issues across the organisation's value chain, stakeholder engagement to contextualise these issues across the different dimensions of sustainability and a holistic alignment of these issues with different sustainability platforms and local regulations.

Practices of organisations adopting international standards during initiation

Organisations within the International Standards category tended to incorporate practices and policies from their international headquarters, holistically integrate different international standards and practices, or clearly go beyond what was required under the minimum standards set by the regulatory context. PH13 is an excellent example of an organisation within the manufacturing sector that extended its initial identification and engagement of sustainability issues beyond what was required by regulatory compliance. Before exploring the broader activities they undertook, it is worth describing the regulatory context that underpinned their identification of sustainability issues.

The organisation was required to obtain an ECC, undertake an Environmental Impact Assessment and comply with the *Clean Air Act* (as well as the standard operational requirements and laws). When examining the environmental aspect, the organisation appeared to focus on how their superior technology could mitigate many environmental issues. This notion was directed from the headquarter operations of one of the joint venture partners, which had significant experience in the industry and had developed comprehensive practices to conform within its home country regulations. Thus, they were familiar with requirements regarding a range of environmental issues, including air emissions from the production process (*e.g.*, smoke and dust), water usage in the production processes and noise, among others).

Respondents from this organisation made detailed references throughout the interviews to the lower environmental standards in the Philippines, which required significantly less of the manufacturing operations. Instead or merely complying with these lower requirements, the organisation leveraged its adoption of superior technology which addressed a range of very specific environmental issues and impacts within their production process. On top of this technical approach to exceeding the local regulatory requirements, the organisation also wanted to ensure that the local community was satisfied that its operations would not have an impact on local environmental conditions. As one respondent reflected:

> It was also a way of telling our neighbours that we care. And we're glad we did it because the surrounding community are happy.

As part of their stakeholder engagement, the organisation undertook mandatory consultations with the local community by holding public hearings. This was conducted through a third-party environmental consultancy group, which did an initial identification and scoping of key issues within the community, as well as documenting key requirements from a regulatory perspective. The organisation drew upon external expertise as it wanted to gather more insights from the local community, and the consultancy group already had excellent connections and insights into the needs of '*these people, the homeowners, the officers, the local government officials, the barangay captain, police stations, Bureau of Fire...*'. This also opened pathways for the organisation to establish more informal communications with different stakeholders as they grappled with locally relevant issues, as well as to get informal feedback on their planning activities.

Beyond the mandatory requirements, where it was evident that the organisation was exceeding local regulations, it also undertook a product life cycle assessment of potential issues and impacts, with a focus on reducing their environmental footprint. As noted above, this focussed not only on leveraging new technologies in the company's processes to reduce energy use but also on reducing emissions and the use of product input resources. The company also looked upstream within its processes, trying to minimise the use of 'new' resources and aiming to re-use recycled inputs into its processes. This had an effect downstream in the post-consumption section of the company's product life cycle, as reducing environmental impact in this way was also linked with the disposal of its product.

From an economic standpoint, the organisation initially appeared to have a very focussed analysis around the financial viability of its operations. It held a series of negotiations with the government to extend incentives for its operations in the form of tax breaks. They sought such tax breaks, as the respondents reflected, due to the competitive nature of their manufacturing sub-sector, which at the time was under significant pressure from large-scale international producers. However, whilst negotiating with the central government, the organisation sought to chart the full value chain of its operations and consider how local partners could be integrated. As one respondent reflected:

> Expanding actually means expanding the scope of our business. We have third party organizations or service providers, such as janitorial, packing, industrial assistance, finished goods movement, so we created employment for them because we expanded the business.

These comments reveal that, although it is a requirement of the ECC to consider the integration of local communities, particularly in terms of employment within their operations, PH13 sought to take this further. It did so by more fully considering the integration of local business partners, both upstream (sourcing production inputs) and downstream (distributors and other service providers). In cases where the local standards and qualifications were not up to the international standards they usually followed, the organisation sought to upgrade and upskill partners and employees alike rather than lower their own standards.

Practices of Compliance Driven organisations during initiation

A dominant feature across organisations classified within the Compliance Driven category was a reliance on local environmental regulations in directing the initiation of sustainability issues. This was specifically linked with the ECC, which was a requirement across sectors in the Philippines. The incorporation of social development programmes was also evident across organisational practices within this category, consistent with the regulatory requirement to implement social development and management plans. Here, organisations were required to contribute an element of their revenues to address social issues, and this usually resulted in the organisations identifying a range of social issues in the area surrounding their operations and selecting the most pertinent ones to address. This often translated into corporate social responsibility programmes to direct their activities in engaging with the community. Beyond this, their planning and analysis was largely constrained to determining whether their operations were going to be financially feasible.

An ideal example of an organisation in the Compliance Driven category is PH24, a large MNE from the utility industry. This organisation specially focussed on the environmental component of its initial identification of sustainability issues. PH24 followed the typical environmental impact 'screening' procedures set by the government (DENR). This was also linked to the organisation's headquarter operations, which had a specialist department dealing with environmental issues within its decision-making processes. It also considered an international standard, ISO140001, on environmental management systems. This international standard was only applied to the organisation's environmental practices.

Overall, however, the organisation emphasised the importance of a compliance approach in its planning and decision-making. A specific team from headquarter operations ensured that it complied with all local laws and regulations. A similarly strong emphasis on local regulatory requirements was evident in the social aspect of its initial planning. This was reflected upon by the Community and Public Relations Officer, who stated; "*the social development program is a requirement of the law, [requiring]...us to engage with community or what we call our social entry...*". While this is a requirement for the organisation, it appears that there was a desire to "*beyond environmental requirements*" (Community and Public Relations Officer).

This led to the development of a Corporate Social Responsibility (CSR) programme, which aimed to respond to local community concerns or requests. By engaging with local communities through a multi-partite team (a multidisciplinary team), the organisation sought to identify significant concerns or areas the local community wanted it to address through its social initiatives. The interview data, together with secondary data collected on this organisation, seem to indicate that this community engagement was more about convincing the community that the proposed power plant was environmentally friendly. This included providing information on the use of water sources, by-products of the power generation, and different types of emissions coming from the operations.

The community engagement outcomes and the development of the CSR programme produced a broad set of areas that the organisation would contribute towards annually (this is in line with government requirements for local contributions). This included five broad categories: (1) Health, Sanitation and Nutrition (*e.g.*, Doctor visits to local community; donation of medicine; dental missions, *etc.*); (2) Education (*e.g.*, donation of educational materials to schools; supporting day care centres; scholarships to local students); (3) Environment (*e.g.*, landscape beautification and coastal clean-up); (4) Livelihood (*e.g.*, skills development training; assistance to local communities); and (5) Special Projects (this appeared to be an open category).

Beyond the environmental and social domains listed above, which were clearly linked with regulatory requirements, economic sustainability largely revolved around decisions regarding investment. For example, the organisation evaluated local market dynamics to determine the supply and demand for the energy sector in the Philippines. However, this activity appeared to be underpinned by a desire to determine the financial feasibility of the proposed investment, rather than to determine how to have a greater, positive economic impact within the communities in which it operated. This position was justified by the CEO of the subsidiary, who explained that this orientation had to be emphasised, as the organisation was not receiving any "*sovereign guarantee… [so] it was [a] fully market based [decision] while other power plant investors had bidding guarantee[s]*".

In summary, the evidence collected during this study showed that a clear Issue Identification process is undertaken by organisations when planning new projects. The study also found that the depth of Issue Identification varied greatly across organisations operating at different levels (categories). Organisations operating within the World Class category appeared to adopt a holistic approach to sustainability assessment during the initiation step, basing their practices and decisions on international guidelines such as IFC, or headquarter policies, where decision-makers considered environmental, social and economic issues. Organisations operating within the International Practices category focussed on social and environmental issues, and considered the impact of the planned project across the whole the value chain. These organisations provided interesting insights into methods of including the local community in the Issue Identification step. Lastly, the data suggests that organisations within the Compliance Driven category, primarily considered environmental issues directed through the regulatory requirements (ECC). Evidence of social engagement was also found, but only through broad CSR goals and linked with SDMP regulatory requirements.

The next section will provide insights into the tools and techniques applied by organisations to identify sustainability issues.

Tools and techniques for the initiation step

This section will explore the key tools and techniques adopted by organisations when conducting the initiation step in a sustainability assessment. Two areas are presented: first, the existing regulatory base that directs the core activities of all organisations when undertaking this step will be discussed. Second, the key tools and techniques utilised by organisations that exceeded the regulatory requirements will be presented.

Regulatory basis

The national regulatory framework in the Philippines provides organisations with specific guidance on the identification of environmental issues and impacts. These are the minimum requirements for all organisations when considering their initiation practices. The prevalence of organisations adopting this as a minimum standard is, in part, due to the sampling frame. All organisations that participated in this study were registered and endorsed by the Board of Investment in the Philippines. As a condition of this endorsement, they were required to conform to all laws and regulations directing their business activities. Regulations in the Philippines require all projects that have the potential for significant impact on the natural environment to obtain an ECC and establish a Multipartite Monitoring Team (MMT). This is associated with the regulatory requirements and managed through the Environmental Management Bureau – Department of Environment and Natural Resources (EMB-DENR). This process is part of a broader Environmental Impact Statement that is also required for new commercial projects.

The national regulation for the Philippines Environmental Impact Statement System (PEISS) classifies projects into one of four main categories. These include environmentally critical projects, non-environmentally critical projects, environmental enhancement or direct mitigation and not covered, as detailed in Table 3.1.

As part of this regulatory process, the first step for an organisation is to determine the classification for their project. All of the projects within this study fall into Category A or B. Therefore, it was mandatory for organisations to obtain an ECC. Upon closer examination, the definition of an 'Environmentally Critical Project' is quite broad and not clearly identified within the PEISS (although examining the EIS Screening Forms[1] provides more clarity on how this is actually defined). The following checklist, based on sectors/types of projects, must be evaluated by organisations to determine whether their project requires an EIS[2]:

- Agricultural Plantation
- Food, Food By-products & Beverages Manufacturing

Table 3.1 EMB-DENR issue requirements

Category		*Applied to*	*Documents Required for ECC/CNC Application*	*Office to Process and Decide*
A: Environmentally critical projects	**A-1**: New	Co-located projects	Programmatic EIS*	EMB Central Office
		Single project	EIS	EMB Central Office
	A-2: Existing and to be expanded, modified and/or rehabilitated	Co-located projects	Programmatic EPRMP*	EMB Central Office
	A-3: Operating without ECC		(In case programmatic monitoring data are available)*	
		Single project	EPRMP in case monitoring data are available EIS if no monitoring data are available	EMB Central Office
B Non-environmentally critical projects		Co-located projects	Programmatic EIS*	EMB Regional Office in the region where the proposed project is located
	B-1: New	Single project	**Programmatic** EIS* IEE checklist	
	B-2: Existing and to be expanded, modified and/or rehabilitated	Single project	**EPRMP**	EMB Regional Office in the region where the proposed project is located
	B-3: Operating without ECC		EPRMP checklist	
		Co-located project	PEPRMP*	EMB Regional Office in the region where the proposed project is located
C: Environmental enhancement or direct mitigation		Co-located or single projects	Project description (Parts 1 and II) *(To confirm non-coverage or further classify as either Category A or B)*	EMB Regional Office in the region where the proposed project is located
D: Not covered			Project description (Part I only) Project prior to 1982 – Proof of project implementation prior to 1982 without expansion/alteration/modification shall also be submitted (if applying for CNC)	EMB Regional Office in the region where the proposed project is located

Adapted from: http://eia.emb.gov.ph/ecc-applications-and-issuance/requirements-for-securing-ecc/eis-screening-forms/.
* **Note**: (*) – optional, subject to laws, rules and regulations.

- Forestry Projects
- Hydropower & Dam Projects
- Mining Projects
- Non-Food Manufacturing
- Sanitary Landfill Projects
- Thermal Power Plants

If a planned project falls under one of the above-mentioned categories, the organisation proposing the project (proponent) must complete an EIS that meets the approval of the EMB-DENR. The current regulatory framework classifies projects according to the nature of its activities, while specific issues are identified during the scoping process. For example, mining projects fall within the EMB-DENR list, and thus mining organisations would be required to undertake an ECC. The specific environmental issues that must be considered under the EIS system would be identified as part of the scoping step. It should be noted that while the ECC grants permission to organisations to pursue a particular project, it is also mandatory for the project proponent to propose an MMT within 60 days of the submission of the ECC. This explains why a higher proportion of mining MNEs in our sample are so focussed on regulatory compliance.

For the next category of projects – non-environmentally critical projects – the following list of broad industry classifications directs organisations towards undertaking an Initial Environmental Examination (IEE):

- Batching and Crushing Plants
- Building Projects
- Cemetery and other Funeral Facilities
- Fisheries, Aquaculture Projects
- Food, Food By-products and Beverages Manufacturing
- Generic – Other types of Projects
- Irrigation, Flood Control & Minor Dam Projects
- Livestock & Poultry Projects
- Non-Food Manufacturing Plants
- Resorts and other Tourism-Leisure Projects
- Roads & Bridges
- Subdivision & Housing Projects
- Waste Management Projects
- Water Supply Projects

If the proposed project falls within one of these categories and an IEE must be produced (which is essentially a simplified EIA), then the project proponent must identify potential adverse environmental impacts and provide an assurance that the project will not require comprehensive environmental studies. This simplifies the process of acquiring the ECC.

For projects classified into the last two categories (C or D), the project proponent must apply for a Certificate of Non-Coverage (CNC), providing assurance to the government that the project does not need any further investigation. This requires a detailed project description and the necessary evidence that the project does not have any adverse impacts on the environment. Since the focus of this study is with large MNEs that have the potential for greater, negative impact, none of the participating organisations had to undertake a CNC, and were instead required to provide much more detail for the EIS.

Whilst the vast majority of industries operate within the framework of the PEISS, mining operations are also subject to the Executive Order No. 79, commonly known as the *Mining Act of 1995*. This national regulation enforces the operational boundaries within which mining activities can take place. A key aspect of Executive Order No. 79 is the requirement to implement a Free Prior and Informed Consent (FPIC) process, which is included in the *Indigenous People's Rights Act* (IPRA; Republic Act No. 8371, Republic of Philippines 1997). Under the *Mining Act*, mining organisations must undertake and obtain the FPIC from local Indigenous populations for the exploration, development and use of natural resources. If an organisation fails to properly engage with Indigenous populations, the project can be stopped or suspended, based solely on the grounds that consultation was not satisfactory. The participant organisations in the current study had either received, or were in the process of receiving, an FPIC. Interestingly, these organisations often used voluntary frameworks and processes that exceeded the requirements of the FPIC to engage with Indigenous populations.

It appears that the current regulatory framework in the Philippines provides clear guidelines for organisational operations, particularly as they pertain to the environment. Under the PEISS regulation, social considerations are only partially addressed through mandatory SDMP. SDMP are social development funds managed by the project proponent and monitored by the EMB-DENR. Evidence suggests that SDMPs are required within large development projects. This study found examples of SDMPs for participant organisations across all three industries, but particularly within the mining and utility sector where there were higher levels of substantial investments and regulatory requirements.

In this review of regulations that influence projects and sustainability assessments, it appears that regulation seems to largely direct organisations towards the PEISS at the initiation step, and is focussed on critical environmental impacts. Beyond this, regulation has provided additional guidance for stakeholder engagement through the MMT, and in the mining industry, through the FPIC. However, while all organisations within the sample complied with national regulations, the data suggests that organisations classified in the World Class and International Standards categories go beyond the national regulatory framework, utilising voluntary techniques developed from internal and external guidelines.

Voluntary techniques

The results so far reveal that most MNEs in the Philippines largely adopt voluntary techniques to direct their initiation step, and thus go beyond the regulatory requirements. In particular, the key voluntary techniques that have been identified through examining organisational practices tend to be qualitative in nature. These tools range from regulatory-inspired checklists to more comprehensive materiality analyses (these were explained in Chapter 2). In addition, it was evident that stakeholder engagement varies from the simple and ad hoc, through to being comprehensive and inclusive.

CHECKLISTS

The evidence suggests that checklists are the predominant tool adopted by organisations during the identification of sustainability issues. While respondents did not directly mention the use of 'checklists' *per se*, the described processes they used are highly aligned with the methods commonly used when conducting checklists. The checklist process essentially entails developing a comprehensive list of established sustainability issues and impacts, then using a range of methods to identify what should be considered within a new project. Some of these lists draw on pre-existing requirements (such as those linked with global sustainability platforms) or policies of the organisation regarding what should be considered, or emerge through the methods utilised for collecting data.

Less-structured methods for developing lists include conducting brainstorming sessions or focus groups. For these methods, decision-makers would identify all of the possible issues they can, which are subsequently refined across the different sustainability dimensions, such as environmental, operational, social *etc.*). This is illustrated below, showing the categorisation of issues across key sustainability categories, adapted from one used by a participant organisation (Table 3.2).

For this study, it was found that organisations adopting more comprehensive practices often used Checklists as a starting point or a method to contextualise the issues, before proceeding to more established lists that may have been derived

Table 3.2 Example of a project checklist

Economic	*Environmental*	*Social*	*Labour*	*Human Rights*
Use of materials	Use of materials	Impact on local communities	Workforce diversity	Child labour
Water usage	Water usage	Land use disputes and compensations	Health and safety	Compulsory labour
Biodiversity disturbance	Biodiversity disturbance	Resettlements	Education and training	Indigenous people
Greenhouse gas emission	Greenhouse gas emission	Compliance with law and regulation	Compensation	Corruption
Energy consumption	Energy consumption			
Rehabilitation	Rehabilitation			

Adapted from a participating organisation.

from their commitments to global sustainability platforms or corporate policies. This more comprehensive approach was evident in a range of organisations (including PH01, PH04, PH05, PH10, PH18), where the checklists utilised were adapted from key international guidelines, such as GRI or IFC frameworks. For example, at PH01, checklists were established through the internal risk management process, taking a multi-disciplinary approach:

> The types of things you'll see on our strategic risk registers are things like major environmental spill and that's assessed. Potential for an employee incurring a serious injury, all the way through to we've only got a five year mine life, all the way through input costs pressures. So we take a very balanced approach to setting up these registers in considering every single aspect of the business, not just from the economic side but also understanding things like socio-political risks all the way through to what potential new legislation is coming at us... So these registers are a lot more holistic than just looking and saying 'what happens if our plant falls over or what happens if the gold price goes to $1,000'.
>
> (PH01)

Through the analysis of the secondary data, various types of risk registers were identified. The key design features of the risk registers usually incorporated the risk type, dimensions and comments. Taken from an organisational perspective, risk dimensions were usually split across the probability of the risk occurring and the severity of its impact if it did occur. Table 3.3 provides a visual representation of an example of a risk register template used by a participant organisation.

STAKEHOLDER ENGAGEMENT

When examining the stakeholder engagement involved in these different approaches, decision-makers interviewed in this study revealed that the most comprehensive approaches enable key stakeholders and technical experts to share

Table 3.3 Example of a risk register

Risk Type	*Dimensions*		*Comments*
	Probability • 5 Almost certain • 4 Likely • 3 Possible • 2 Unlikely • 1 Rare	**Severity** **1 to 10 Scale:** **1 Insignificant – 10 Catastrophic**	
Health and safety			
Environmental damage			
Raw material market price			

Adapted from participating organisations.

their insights into key issues that need to be considered. They also revealed that stakeholder identification and engagement was central to the initiation activities. For example, in the case of PH05, determining the stakeholders that would be involved was a core process undertaken, before considering any sustainability issues. Their process considered its own involvement as well as the methods of engagement, potential impacts and interests of stakeholders to be included. This was explained by a decision-maker:

> [O]ne of the first processes you go through is identifying first of all your stakeholders and then you start going through a process of profiling them. How much impact do they have, how much interest do they actually have and once you start getting through that process of profiling them, then you start sitting down and thinking more strategically as to how we go about the engagement.
>
> (PH05)

The process adopted by PH05 provides greater potential for extracting and utilising stakeholder knowledge to inform the initiation processes and development of sustainability checklists. The involvement of stakeholders enhances the organisation's ability to identify and consider issues/impacts in a way that may not be possible through traditional technical methodologies and may be specific to the cultural, religious, ecological or economic context of the operational area.

Several structured techniques for engaging stakeholders were evident in organisations involved in this study. For example, where relevant stakeholders were identified, engagement and communication strategies developed and reported upon, and the effect of the ongoing identification of potential issues or impacts was incorporated systematically into business planning. High levels of stakeholder engagement and inclusiveness was reflected by the Community Engagement Manager of PH07:

> So, we are very participatory and consultative and understand the concerns of the residents, local executives, barangay officials, [a specific person de-identified], peoples organisations, [a specific organisation de-identified], elders organisations.
>
> (PH07)

In examining the methods for undertaking stakeholder engagement as part of the initiation step, it was also evident that some organisations use local development teams to identify appropriate stakeholders to be included in the process. This was aimed at obtaining better local knowledge, leveraging personnel who better understand and have lived experiences of being in the local community (both internally and externally to the organisation). Essentially, this is viewed as a method for bridging the gap between the local and country-specific context, and the global strategies, approaches or knowledge of the organisation. Acquiring this country-specific knowledge was viewed by participants as a contributing factor to successful project development. A decision-maker of PH19, for example, shared this 'bottom-up' approach of first engaging with the context of where the organisation planned to operate:

> The process is started by the business development people on the ground or in the country that is being considered for expansion. The report of the local business development team goes up to a business development team in the central office [bottom up]. A series of exchanges of data and questions happens between the two groups. Local knowledge from key stakeholders, push for the new business and quality assurance are with [the] local team.
>
> (PH19)

Decision-makers also shared the idea that a 'correct' and 'accurate' identification of stakeholders was often aimed at improving the quality of the initial process. A range of other organisations adopting comprehensive practices used systematic tools that enabled them to screen for possible sustainability issues by first identifying key stakeholders. This was particularly the case with organisations adopting the GRI standards and materiality analyses. The materiality analysis usually unfolded through four key steps:

1 Stakeholder Identification
2 Indicators Identification
3 Survey
4 Ranking Matrix

MATERIALITY ANALYSIS

Materiality analysis was found to be an effective tool for the identification and selection of the most important issues to core business activities and key stakeholders. This included collecting information from both internal and external stakeholders, and identifying the full breadth of key issues that they raise. Each issue is weighted for its importance to both internal and external stakeholders. Those issues deemed most important became the focus throughout the process. Organisations engaging in this materiality analysis tended to execute the first two steps during the initiation step (stakeholder identification and indicator identification), before completing the last two activities during the scoping step (survey and ranking matrix).

STAKEHOLDER CATEGORISATION

Evidence of stakeholder categorisation was found across participating organisations that often engaged with two types of stakeholders:

- Internal stakeholders: includes those directly involved and affected by the proposed project. This may include shareholders, local communities and economic actors, local government and NGOs operating within the region of operations.

- External stakeholders: includes those playing an indirect role in the project, but who can provide specific guidance. Such stakeholders were often represented by national or international project partners and international NGOs.

As a concurrent activity, while undertaking stakeholder categorisation, organisations often begin identifying key sustainability indicators that can be evaluated subsequently in the scoping step. In identifying such sustainability indicators, engaging with these stakeholders groups has been highlighted as essential. This view was shared by multiple respondents, including the key decision-makers of PH12, who emphasised that using such processes is vital for identifying sustainability 'threats' or 'risks' and the likely success of a project:

> Stakeholder engagement is absolutely vital and [so is the] materiality [assessment] and reporting on the things that are of most material risk and importance to the organisation.
>
> (PH12)

This is not, however, a static process that is only undertaken at the start of a sustainability assessment or prior to the commencement of operational activities. Rather, it is a process that is ongoing, for those organisations that are adopting these more comprehensive practices. A materiality analysis helps to frame this engagement with stakeholders, although constant attention to stakeholders is needed in order to renew and reassess new sustainability considerations as operations continue. As the operational manager of PH05 reflected, the cyclical nature of stakeholder engagement is 'never-ending':

> It's a never ending cycle. That's why a stakeholder engagement is so important. You can be blind to potential risks and to potential opportunities in the absence of actually engaging with people but I think that's where a lot of companies have gone wrong. They walk into an area just assuming what the stakeholders would want or would want to see out of a potential project and that's where you can get it horribly wrong.
>
> (PH05)

A range of organisations expressed their belief that negative consequences would arise if they failed to engage with stakeholders during the initial stages of their sustainability assessment. This is particularly the case when particular stakeholders would be affected by the proposed operations of the organisation. In these cases, establishing trust and ensuring effective communication is critical. For example, this was highlighted in the Issue Identification activities and reporting undertaken by PH07, where it was reflected by key decision-makers that:

> [e]xperience is showing that transparency could be the foundation on which trust could be built, and in the process, the stakeholders are discovering that mutual gains could be identified.
>
> (Screening report, PH07)

It appears that voluntary engagement across organisations has various degrees of complexity. For example, analysis reveals that some organisations incorporate social and economic factors into simple checklists whilst having limited engagement with stakeholders. At the other end of the spectrum, a range of organisations showed evidence of using detailed risk management-based checklists or those associated with global sustainability platforms (*i.e.,* GRI standards). Such activities reflect a more comprehensive approach towards the identification of potential adverse effects and issues associated with projects. It is also clear that organisations deploying local teams to identify sustainability issues enjoyed strengthened stakeholder engagement and gained more insights.

A closer inspection of 'who said what' revealed that organisations operating within the World Class category largely utilised materiality analysis, and so had a comprehensive framework to identify key stakeholders and sustainability indicators. These organisations revealed that the materiality analysis provided the foundation for a strong and stable stakeholder engagement process that was key to a successful project initiation.

Summary

In summarising the findings of the first step of the sustainability assessment, it is evident that, in general, organisations identify sustainability issues first and foremost through an examination of, and compliance with, regulatory frameworks. The revised version of the PEISS offers organisations relatively clear guidance regarding the environmental issues and impacts that need to be considered. More specifically, it provides organisations with a clear project activity-based checklist to classify the critical environmental issues and impacts of the project. Although the participants of this study were large MNEs, and were thus required to address more regulatory requirements, many move well beyond the minimum requirements when identifying sustainability issues, particularly as they pertain to social and economic aspects of their operations.

This broadened approach to addressing initiation practices is driven by voluntary actions by organisations. Practices rely heavily on the development of checklists of potential issues that should be considered across different sustainability dimensions. The more comprehensive practices, linked to the use of materiality analysis, demonstrate a concurrent process organisations undertake to engage with stakeholders and to identify issues and associated indicators. This indicates that higher level practices are increasingly moving towards more participatory approaches, driven by the voluntary activities of organisations.

The next section explores the findings of this study relevant to the scoping step, which is the second step of the Issue Identification and Prioritisation Stage.

Scoping step

The scoping step builds on the identified issues established during the initiation step. It prioritises and selects the issues of most significance to the intended project. It allows organisations to focus on the type of issues and impacts that they need to measure, monitor, evaluate and report upon, based on the significance of the issues to stakeholders. It provides a basis for determining the breadth of development impacts considered and addressed, as well as providing a basis for determining the potential quality of the investment for local development.

This section will present the main results of the scoping step. The same structure for presenting the results used for the initiation step will be used here, and for all subsequent steps. Accordingly, this section will first present the classifications of organisations based on their sustainability practices during scoping. Next, the management practices of organisations across each classification will be explored in depth. Further insights will be provided into how participating organisations refined the previously identified sustainability issues through exemplar cases. Following this, the next section will identify and describe the main tools and techniques used by organisations to scope and prioritise key sustainability issues.

Practice classification of MNEs – scoping

When considering the breakdown of organisational practices for scoping, it is evident that the categories of World Class and International Standards dominate their scoping decisions and activities. Some 38% (n = 9/24) of organisations were classified within the World Class category. Likewise, approximately 38% (n = 9/24) of organisations were classified as belonging in the International Standards category. This illustrates an overall prevalence of approaches exceeding compliance by organisations within the sample.

A smaller percentage of organisations (25%, n = 6/24) were classified in the Compliance Driven category due to their scoping practices. This remains a significant proportion of organisations that only comply with the minimum standards set by regulations or have limited considerations beyond these regulatory requirements. Figure 3.5 provides a visual representation of the overall results.

From Figure 3.6 below, it is immediately evident that the utility industry is dominated by World Class practices, while both the mining and manufacturing industries have a higher proportion of organisations falling within the International Standards and Compliance Driven categories.

For the mining industry, 25% (n = 2/8) of organisations were classified into the World Class category (the same two organisations as for the initiation step). The other two categories had an equal number of organisations, with 37% in both. While this is a decrease in the overall number of organisations within the Compliance Driven category compared with the initiation step, there remains a significant number of organisations focussed on only meeting compliance requirements for the key issues at this step. This is particularly the case around the environmental

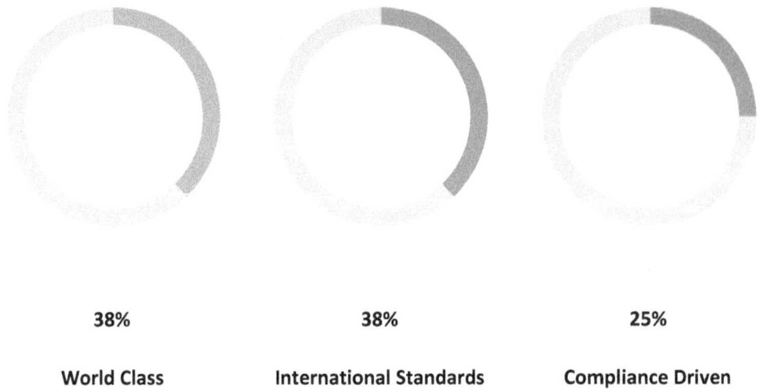

Figure 3.5 Practice classification – scoping.

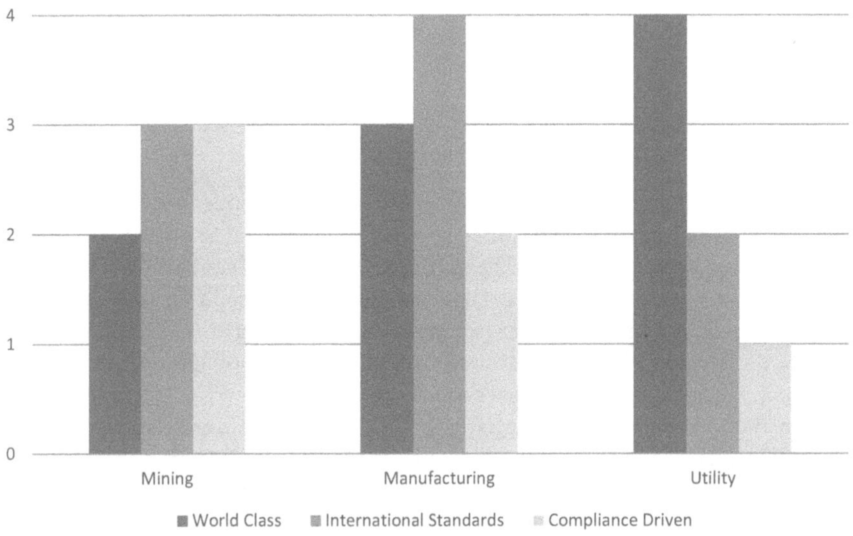

Figure 3.6 Practice classification per industry – scoping.

and social/community dimensions, with significant alignment between organisational practices and the regulatory requirements of the ECC and SDMP.

In terms of the manufacturing sector, a similar pattern emerged, with the same organisations classified at World Class levels for both the initiation and scoping steps. This remained at 33% (n = 3/9) of organisations. However, a shift was evident in the greater number of organisations in the International Standards category compared with the initiation step. Approximately 44% (n = 4/9) of organisations were classified within this category. The remaining two organisations within the manufacturing sector fell into the Compliance Driven category.

Organisations in the utilities sector again dominated the World Class category, comprising 57% (n = 4/7) of the organisations. It appears that organisations operating at this higher level tend to do so across the initiation and scoping steps. Moreover, similar tools and techniques are adopted, in particular, the materiality analysis. The remaining organisations were split across the International Standards (14%, n = 1/7) category and Compliance Driven (28%, n = 2/7) category.

The results presented next will now turn to a more comprehensive examination of organisational practices during scoping across each of the categories.

Management practices during scoping

This section will examine the organisational practices adopted for scoping across the three levels of classifications. It will begin by looking at the general practices of organisations, before providing a detailed examination of exemplar cases of organisations for each category. This will include examining the background behind their investment and the general influences directing their practices before considering the specific scoping practices that they implement.

World class practices during scoping

As was evident in the examination of World Class practices for the initiation step, this step is again dominated by the broader sustainability frameworks, policies and procedures being implemented by organisations. Two key elements emerged as being important aspects in directing their practices: the role of the corporate headquarters and its commitment to global sustainability platforms.

This is particularly evident in PH21, a medium-sized utility company operating in the Philippines. This organisation received significant investment from a regional multinational that played a central role in directing scoping practices at the subsidiary level. According to the subsidiary president and CEO, the organisational philosophy of the headquarter operations is critical in directing how they approach the identification of, and approach towards, sustainability issues. As part of their planning processes for operations, the organisation focussed on a transfer of knowledge and technology that extended beyond a cursory management approach. Rather, it is more about allowing the subsidiary partner to be independent and to see this extend to the local context. The president and CEO reflected on technology transfers from the headquarter operations:

> In every sense, not only technical technology, [but also] … management technology, HR technology, CSR technology, and [in] every sense we need to transfer technology, so that by the year 2028 [the headquarters] will transfer to [subsidiary]. We can primarily give entire assets, including human, to the Philippines and we probably be discussing reaching high. So this is something that I can tell.

The 'transfer' approach is embedded into the organisation's strategy, which emphasises integrating international and global standards into all their operations. This ranges from the management and operating systems to health, safety and environment practices, through to the development of human resources. This is reflected in their aspiration of achieving the highest possible standards of '*good corporate citizenship*'. This starts with ensuring that the investment is financially viable and that the organisation is able to implement its desired strategy.

Once this was evaluated, the organisation ensured that the minimum standards of the government were being met. As part of this, the CEO recognised that there were 50 key conditions that the organisation needed to meet under local regulatory requirements. This included seven that were linked to the ECC, 17 that were linked to local government endorsement conditions (which included environmental and social requirements) and 26 additional conditions for its operation. Beyond this, the organisation planned to operate in an area where an indigenous community would be displaced by its operations. It engaged in a Free, Prior and Informed Consent (FPIC) process to ensure that the affected community had the opportunity to either consent to the land use or refuse permission for operations to go ahead. The regulatory requirement involved a range of different sustainability-related issues that were non-negotiable and needed to be addressed before the organisation was able to operate.

The organisation also adopted the Global Reporting Initiative (GRI) guidelines, that were pertinent for the utilities sector, which contained a range of issues that would need to be addressed. However, another key component of adopting the GRI guidelines is conducting a materiality analysis to determine the most important sustainability issues for key stakeholders. In its sustainability report (a GRI requirement), the organisation delineated the 'boundary' of what was to be evaluated, which factored in the surrounding area directly affected by operations as well as neighbouring areas that should be considered for biodiversity and habitat protection.

The effect of the materiality analysis will now be examined to highlight how this directed the organisation's selection and prioritisation of issues, a key component of the scoping step. The identification of material issues was informed by international standards and stakeholders. For example, a list of issues was generated from 110 sustainability issues extracted from the GRI standards. Each item in the list was then scaled according to stakeholder evaluation of their importance. Issues were highlighted as 'material' when they reached a certain threshold of stakeholders identifying them as being important. These issues were then prioritised and selected as areas to address for the project (and for the next step, to determine potential impact and mitigation strategies). To do this, the organisation placed each issue into one of the three sustainability dimensions. An example is provided in Figure 3.7.

This was not only implemented at the start of the operations, but was a cyclical process that was regularly updated to reflect the engagement and feedback the organisation received from its stakeholders. Beyond this, the organisation established key material issues across a range of different categories linked to the

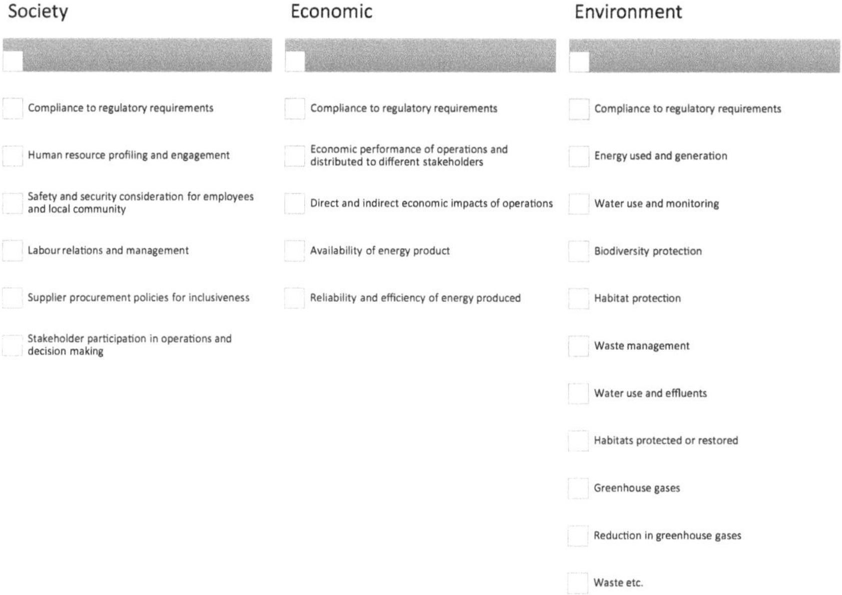

Figure 3.7 Extract of the GRI sustainability categories adapted to PH21.

GRI guidelines, focussing further on the top five issues within each category. This included economic, societal, environmental, product responsibility, labour, electric utilities and human rights. For each of these categories, the key issues were linked with the specific criteria within the GRI standards (Figure 3.8).

While these initiatives were aimed at addressing the most critical material issues, this was only one part of the broader sustainability practices of the organisation. It aimed to meet a checklist-style of key sustainability issues, linked with local regulatory requirements and a global sustainability platform, but also followed very detailed processes for periodically identifying the most important sustainability issues on which to focus specific initiatives.

International standards during scoping

Organisations within the International Standards category generally exceeded expectations set by the government in prioritising different sustainability issues. This is usually associated with the adoption of a range of international standards, or a move towards beginning to adopt global sustainability platforms such as GRI. PH07 is an example of a mining organisation that is both exceeding a compliance-driven perspective and attempting to incorporate more accepted international and global platforms for addressing sustainability issues.

Decision-makers of PH07 revealed that the organisation first orientated activities around a compliance perspective, and addressed two critical elements

Figure 3.8 Extract of the GRI sustainability criteria adapted to PH21.

essential for gaining a 'license to operate' in the Philippines: a focus on achieving approval from local communities on environmental and social perspectives. The Vice-President of Community Relations described how the organisation views these two dimensions as inherently interlinked:

> We cannot separate the social and environmental aspect. [The organisation] views it as something that goes hand-in-hand. We cannot talk of social development without dealing with environment, and we cannot conserve, protect the environment without addressing the social aspects. To see to it that there is congruence between our social development programs and environmental management programs. The real work is really in the communities. Because we want them to actively participate. The way we plan things, and implement them, we are just like a facilitator, while it is the community that decides on the project.... Our role is also to make sure that there is active and meaningful participation of our stakeholders. That is very very important to us.

While this statement is oriented around the implementation of programmes to address both social and environmental issues, it also reflects the interconnections between these dimensions. This is particularly evident in the way that PH07 views the consideration of sustainability across both areas in setting up its operations. Indeed, in planning its operations and engaging with sustainability, the organisation appears to be moving towards a materiality analysis, which sets the broad context for identifying the most significant sustainability issues within its operations. As the organisation moves towards the GRI sustainability standards and begins to report on its sustainability performance, it is going 'beyond compliance' in its operations.

Notwithstanding these positive moves towards improved sustainability outcomes, there are also some areas that the organisation could improve upon. For example, although PH07 was able to identify a range of material issues, it was not clear as to which stakeholders had determined their importance relative to the organisation. Nonetheless, they had identified nine broad categories of focus: facility protection, community development, labour practices, health and safety, resource management, waste, air quality, energy and water management. Under each of these categories, the organisation provided further detail through associated indicators. While this seemed to be quite comprehensive, it is important to note that none of these areas are externally audited. However, since a range of indicators are linked to government requirements, it could be assumed the government undertakes checks to ensure that the development project is in line with what is required.

Furthermore, the consultation underpinning the process of determining material issues appears to be in the early stages of development, with more systematic processes needed to refine how this occurs. For example, their engagement currently revolves around consulting only with local leaders of the community (including government officials) and residents, although there is a lack of detail on how this occurs. Those interviewed revealed that the organisation tries to validate the issues identified through this process by living in the location themselves.

In general, the company's activities around prioritising issues seem to be reactive, rather than having genuine global standards in place. For example, when it encountered a major environmental issue in its operations, the organisation's response was minimalist, and simply complied with government requirements. This was expressed succinctly:

> In [year] there was a tailing dam spill. We did what was required by law. We are done with the clean-up.

This sentiment does not appear to align with having responding to material issues around waste management and ensuring that appropriate prevention measures are in place. Hence, while the organisation is moving in the right direction towards adopting practices aligned with global sustainability platforms, it appears that it still has some way to go before it can be genuinely recognised as performing at these standards. This situation is confounded as the organisation's practices are not externally audited to validate its actions.

Compliance Driven standards during scoping

A common approach adopted by all participating organisations was to determine the business case for the investment undertaken; this is somewhat intuitive, as the emphasis within the private sector is on generating profitable ventures. However, this focus on economic feasibility appeared to be much more prevalent for organisations within the Compliance Driven category, where it remained an underlying focus across the evaluation of which issues are prioritised.

It was also evident that organisations that were Compliance Driven placed a heavy emphasis on using ECC compliance processes to determine the most important issues to prioritise. This was particularly evident in PH10, a manufacturing organisation, where the initial identification and prioritisation of issues centred on developing a business case for the proposed investment. This included undertaking a project study and due diligence for market development within the Philippines. This very business-centric approach was also reflected in the composition of the team that was to undertake this work, as it included staff with finance, accounting and legal expertise to evaluate the Philippines context for the new venture. Once the business case had been developed, and the preferred model of the new venture was decided upon by management within the headquarter operations, their focus then turned to technical priorities for establishing the factory. This process is described by one of the key executive team members within the subsidiary:

> I will then make [several] options for the proposal for them [headquarter decision makers] to select from. After they have selected the proposal, then we will go through the details. So we start drafting the proposal, the details of it, and the requirements... we will ask them in terms of, say for example, [a] manufacturing factory... We have to be very familiar with the technology because we could not just design something if we are not familiar with the process. Most often, we have some consultants hired by the company that will be working hand-in-hand with our Engineering Team.
>
> (PH10)

This approach reflects a general investment style decision-making process, where the organisation first focusses on the type of investment before proceeding to specifics of the type of operations it will implement. In this case, the focus revolved around the specifications of the factory, including the equipment to be utilised. As one respondent explained:

> So we have to know the details of the process before we can come up with a design aspect of the equipment because we have to select and I have to tell them that 'this is the capacity of this particular equipment' - so this is where the design comes in. Then after that, we go through the details of the plant, where to put up the factory and some requirements of the process which will require purely on the capacity of the equipment that we will be putting in that factory.

Once the technical specifications and business case had been established for the investment, the organisation then proceeded to consider local regulatory requirements. This included the basic requirement to have its technical specifications approved but also included a heavy emphasis on the environmental requirements set by EMB-DENR. This is articulated by one of the respondents, who details this process:

> Then talking of the considerations, we have to comply [with government regulations]. We can't directly implement the project unless there are government compliance documents that we have to comply to. So, we have to have it applied to the city engineers for approval, the mechanical plans, electrical plans, sanitary, ECE [Electronics and Communication Engineering] plans. So, all the blueprints will be subject for approval from the City Engineering. Then after that, if we have to put-up Pollution Control Facilities such as Wastewater Facilities, we also have to comply with all DENR requirements.

Since regulatory requirements were largely centred around environmental issues, the key issues identified and prioritised were also largely centred around environmental issues, including water use and treatment, air emissions, and the use of hazardous materials. These are all linked to the DENR requirement and ECC certification required for the organisation to operate. One respondent outlined the process of applying for the ECC, which focussed the organisation on examining environmental issues that the government required to be addressed:

> If the facilities involve the discharge of pollutants, such as wastewater, air or solid waste – we need an approval. In case there would be pollutants in the form of water discharges, or pollutants that have emissions, we also have to give a proposal to them [i.e., DENR]. Some projects like [the] wastewater treatment facility and pollution control facilities on boilers, electric generator sets, etc. For solid waste, how do we transport the solid waste? How do we keep that one? How do we recycle the solid waste? [This information is included in the] proposal [that we submit] to DENR.

In response to the organisation's application for the required licences, the government made several recommendations, for example, that the organisation needed to develop a new wastewater treatment facility to meet the specifications of the new regulatory requirements. This was largely because it had purchased an existing facility that it was planning to upgrade. The existing facility had not been updated to reach the new standard set by the government, so greater scrutiny was applied as part of ensuring the organisation complied with these new standards

Social issues were limited largely to the mandatory regulatory requirement of employing a certain percentage of local labour. One respondent described how the organisation complied with what was required:

> We went through the [standard] process. We went to the barangay first, and then we were invited for the [public] hearing. After that, it [the project] was approved by the Barangay although there were some conditions that we had to comply with. For example, they [i.e., the Barangay] wanted some of the locals to be employed at a percentage [of the total workforce]. [But hiring] depends also on the qualifications of the people, and also their skills and the experiences of the applicant.

Other broader issues that were considered during the planning stage as part of the regulatory requirements were not clearly linked with sustainability assessment practices for scoping. For example, basic building specifications like the structural design, mechanical and electrical designs, and computer and telephone system. The organisation made it quite clear that this was a very technical process, not requiring the active participation of stakeholders. Public hearings were only part of the process because this was a government requirement, and only to provide a basis for officials and local communities to suggest any further key issues that needed to be considered as part of the organisation's planning.

The rest of the issues considered during this stage were mostly business-related; about building a clear business case for the project. This included matters such as the availability of labour (the organisation acknowledged that it would need to conduct training to upskill locals so that it could meet international standards), access to electricity, shipping and broadband connection, among others. The economic orientation was clearly articulated one of the respondents:

> Our main concern was the economic impact of our investment and how we could benefit the stakeholders.

Overall, when examining this organisation's practices at the scoping step, it was quite clear that the key process of prioritising issues was directed towards the regulatory requirements of the government. Further consideration and prioritisation of key sustainability issues within its operations was not evident from the interviews or secondary data collected on the organisation.

The next section will provide further insights into the specific tools and techniques used by decision-makers to undertake the scoping process.

Tools and techniques used during scoping

This section will first describe the existing legislation that regulates the scoping step and directs organisations towards implementing certain processes and practices when scoping issues. The PEISS, in particular, provides project proponents (organisations) guidance across the selection of sustainability issues, which are mainly centred on environmental issues and impacts.

This section will then explore practices voluntarily implemented by organisations to more holistically refine and prioritise the selection of sustainability issues. As was evident in the initiation step, results here indicate that organisations' more comprehensive practices focus heavily on the use of advanced tools that favour stakeholder engagement throughout the scoping step. A mixture of qualitative and quantitative based tools and techniques are practices by MNEs during this step.

Regulatory basis

The scoping step is largely influenced by environmental regulation. The current EIS integrates a comprehensive scoping procedure based on public consultation and technical knowledge. The DENR Administrative Order 2003-30 defines scoping as follows:

> The stage in the EIS System where information and project impact assessment requirements are established to provide the proponent and the stakeholders the scope of work and terms of reference for the EIS.
>
> (AO 2003-30 EMB-DENR)

The EMB-DENR handbook details this procedure, dividing the scoping process into a *pre*- and *post*-scoping process (see Figure 3.9) As mentioned earlier, the PEISS focusses only on environmental issues and impacts, and this is translated into the selection of the Environmental Impact Assessment Review Committee (EIARC), which comprises mainly independent technical experts and professionals selected by the EMB. The technical scoping mainly relies on established lists and thresholds, with the support of technical experts. While containing many similarities to checklists, established lists are more refined and identify key

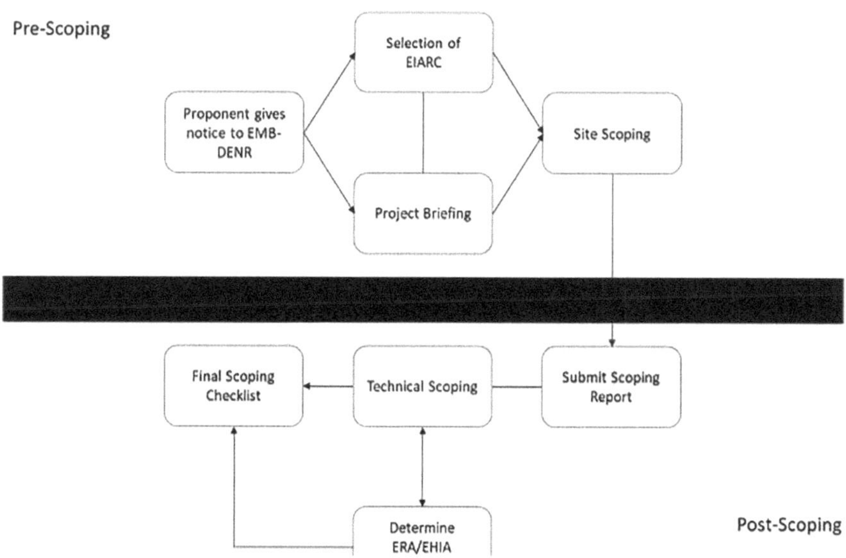

Figure 3.9 Scoping under the PEISS (EMB-DENR handbook).

sustainability indicators (in this case, environmental). This provides guidance to organisations as they need to address each item on the list of requirements.

Through further analysis of the scoping procedures within the EIS system, it is evident that for this step, organisational practices are focussed around the use of established lists and quantitative thresholds. The project proponent must evaluate how the project performs against predefined industry indicators established by the EMB-DENR throughout the project's duration.

Based on our analysis of the submission documentation provided by the EMB-DENR for the mining sector, organisations are required to demonstrate compliance on very specific environmental issues (for example, water disposal, soil erosion, soil fertility) (see Table 3.4). Organisations are required to gather expert knowledge on these issues if the project exceeds set thresholds. Interestingly, the required thresholds are often established through extensive baseline studies completed during the impact analysis step (which follows the scoping step). The methodology applied for such measurement must be defined during the scoping step, which is subsequently approved by the EMB-DENR if it complies.

It appears that the final scoping checklist developed by organisations relies heavily on established lists (from government regulations) as well as technical expertise. However, little evidence was found of any extensive stakeholder engagement by MNEs. While the EIARC can include members from local communities to further strengthen the 'local' dimension of the project, no structured stakeholder engagement process was identified with participating organisations. Some insight as to this situation was revealed by a respondent from PH10, there is evidence that when seeking approval from the EMB-DENR, organisations will strictly comply with their requirements:

> So, all the blueprints will be subject for approval from the City Engineering. Then after that, if we have to put-up Pollution Control Facilities such as Wastewater Facilities, we also have to comply with all [EMB-] DENR requirements.
>
> (PH10)

While this regulation does not require extensive stakeholder engagement during the scoping step, organisations tend to take some initial actions towards establishing an MMT (Multipartite Monitoring Team). Decision-makers, when securing the ECC, must establish an MMT within 60 days of the approval date. As this is often depicted as a lengthy and contentious step, MMTs are often selected during the scoping step of a project. MMTs must be inclusive of key stakeholders and take local authorities and communities into consideration. Their role is to monitor a project's impacts post implementation. An earlier integration of MMTs allows organisations to more accurately identify and engage with key stakeholders throughout the project's lifetime. As articulated by the community managers within PH14, early engagement of stakeholders occurred during their project planning phase:

Table 3.4 ECC application form for new projects

List of Key Impacts	*Baseline Data Parameter Requirements*	*Required Assessment Methodology/Approach*	*Baseline Conditions*		*Impact Analysis*		*Mgmt. Plan*		*Monitoring Plan*		*Remarks*	
During scoping: Unless otherwise specific as agreed during scoping, all items listed are required. Write specific instructions (if any) on the blanks/spaces provided.			Page	Checkbox	Page	Checkbox	Page	Checkbox	Page	Checkbox		
	Map; Results of petrographic and minegraphic analyses; Results of geochemical analyses of rock samples (applicable areas); Hazard maps											
1.3 Pedology												
1.3.1 Soil erosion/ loss of topsoil/ overburden	Summary of soil investigation Report on soil type and quality; Erodibility potential; Bank stability	USLE / similar modelling when applicable										
1.3.2 Change in soil quality/ fertility	Laboratory results on soil sample analysis for N, P, K, pH, organic matter, micronutrients and trace metals e.g., Pb, Hg, As, Cd, Cr hexavalent, etc.	Physical analysis (water holding capacity, texture aggregate stability of dam); Secondary data: chemical analysis										

(Continued)

List of Key Impacts	*Baseline Data Parameter Requirements*	*Required Assessment Methodology/Approach*	*Baseline Conditions*		*Impact Analysis*		*Mgmt. Plan*		*Monitoring Plan*		*Remarks*	
***During scoping**: Unless otherwise specific as agreed during scoping, all items listed are required. Write specific instructions (if any) on the blanks/spaces provided.*			Page	Checkbox	Page	Checkbox	Page	Checkbox	Page	Checkbox		
1.4 Terrestrial Ecology												
1.4.1 Vegetation removal and loss of habitat	Flora and fauna species inventory or survey report;	Quadrat sampling for flora use mist nets, traps, transect for fauna										
	Historical occurrences of pest infestation, forest/grass fire and/or similar incidences											
1.4.2 Threat to existence and/or loss of important local species	Summary of endemicity / conservation status	Include discussion on overall impact to flora and fauna										
1.4.3 Threat to abundance, frequency and distribution of important species	Summary of abundance, frequency and distribution											
	Economic importance and uses of significant flora and fauna											
1.4.4 Hindrance to wildlife access	Sampling/survey map in relation to the project site											
2.0 The Water												
2.1 Hydrology/Hydrogeology												
2.1.1 Change in drainage/ morphology	Drainage map; historical flooding/drought occurrences	Flood simulation/ modelling, consider extreme weather										

> It is a requirement of the DENR. And today every ECC has a built-in clause that you are to have an MMT. It's part of the ECC. Even before the plant operates … we should already organize the MMT.
>
> (PH14)

Furthermore, organisations have also revealed that early engagement with stakeholders during the scoping step creates a positive environment (trust and communication) that is beneficial for both the organisation and stakeholders. Indeed, it was found that the organisations in this study tend to have a more proactive approach towards the selection of members of the MMT. This is largely through exceeding the requirements of the government and implementing a variety of tools and techniques to engage with stakeholders as part of the scoping step. These tools and techniques will now be examined.

Voluntary techniques

Beyond the regulatory basis for scoping, it was evident that organisations have implemented a range of specific tools and techniques during the scoping step. Established lists are a powerful tool for identifying a range of issues, but are limited in their ability to facilitate appropriate engagement with stakeholders. They tend to follow a top-down approach, where the decision-maker converts the regulatory requirements into key issues and impacts to address. Participants in this study revealed that MNE's in the Philippines typically adopt more advanced, participatory practices, allowing for greater flexibility and a better integration of key stakeholders.

Participatory practices adopted by participating MNEs were found to be mostly qualitative in nature, but can integrate a quantitative aspect when comparing sustainability indicators. Two principle methods were identified as being used by organisations to guide their more comprehensive practices for evaluating and refining key sustainability issues: Environmental and Social Impact Assessment (ESIA) and materiality analysis. The next section will begin by exploring ESIAs, which are a more comprehensive approach to social and economic issues. ESIAs also provide a better basis for stakeholder engagement through traditional Impact Assessment procedures. This will be followed by results that capture organisational practices around the use of materiality analysis, which will provide clarity on how such practices unfold during the scoping step and guide decision-making when selecting key sustainability issues.

ENVIRONMENTAL AND SOCIAL IMPACT ASSESSMENTS

As previously highlighted, PH01 demonstrated comprehensive practices when conducting the initiation step of their sustainability assessment. They did the same when conducting the scoping step, where it was found that decision-makers demonstrate a well-established refinement and prioritisation of sustainability issues.

As explained previously, the mining industry falls under the Category A classification of the ECC and therefore needs to have its environmental impacts carefully assessed by the government. This has been translated into an extremely comprehensive '*world class*' ESIA (as respondents described it). Table 3.5 below depicts the three main steps of the ESIA undertaken. Phase 2 of the ESIA is focussed on issue scoping, as well as on disclosing the main information about the planned mining activity to stakeholders. As seen in this ESIA, there can be a large number of stakeholders (local and surrounding communities, local businesses, infrastructure partners, education partners and local NGOs).

During interviews with key executives within the decision-making team, it was highlighted that the management of social issues was at the heart of the sustainability assessment and indeed, the project itself. The planning process had a strong community orientation, as the development was planned in an Indigenous area. At the time of the interview, the organisation was still seeking final FPIC approval. The FPIC approval would guarantee financial compensation to the Indigenous population for potential impacts arising from the project. However, in addition, the MNE's decision-makers were concerned about the management of a significant influx of wealth into the surrounding communities as a result of their operations. Respondents emphasised that the management of socio-economic development is the key to ensuring a successful project.

RISK MATRICES

Analysis of the interview data revealed that organisations that were classified as being World Class comprehensively incorporated environmental, social and economic issues within their scoping practices. In so doing, a number of organisations revealed that risk matrices provided them with a foundation to identify

Table 3.5 Example of an ESIA scoping process

Phase 1	*Planning*	This phase included the development of an EIA Stakeholder Engagement Plan and the identification of stakeholders	✓
Phase 2	*Issues scoping*	This phase involved an information, education and communication campaign with key stakeholders from [date removed] and culminated in public scoping meetings in each of the four municipalities covering the Mine Project site. The objective of this phase was to provide information on the Mine Project and the EIS and ECC processes, and to elicit stakeholder issues and concerns about the Mine Project. More than [number removed] people were consulted during this phase.	✓
Phase 3	*Issues response and feedback*	This future phase is designed to respond to issues raised by stakeholders, including feedback on the results of the EIA studies.	×

and prioritise such issues and prioritise key issues. This was partly captured by the comment from a respondent from PH05 stated:

> The risk matrix goes all the way up to catastrophic failure and to a probability that it will happen on a daily basis. So, if we have a risk get up into that quadrant then some serious decisions need to be made.
>
> (PH05)

Further analysis of the practices implemented by PH05 revealed that the organisational risk matrix was based upon international guidelines, including the IFC performance standards. The performance standards have been created to improve the environmental and social performance of IFC-supported projects through a risk-based approach. The IFC (2012) performance standards are focussed around eight key sustainability areas:

1 Environmental and Social Assessment and Management System
2 Labour and Working Conditions
3 Pollution Prevention and Abatement
4 Community Health, Safety and Security
5 Land Acquisition and Involuntary Resettlement
6 Biodiversity Conservation and Sustainable Natural Resource Management
7 Indigenous Peoples
8 Cultural Heritage

When frameworks such as the one developed through IFC are applied, the general scope of the project is also expanded to incorporate social and economic dimensions. For example, key decision-makers from another organisation, PH19, provided some insights into how sustainability considerations are broadened when incorporating the IFC framework:

> We began with the template of the IFC operational policies guidelines, but then we were engaging ourselves with the other financing institutions like the [de-identified]. So, we looked at IFC as well and then the environment and social governance got expanded to meet requirements of all these lenders.
>
> (PH19)

Extending beyond the use of IFC guidelines and ESIA protocols, it is evident from a range of organisations that the use of materiality analysis (adapted from the GRI guidelines) was also critical in guiding scoping practices. The next section will explore the use of this tool, and provide further insights into how it has been applied.

MATERIALITY ANALYSIS

The materiality analysis tool appears to dominate the practices of organisations within the World Class category. Organisations reflected that by conducting a materiality analysis, they were able to bridge the gap between stakeholder engagement and issue prioritisation. Essentially, the use of materiality analysis allows for the identification of key stakeholders and enables organisations to engage with these stakeholders to understand the most important or 'material' issues that should be focussed on in their planning processes.

During the scoping step, the key underlying strategy of the materiality analysis is to conduct surveys across the identified key stakeholders to determine the most important issues and impacts for the organisation to consider. These surveys allow decision-makers to both identify and rank key sustainability issues, not only evaluating these against priorities identified by external stakeholders, but also linking them to important stakeholders within the organisation. This process is not limited to conducting surveys, as it can also integrate the experience of, and feedback from, local teams on the ground. A materiality analysis should be seen as a summary tool, that integrating key sustainability issues and impacts for external stakeholders and the project proponent (within the organisation) with equal consideration.

Experience is a key basis for undertaking a materiality analysis, with many organisations utilising previous project experience in other countries as a basis for guiding how they implement it for their current project. Community managers within PH06 reflected on the importance of their previous experience, stating that:

> Experience is what helps us do things the right way; there are no formulae that can take care of the soft issues. Understanding and getting the right people to work on it, right from the beginning, is what helps.
>
> (PH06)

Through a closer analysis of the influencing factors in implementing a materiality analysis, it is evident that many organisations do this through leveraging international commitments and frameworks linked to the GRI organisation. The GRI framework for conducting a materiality analysis provides a visual method to prioritise impacts based on the magnitude of their potential impact, as well as due to their relevance to different stakeholders. Essentially, the results of undertaking this stakeholder engagement, both within and beyond the organisation, allow the creation of a ranking matrix to visually depict key impacts that should be considered. Figure 3.10 below provides an example of such matrices in action, with the points representing sustainability indicators and the two-axis representing the respective significance for stakeholders (Y-axis) and environmental and social impacts (X-axis).

In examining this process further, the organisation essentially takes the information from both internal and external stakeholders and ranks the screened issues according to their importance. Once issues are ranked, results are graphically represented. The issues in the top right of the matrix should be considered as a priority, with both high likelihood and impact. Figure 3.11, below, which has been adapted from the GRI guidelines, provides a visual understanding of how such matrices are used.

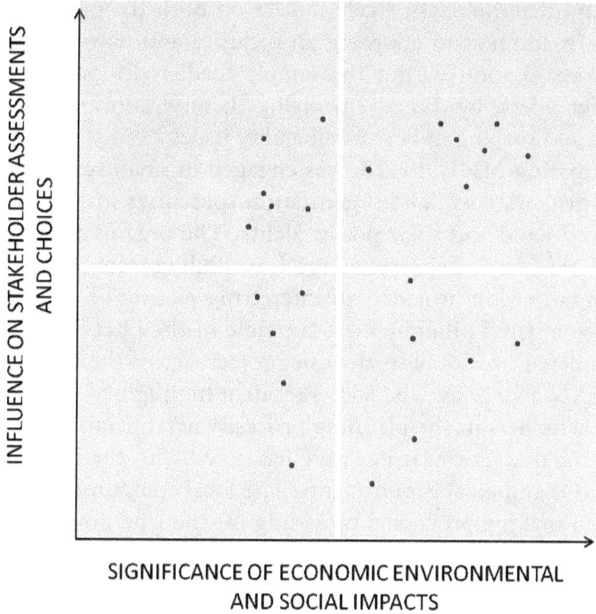

Figure 3.10 Example of a GRI materiality analysis.[2]

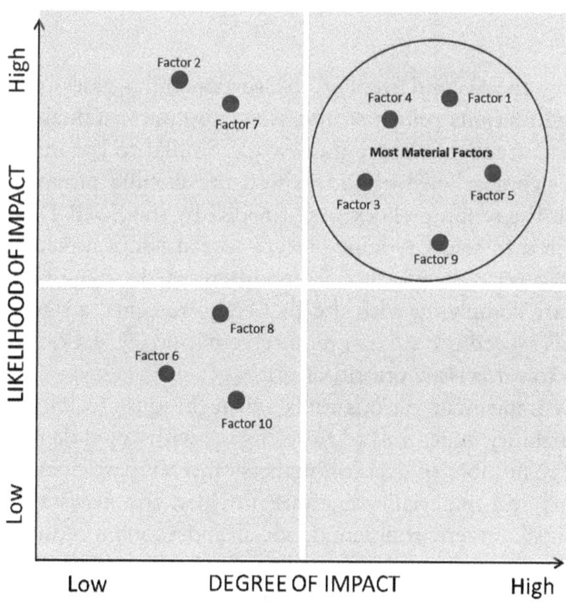

Figure 3.11 Example of GRI materiality analysis results.[3]

By applying such methods, decision-makers were able to refine the issues of importance and determine the likely impact on both the organisation and its stakeholders. In addition to adopting an inclusive and participatory tool such as this, one organisation within the sample further demonstrated how they included stakeholders, by directly involving them within its project planning team/process and scoping of key sustainability issues.

One participating MNE, PH23, was engaged in small-scale power production and off-grid systems. The organisation specialises in biogas production facilities as well wind and solar power plants. The organisation was classified within the World Class category, and receives funding from the IFC and World Bank. The organisation provided an interesting picture of the renewable energy landscape in the Philippines. At the time of the interview, the organisation had completed a series of small-scale projects across the Philippines as well as other ASEAN countries. The Vice-President highlighted the importance of including stakeholders in the planning process when operating at higher environmental standards. Social issues were identified with the help of local communities, NGOs and local governments. The local communities were involved in the decision-making process in providing off-the-grid power solutions. The Vice-President reflected:

> In [location], we have a micro-grid ...which is being managed by the people there: the NGO and the community... When we do design, we do a holistic approach. We go bottom up. Not only with the Mayor or selected participants but real community members.
>
> (PH23)

In summarising the second step of the sustainability assessment, this study found that organisations prioritise and select specific sustainability issues with the help of the current regulatory framework. Similar to the initiation step, the PEISS provides comprehensive guidance on the scoping of environmental impacts. Through the scoping checklists provided by the EMB-DENR, organisations are required to select specific project-related issues linked to their sector of activity. However, the evidence from this research suggests that, while all organisations are complying with the ECC requirements, a significant number of organisations exceed the current requirements and legislation, adopting a holistic approach towards issue prioritisation.

Indeed, they implement various tools and techniques to select the most important sustainability issues and to fully engage with key stakeholders. Insights shared by a large number of decision-makers of MNE participants suggests that risk assessments and materiality analysis provided the necessary guidance for them to prioritise key environmental, social and economic dimensions. Additional comments from respondents suggest that such tools allowed better stakeholder engagement throughout their scoping processes.

Summary of second stage

In summary, this study confirmed previous findings as it identified two key steps commonly undertaken by MNEs in the Philippines: initiation and scoping, as part of stage one of a sustainability assessment. Evidence suggests that both steps are guided by the current regulatory framework, providing organisations with a set of tools to identify and select sustainability domains and issues that should be integrated into their assessment.

The current legislation (*e.g.*, PEISS) provides a range of checklists and established lists for organisations to complete for the first stage of the sustainability assessment. An examination of the documentation provided by the EMB-DENR suggests that such tools are limited, as they tend to identify and select only key environmental issues. However, this study identified that a large number of organisations are operating beyond the regulatory requirements, and are adopting a more inclusive approach towards improving the sustainability of their operations across both initiation and scoping.

It was found that organisations adopting superior practices typically applied international standards such as ISO 9001 or ISO 14001 to strengthen their participatory approach to Issue Identification and Prioritisation. In addition, organisations that were classified as being World Class revealed they adopted specific guidelines to inform their practices during initiation and scoping, including the use of risk assessment and materiality analysis to guide their decision-making process. These specific guidelines were often adopted due to different international commitments of the headquarter operations that were linked to institutions such as the World Bank, IFC or GRI. This provided the foundation for strong stakeholder engagement (consistent with global standards) across this first stage and clear tools and techniques being implemented beyond regulatory requirements.

The next chapter will present the findings from our analysis of MNE practices during the second stage of the sustainability assessment: Impact Assessment.

Notes

1 Screening forms from the EMB-DENR available at: http://eia.emb.gov.ph/ecc-applications-and-issuance/requirements-for-securing-ecc/eis-screening-forms/.
2 Adapted from the Global Reporting Initiative: https://www.globalreporting.org/resourcelibrary/GRI-DefiningMateriality2016.pdf.
3 Adapted from the Global Reporting Initiative: https://www.globalreporting.org/resourcelibrary/GRI-DefiningMateriality2016.pdf.

4 Impact assessment stage

Introduction

This chapter presents the findings for stage two of the sustainability assessment: impact assessment. Organisations use the key sustainability issues identified and prioritised in stage one to now determine their potential impact and to develop potential alternative or mitigation strategies where needed. Two key steps form the basis of this stage, impact analysis and alternative selection, and results will be presented for each step (see Figure 4.1).

The following sections present the results from analysing organisational activities of participating MNEs during stage two of sustainability assessments. The structure will follow that used in presenting stage one results (Chapter 3), including classification of organisational practices, explanation of management practices and exploration of the tools and techniques utilised by organisations.

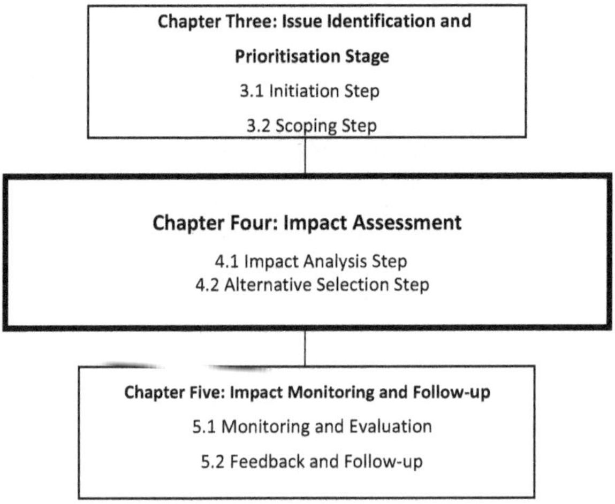

Figure 4.1 Data results chapter overview.

Impact analysis step

Impact analysis is the third step of a sustainability assessment. During this step, it is theorised that decision-makers focus on predicting the impacts and significance of selected sustainability issues over the operational activities and life-time of a project. Impact analysis is a technical step, wherein the significance of the scoped issues is assessed by the organisation. The complexity of measuring the socio-economic and socio-environmental impacts, a key requirement for this step, makes this one of the more challenging steps within a sustainability assessment. The following sections present the results of the analysis that was conducted with interview data and secondary data sources, providing insights into practices of the organisations within this sample.

Practice classification

The classification of organisations that participated in this study reveals that both World Class and International Standards categories dominate practices during stage two. With 38% (n = 9/24) of organisations being classified into both categories, World Class and International Standards, it appears the majority (three-quarters) of organisations are exceeding the local regulatory requirements and minimum standards set by the Philippines' government. On the other hand, 25% (n = 6/24) of organisations were classified into the Compliance Driven category, indicating a tendency to only meet minimum standards (see Figure 4.2).

For this step, the classifications were similar to those of previous steps so that the same organisations, in their respective industries, were classified the same. This suggests they use similar tools and techniques to implement the first three steps of sustainability assessments.

One interesting finding is that organisations within each category tend to perform at a similar level across the first three steps, especially for those in the World Class category. Evidence points towards a generally consistent implementation

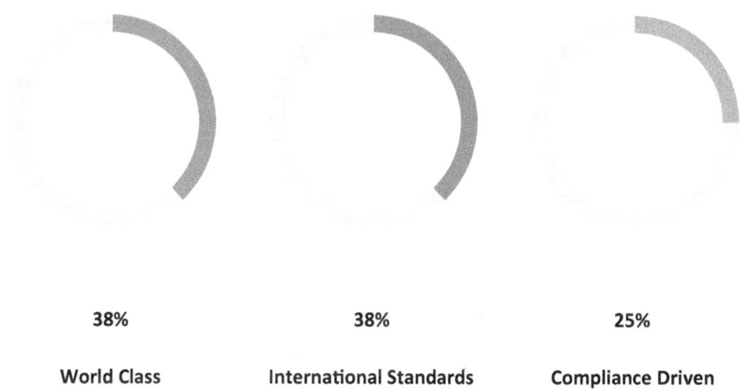

Figure 4.2 Practice classification – impact analysis.

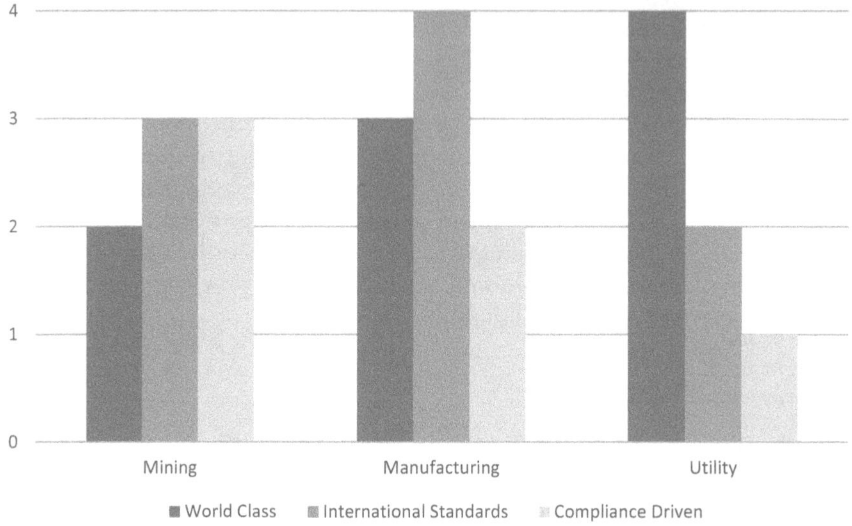

Figure 4.3 Practice classification per industry – impact analysis.

of standards across the first three steps, fuelled by corporate headquarter policies and practices, and their commitment to global sustainability platforms.

Taking a closer look at classifications, Figure 4.3 below illustrates the number of organisations per category by industry. As noted earlier, World Class and International Standard categories dominate the classifications.

However, mining organisations were dominant in the Compliance Driven and International Standards categories. Mining organisations made extensive reference to the legally mandated requirements within their operations. Conversely, utilities organisations adopted World Class practices more so than those in other industries, while only one MNE was Compliance Driven. Manufacturing organisations was more evenly spread across the categories, though more adopted International standards.

The next section examines organisational practices in detail, which includes presenting findings from exemplar cases for each category.

Management practices

The following section is oriented around a more detailed explanation of the management practices and sustainability considerations of organisations within each category. This includes a detailed exploration of the frameworks or foundations of organisational practices in each category, as well as a general overview of the key activities undertaken. Presentation of the results will begin with activities of MNEs within the World Class category, followed by those for the International Standards and Compliance Driven categories.

World class

In examining the practices of organisations within the World Class category for the impact analysis step, it became evident that they not only have comprehensive processes for determining impacts but are also committed to a range of global sustainability platforms. A range of industry-specific sustainability commitments was evident for the organisations within this category, as well as a commitment to key global platforms such as the Global Reporting Initiative standards (GRI), United Nations Global Compact (UNGC), Carbon Disclosure Project (CDP) and International Finance Corporation (IFC) social and environmental sustainability, among others. Organisations also referred regularly to the effect of international commitments in driving internal change, including setting new corporate strategies and objectives around sustainability and sustainable development.

This is particularly evident when looking at PH05, a major mining operation within the Philippines, as well as globally. Before outlining the actual sustainability considerations linked with its impact analysis, it is worthwhile exploring its broader processes, which reflects an orientation (evident across all organisations within the sample) towards an initial focus on determining the financial feasibility of its operations. This provides the basis for determining the initial impact of its investment and is centred on determining the likelihood that any proposed investment undertaken by the organisation will be able to generate a sufficient financial return. As a respondent from PH05 reflects:

> We started coming to the realisation; well it truly is about the triple bottom line. If we're not making money we're inherently unsustainable; the shareholders would pull out; eventually we'll go belly-up; and then you can forget about all the fancy work done in terms of shared value, in terms of ensuring employees are safe and providing for wellbeing and making sure that we operate responsibly with regards to the environment management. If you're not making money, all that becomes impossible. You can have all the best intentions in the world but a lot of these things do require finances and a viable business concern to be able to pursue them.

Once the organisation has determined that the proposed project represents a sound investment, it then proceeds to an examination of the local context. Contextual examination covers the regulatory context within which it will operate, including:

- Specific laws linked with the financial feasibility of the operations (*i.e.*, tax rates, repatriation of profits *etc.*);
- Key social challenges in the country;
- Key risks entailed by operating within the country.

This forms a very general strategic country assessment that the organisation undertakes before committing to the investment. After the initial financial and contextual analysis, the organisation then conducts a more holistic assessment of the proposed project, and this is where the substantive sustainability issues are first considered. Assessment of sustainability issues and impacts builds from the key international commitments the organisation has to global sustainability platforms. PH05 has committed to a range of sustainability platforms, including an industry-specific standard, GRI G4 guidelines, UNGC, the CDP, the IFC social and environmental standards, a range of ISOs and AA1000 for stakeholder engagement.

Overarching these commitments, and in an attempt to better integrate these commitments into its operations, the organisation established a broad sustainability framework. This sustainability framework integrated the full range of sustainability issues and impacts that were linked with its international commitments, and this then funnelled down to a range of policies that aimed to assist in the implementation within their operations. As a key executive from the headquarter operations of the organisation reflected:

> One of our big challenges was how we actually translate all these policy statements and the framework into action on the ground. So, we actually went into a process of re-crafting essentially the DNA of the company. So it was at that point that we came up with the vision which is to be the global leader in sustainable mining… And then we went about setting up a series of values for the organisation… The idea behind the values is that they would link directly back to what we say in our policy statements but be a much easier, more understandable format rather than people sitting down and reading policy statements.

These values enabled the organisation to better translate its international commitments – through its sustainability framework and policies – into operational changes. From a strategic point of view, it is clear the organisation has attempted to transform how it engages with, and operationalises, its commitments to sustainability and sustainable development. Looking more specifically at how it translates this process into its impact analysis, the organisation has implemented a risk management approach to impact assessment. This type of assessment is linked with ISO31000 and translates into the organisation evaluating the entire life cycle of its operations, from exploration to closure, identifying key sustainability risks within its operations. For example, one respondent revealed:

> We've got a process as well embedded in the organisation, a risk management process. We've fashioned that whole enterprise-wide risk management system around ISO31000 and that allows us to sit back and look at potential risks strategically… Obviously we've got matrices in place that work on a probability versus severity basis that eventually kicks out a risk score for us. On a quarterly basis we revisit those strategic risk registers and go through each and every single risk. Obviously if something is starting to move up the risk register then that could trigger for us to start addressing the issue.

> Conversely, we also look at things on an opportunity matrix, which is really turning a risk matrix upside down and looking and saying, 'well what's the potential upside' and starting to track that. We use that as a strategic tool just to understand where we are in the process and how we're going on our priorities.

Aligning with this approach, the organisation also undertakes a materiality analysis across all its operations, from both a global and local level, identifying the key issues for its operations. This is integrated into its risk management approach, along with all the other key issues and impacts linked with the requirements specified in its different sustainability platforms. What is evident from both the interviews and secondary data (including the organisation's reporting requirements) is that the organisation has a complex and interlocking set of sustainability issues it evaluates in its operations.

All of the aforementioned assessments and approaches forms part of the baseline activities PH05 undertakes in its operations, both as part of its initial evaluation of a proposed investment location, and as an ongoing process annually. The baseline activities also contribute towards its initial environmental and social impact assessments, undertaken as part of the regulatory requirements for its operations. In charting all of these activities, and the full range of issues and impacts that the organisation evaluates, a complex map begins to form of all the areas evaluated.

With a focus on material issues alone, impact areas that may require attention can be produced (see Figure 4.4). This accounts for the most material issues across the organisation's global operations, and how these are attached to indicator categories wherein each material issue is broken down into measurable areas. While this is not graphically presented through the organisation's reporting activities, data has been aggregated here to allow for a clearer presentation of PH05's activities to identify and measure different issues and impact areas within its operations.

There is significant complexity involved in evaluating the issues and impacts the organisation considers as part of its impact analysis processes. Nevertheless, it is evident that the organisation establishes a comprehensive basis for determining the impact of its operations across a broad set of sustainability issues. This is linked with the most important material issues for the communities in which it operates. The entire process is also externally audited by an international consulting firm, to ensure that it is accurately reflecting the organisation's activities.

International standards

Organisations within the International Standards category clearly exceeded the regulatory requirements specified under Philippines' laws. This included the requirements specified under the environmental compliance certification and environmental impact statement and, to a lesser extent, the social development management program. Some organisations were also starting to implement GRI

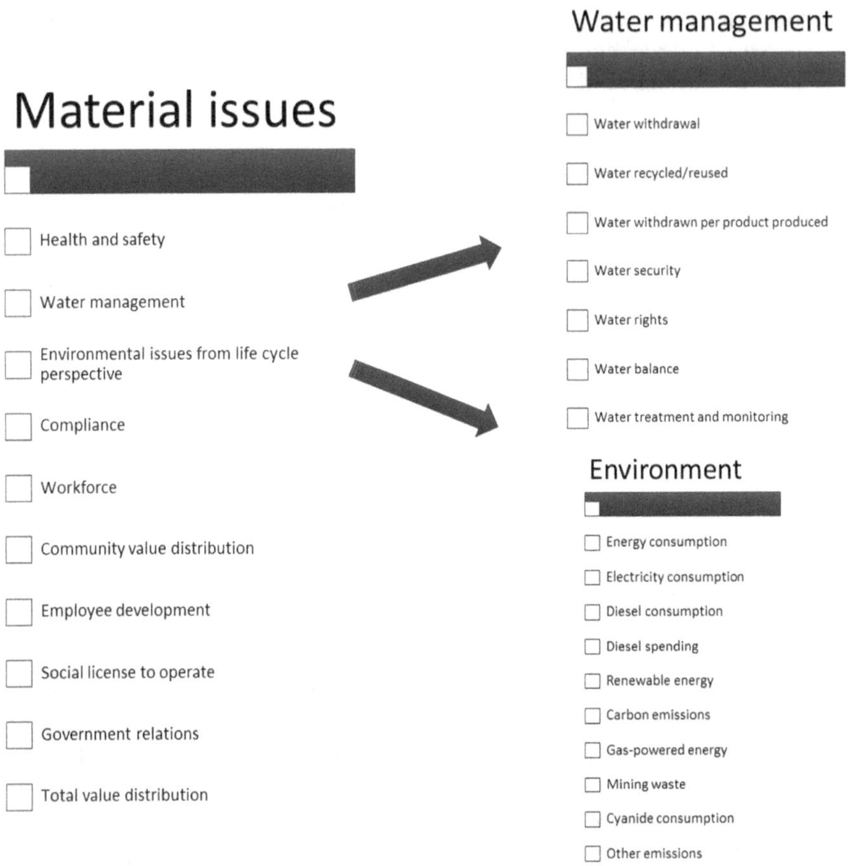

Figure 4.4 Material issues categories.

standards, with the introduction of reporting in accordance with the specifications outlined by GRI. However, despite this move, these organisations appeared to be either (1) still transitioning towards full adoption of these standards or (2) maintaining a focus solely on the environmental aspects of their operations.

PH18 is an excellent example of an organisation that has increasingly moved towards the adoption of a global sustainability platform, although it still has some way to go before it comprehensively accounts for the full breadth of sustainability issues in its impact analysis. As has been frequently recognised across all levels of organisations within the sample, the economic (financial) analysis of the operations was a key point initially evaluated by PH18 through an impact analysis. As it was evaluating the potential of taking over existing facilities, the organisation was focussed on identifying and evaluating the assets and cash flow of the existing operations. This included economic and financial modelling of the assets to determine the potential of their investment for returns. Once this was completed, results were presented to the investment committee within the headquarters before proceeding to the board for approval.

Despite the orientation around determining the economic feasibility of the operations, interviewed participants also emphasised that the local community and government were engaged significantly during this initial process of evaluating the investment potential. This included establishing communications channels to allow the local community to understand what the organisation was planning, as well as opening a pathway for determining key social and community issues that needed to be considered during its investment. Underpinning this engagement, the organisation conducted a baseline study to determine where it would need to target social programmes. As part of this study, the organisation sought to identify the necessary information that would direct its programmes as well as general business information, such as the local community's perception of existing operations and knowledge of the brand, among other areas.

There was an emphasis by the key decision-makers on determining a comprehensive basis for what the community wanted through expressed opinions, but as well as what was needed to improve community development. While this appeared to be a participatory approach to community engagement, it still largely sat within the realm of a basic CSR programme, aimed at contributing the necessary funds (linked with the SDMP) towards pertinent areas identified by the community. Nevertheless, the organisation made efforts to better understand the local communities affected by the operations it was planning to conduct, as one respondent commented:

> There were a lot of communications with the local government and the community in terms of acceptance. What we did was a lot of engaging stakeholders within the local government and key influencers within the local organisations. Our target was really to be more inclusive because when it comes to community relations, there may be some information gaps along the way and we wanted to address those... We wanted our programs to be relevant based on where the community was, at that time. And all our programs are aligned not just based on what they need but also based on the baseline.

Despite the professed focus on community engagement and issue identification as part of the organisation's impact analysis, it appeared that the main thrust of its evaluation was still concerned with the technical specifications of its operations. Evaluation was largely focussed on how to improve the output of the facilities, including evaluating the technical and technology aspects of the operations, as well as the labour resources involved. The participants interviewed emphasised issues around the maintenance standards of the plant, the need to upgrade the facilities to improve power output, and the need to bring in foreign expatriates with the expertise to improve the efficiency of the operations. As one respondent said:

> We repaired a lot of stuff and we made stuff designed to have the power plant go to [full capacity] and we have put it back in the service. With regards to

> the people, we had a fairly significant number of expats here initially – both full-time expats and people that came in just to support the turnaround efforts. Over time, we significantly reduced the amount of expats. I think we have about four or five at the plant today. Our intention is to get to a point when maybe we do not need any or we may need only one or two at some point. The number of folks that were working at the plant has gone down. We look for people to be more efficient and we put processes in [place]. We did a lot of orientation and training ... [with] the employees.

When examining the data collected on PH18 regarding its global operations, it became clear that the organisation was working towards adopting the GRI G4 standards across the board. While a range of different material issues were identified in its global operations, it was not clear how they funnelled down to its activities in the Philippines. What was clear, however, was that the organisation appeared to have a major focus on evaluating two key aspects of its sustainability performance – labour resources and environmental performance.

For its environmental management, for example, the organisation has a comprehensive set of management and technical standards for all its operations, including pre-operational activities. It undertakes an impact analysis to evaluate its impact across different issue categories and indicator groups. Its environmental performance, although focussing on the four key areas of Water, Effluents and By products, Biodiversity and Air Emissions (see Figure 4.5), also includes a wide range of different systems to ensure that it has appropriate methods to identify its impacts and management of environmental requirements, including spill management, hazardous waste management, biodiversity protection and chemical management. This extends to analysing its suppliers and contractors and the activities that they implement around their environmental performance.

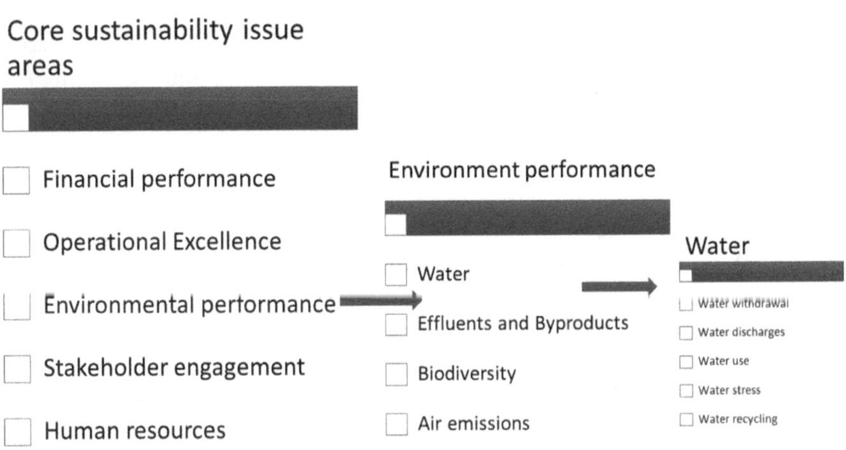

Figure 4.5 Example of GRI environmental categories and indicators.

A similar comprehensive approach is evident within the human resource section of the organisation's reporting, which details a comprehensive set of human resource measures for determining impact within the organisation's operations. This extends across basic employment statistics covering gender, location, training, health and safety indices, to more comprehensive programmes of employee engagement. The major limitation of its approach appears to be the aggregated nature of its reporting and the information provided. It was very difficult to see how the organisation was measuring its impacts across social dimensions, beyond basic CSR programmes, and the economic impact beyond its financial performance and returns on investment.

Compliance driven

In terms of the organisations within the Compliance Driven category, it was evident that the environmental regulations of the Philippines were again predominant in directing activities for these organisations. This includes the initial ECC requirements for impact determination and the ongoing monitoring conducted by DENR. Organisations in this category were aiming to meet these regulatory requirements as a focal point of their impact analysis processes. Scant evidence was available of these organisations extending their analysis to socioeconomic considerations, beyond basic financial analysis conducted to ensure a profitable venture. The other key characteristic within these organisations was a lack of transparency in reporting (such as through their websites) beyond the monitoring reports required by the government.

A suitable example of a Compliance Driven organisation was PH16, a specialist manufacturing organisation. According to participants interviewed from PH16, the plant it has in the Philippines is a replication of the plant it has within the headquarters' home country. The company was successful in securing a tendering bid, at the lowest cost, with a major global manufacturer already operating in the Philippines. It has developed a close relationship with this manufacturer, including establishing its factories on their premises. The products manufactured by the organisation are specifically built to input the production processes of its manufacturing partner.

When examining PH16's initial investment decisions and planning, the team involved in setting up the operations was very much oriented towards technical feasibility. This appears to have largely involved the owners and a core set of engineers examining the feasibility of the technology needed to be developed for its contract partner. No broader feasibility study was undertaken by this team as part of the process to determine and measure key impacts linked with sustainability issues.

Once the decision had been made around the technical specifications and capability of the organisation to deliver the contract as specified by its partner, PH16 then hired third-party consultants to assist in compliance with all regulatory requirements. This included an ECC. As one respondent explained:

> This company's [third-party consultant] mandate is to be 100% compliant always to regulations. We do not engage in erroneous activities and every compliance requirement that we become aware of had to be complied with.

Compliance with local regulatory requirements was a key orienting factor when establishing operations for this organisation, including when to engage externally with communities that may be affected. This was reflected by one participant when asked about the involvement of surrounding communities:

> No, because we are coming in to an existing manufacturing site. I would assume that our impact is minimal. There were already industrial activities here… normally, it's handled by [the contract partner] because this is their place and we are just guests inside it. They generally prefer to be the owners of the site. They control the security and activities within the local council.

When questioned about whether they needed to form any multidisciplinary teams to engage with sustainability issues (which is a common aspect of the ECC requirements), they made it clear that this was not necessary. The fact that they did not have to use a Multipartite Monitoring Team (MMT) meant there was limited engagement with any issues beyond what was specifically mandated by the government. This is captured by the following quote from one participant:

> We also don't have an MMT and we do not engage the community. Perhaps it is because this facility is not ours. It is [contract partner's]. I guess [contract partner] has many community services undertaken…

Despite the narrow focus of the initial impact analysis for its operations, the organisation did consider different key environmental issues associated with its operations. This includes the use and recycling of water in its production processes, oil for its machinery, air emissions and noise. One participant explained that this was generally a cursory process and was solely aimed at meeting requirements set by the government:

> Our water consumption is very small. We have a closed circuit so any water we use for our machinery is condensed back in the equipment… We have a technology for recycling water. We have a closed manufacturing system, so we do not make any discharges. If we lose water, [it is] through evaporation of cooling fans. Yes. Even the waste from the machine's oil that we change, we have to get that certified and sent to an accredited recycling agent. The accreditation by DENR is a recent activity. We make noise but it is minimal. Yes, we do check the noise levels. We do noise monitoring every year as part of the compliance. We check the whole factory…

Beyond key environmental issues, especially those required through a compliance perspective, the organisation also considered other issues around health and safety linked with its operations. This was again influenced by external forces, with the contract partner requiring that PH16 meet European standards for its production processes. As one respondent stated, '*That is the certification that we are pursuing because it is the requirement of [the contract partner]*'. This was linked with its adoption of ISO9001 for quality management systems and ISO180001 for occupational health and safety.

In examining other activities aimed at engaging and potentially measuring impacts beyond its operations, the organisation also had a corporate social responsibility programme established. Very little detail was provided on this programme, and it did not seem to translate into any systematic evaluation on sustainability issues beyond those identified above. Rather, it appeared to be more of an emphasis on developing a strategy of how PH16 considers its customers, suppliers, environment and employees. Most of this appears to be linked with local regulatory requirements or engaging with the organisation's staff. One respondent detailed this further, saying:

> Most of our [CSR] activities are focused on the staff themselves. Each year, we try to expand quietly, without the Head Office noticing, the range of benefits the staff receives... Like now, we offer educational benefits, so we pay for the [employees'] children's schooling expenses. We expanded health to cover dependents and we slowly expanded on that. The quality of life of our staff has been better [because of these additional benefits].

While these efforts seem worthy in terms of providing better conditions/benefits for employees at the subsidiary, there was no evidence to indicate any additional processes were being put in place to measure other impacts. One final aspect that was identified through secondary data, including PH16's website, was the adoption of a CO_2 reduction programme, aiming to measure and reduce the emissions from its material consumption, manufacturing and logistics elements of its operations. The programme is targeted at generating significant reductions across its operations by 2020. No evidence was found to demonstrate that PH16 was actually implementing an impact analysis process to measure emissions.

The presentation of our analysis will now turn to examining the key tools and techniques being implemented by participating organisations.

Tools and techniques

The earlier section detailed how the impact analysis step requires decision-makers to evaluate very specific impacts within their activities. To do so, decision-makers rely on a range of methodologies which enable them to integrate uncertainty into the decision-making process. Insights from participating organisations revealed that formal tools and techniques are implemented to assess these impacts. Due to the complexity, and need for replicating similar processes across operations and timelines, these techniques are often quantitative in nature. The Philippines regulatory framework provides a solid foundation for the assessment of environmental impacts. Through the EIS system, key tools were identified to conduct these assessments, including:

- Baseline studies – baseline studies have been found to be extensively applied throughout the assessment processes. Baseline studies are mandatory and assess the biosphere and hydrosphere at the beginning of the study. The decision-makers then forecast the possible significant impacts through the use of expert knowledge and modelling.
- Quantitative models – assess anthropogenic impacts through the measurement of key indicators (loss of ecosystem value, CO_2 emissions, air quality and water quality). Quantitative modelling can be utilised to forecast the impact on the biosphere. Such measurement approaches have often been referred as environmental 'load' or 'pressure' measurements.
- Life Cycle Assessment (LCA) – LCA is predominantly applied throughout the mining and manufacturing sector, allowing organisations to assess environmental impacts throughout the life cycle of their operations.

Looking further into assessment tools and techniques, analysis suggests that organisations operating more comprehensive practices tended to implement tools and techniques allowing them to assess impacts across the social and economic dimensions as well. Insights shared by key participants revealed two main methodologies are commonly used to assess these impacts:

- Cost-Benefit Assessment (CBA) – identified as the predominant method for organisations at all levels of classification. CBA allows organisations to integrate sustainability issues through a financial evaluation.
- Risk Assessment – found to be a prominent tool used by organisations to assess sustainability issues. The main characteristics associated with risk assessments are their flexibility and integration into the decision-making process.

The next sections will further detail the tools and techniques identified above, including the regulatory guidance provided by the government.

Regulatory basis

Baseline studies are a key element of the assessment of impacts. Evidence from the analysis of organisational practices indicates that these studies have been utilised in many of the cases where decision-makers assessed the environmental impact of their planned activity. As mentioned in the previous section, baseline studies are a mandatory part of the EIS and are needed to obtain the ECC. Baseline studies aim to provide a greater understanding of the 'state' of the biosphere, geosphere and hydrosphere before the planned activity begins.

As previously detailed, the EIS documentation for mining activities requires the use of various tools and techniques to assess the baseline. The example below (Figure 4.6) illustrates how the hydrosphere and biosphere are assessed

List of Key Impacts	Baseline Data Parameter Requirements	Required Assessment Methodology/Approach	Baseline conditions		Impact Analysis		Mgmt. Plan		Monitoring Plan		Remarks	
During scoping: Unless otherwise specific as agreed during scoping, all items listed are required. Write specific instructions (if any) on the blanks/spaces provided.			Page	Checkbox	Page	Checkbox	Page	Checkbox	Page	Checkbox		
	Map; Results of Petrographic and Minegraphic Analyses; Results of Geochemical Analyses of Rock Samples (applicable areas); Hazard maps											
1.3 Pedology												
1.3.1 Soil erosion/ loss of topsoil/overburden	Summary of Soil Investigation Report on soil type and quality; Erodibility potential; Bank stability	USLE / Similar modeling when appicable										
1.3.2 Change in soil quality/fertility	Laboratory results on soil sample analysis for N, P, K, pH, organic matter, micronutrients and trace metals e.g. Pb, Hg, As, Cd, Cr hexavalent, ect.	Physical analysis (water holding capacity, texture aggreagate stability of dam); secondary data: chemical analysis										
1.4 Terrestrial Ecology												
1.4.1 Vegetation removal and loss of habitat	Flora and fauna species inventory or survey report;	Quadrat sampling for flora use mist nets, traps, transect for fauna										
	Historical occurrences of pest infestation, forest/grass fire and/or similar incidences											
1.4.2 Threat to existence and/or loss of important local species	Summary of endemicity / conservation status	Include dicussion on overall impact to flora and fauna										
1.4.3 Threat to abundance, frequency and distribution of important species	Summary of abundance, frequency and distribution											
	Economic importance and uses of significant flora and fauna											
1.4.4 Hindriance to wildlife access	Sampling/survey map in relation to the project site											
2.0 THE WATER												
2.1 Hydrology/Hydrogeology												
2.1.1 Change in drainage/morphology	Drainage map; historical flooding/drought occurrences	Flood simulation/modeling, consider extreme weather										

Figure 4.6 EIS impact analysis guidelines.

through this process. The documentation requires an in-depth understanding of and information about the assessment of changes across soils and local fauna and flora.

The project proponents are also required to provide a comprehensive assessment of how changes in the physical and chemical parameters by the project will affect soil fertility. To do so, project proponents must first collect baseline data on the water-holding capacity of soil, soil texture classifications, and an in-depth chemical analysis of key chemical components such as nitrates, phosphorus and potassium. These components are selected by the EMB-DENR as key markers of fertile soils.

Decision-makers confirmed that a large amount of data is collected for baseline studies. For example, one respondents from PH03 revealed:

> That's normally how we start planning our projects. Normally we go back to the communities, get necessary data, start collecting baseline [data].

Evidence from the analysis of data suggests that baseline studies are a crucial component of assessments, as they form the 'point of reference' for the entire process. From the perspective of decision-makers, a baseline study determines current levels of areas relevant to potential impacts at a certain point in time, which sets the context for all evaluation activities.

Each sector within the sample, and more broadly across the EMD-DENR classifications, has different impacts from an environmental perspective. The baseline requirements from the EMD-DENR therefore vary greatly from industry to industry. For example, the mining sector has a specific focus on pedology (soil) and biodiversity losses, while the manufacturing sector is required to investigate waste release and water consumption. The EMB-DENR guidelines[1] on impact analysis differentiate the baseline requirements across the following sectors:

- Agricultural Plantation
- Food, Food By-products & Beverages Manufacturing
- Forestry Projects
- Hydropower & Dam Projects
- Mining Projects
- Non-Food Manufacturing
- Sanitary Landfill Projects
- Thermal Power Plants.

It is clear from the analysis of organisational practices that many organisations contract independent technical experts to provide an objective overview of the current state of the ecosystem. These independent technical experts also tend to carry out the entire baseline study, providing an objective and auditable process for organisations. To guarantee the validity of the baseline study, organisations usually also seek approval of a panel of experts through discussions with stakeholders. The main ecosystem issues are taken into account, which are usually structured around the findings of the scoping step. Interviews with key decision-makers revealed that organisations usually focus on:

- air-related impacts
- water-related impacts
- biodiversity-related impacts

This focus was also emphasised in the PEISS handbook for practitioners, which details the importance of baseline studies when defining significant impacts, with a specific focus on the environmental impacts. This environmental focus is evident in the Revised Procedural Manual for DAO 2003-30:[2]

> [I]mpacts which damage the environment to the point that the environmental resource loses its capacity to sustain life or to continue functioning within baseline levels and efficiency.

The current PEISS defines baseline levels, but also provides some guidance on the applied methodology to forecast and predict the significance of future impacts. It appears that the key methods provided by the PEISS are based on quantitative modelling. The next section explores the use of quantitative models as part of the impact analysis step.

Quantitative models

Impact assessments are heavily reliant on quantitative methods and models. Quantitative methods for impact forecasting were used extensively in organisations that participated in this study and spanned across all industries. To implement predictive models, the decision-maker must translate significant impacts into measurable indices. To assist with this task, specialists usually undertake this process, who can be internal or external to the organisation.

A limited number of organisations have extrapolated these quantitative methods into mathematical modelling in an attempt to predict future significant impacts. For example, advanced practices were evident within PH01 through the analysis of its project reports, which detailed how it undertook its air quality assessment.

> Air quality guidelines have been adopted for the Project. These include [de-identified] and relevant international air quality standards. A detailed air quality modelling assessment was undertaken for the Project involving [number] model scenarios. [de-identified] included all relevant air emissions including particulate matter, metals, sulphur dioxide, nitrous oxides and volatile organic compounds.

These sorts of 'advanced practices' are not the norm, however, with many organisations ***not*** undertaking comprehensive modelling. This arguably inhibits their ability to determine the intangible costs (such as those incurred through environmental impacts) and compare that with the overall costs of their operations. Decision-makers with experience in the field emphasised this point, noting that intangible costs arising from environmental and social impacts are the biggest threat to the economic viability of projects. Past projects have suffered from poor financial planning and underestimation of the environmental and social costs.

Beyond this general environmental modelling, it was also evident in the manufacturing sector that organisations in the World Class category were relying on advanced quantitative techniques. Specifically, the key methodology most frequently used was a LCALCAs can be adopted in various contexts but are generally a component used to help account for carbon emissions in operations and linked with the adoption of ISO14000 or CDP guidelines. This is demonstrated, in part, by internal documentation from PH12:

> Through this project, emphasis on four specific dimensions was given during the product research and development stage including [sector of activity], economic, environment and social aspects. The product life cycle assessment (LCA) was applied according to the ISO 14000.

Organisations within this study labelled LCA differently (*e.g.*, cradle-to-cradle analysis, product life analysis or input-output analysis), although all engaged with the concept of shifting the assessment process from the operational level towards the product level. This enabled greater transparency and accuracy when calculating environmental impacts. The analysis of organisational practices indicates that LCA usually revolved around three main topics:

- Water – the water usage from raw material extraction to product disposal is calculated.
- Energy and raw materials – the emissions of greenhouse gases, as well as the use of natural resources as raw materials along the product life cycle, are calculated.
- Waste – the amount of waste generated by a single product is taken into consideration.

LCAs are complex tools and often require the use of research partners and experts. It is an attractive tool to use as it provides a more accurate environmental footprint of a product. LCA tools also present the advantage of enabling the comparison of past projects with planned future activities. When implemented properly, decision-makers can rely on data from previously established projects. As a result, decision-makers can rely on previous knowledge to inform their current impact analysis practices. Figure 4.7 below presents the LCA across a three-year period of a participating manufacturing organisation.

Building on quantitative modelling techniques, such as the LCA, for assessing environmental impacts, organisations operating beyond regulatory requirements also provided interesting insights into more holistic tools, providing an inclusive

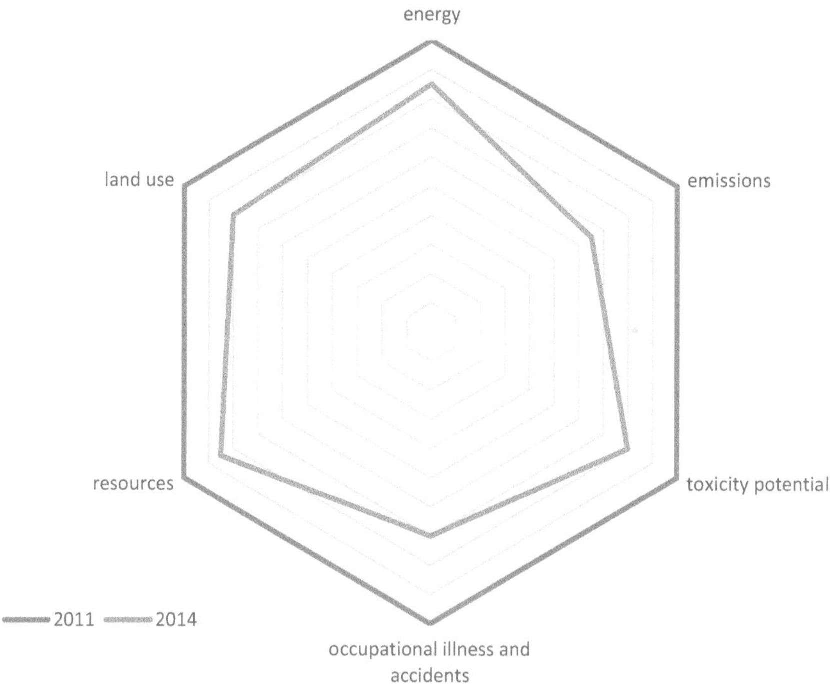

Figure 4.7 Life cycle assessment. Adapted from a participating organisation.

assessment across the social and economic dimensions. Such tools are explored in the next section.

Cost-benefit analysis

In examining the broader practices of organisations across the sample, it appears that Cost-Benefit Analysis (CBA) is a commonly used assessment tool. This tool has been mainly identified in organisations operating with more comprehensive practices, particularly those seeking to measure both social and environmental dimensions. Evidence suggests that the CBA is usually applied through both steps of the impact assessment stage. This section will first analyse how the CBA is utilised during the impact analysis step.

The CBA is usually carried out by decision-makers to provide a standardised measure of significant environmental and social impacts. Usually, the issues identified in the scoping step are integrated into a CBA measurement model. This measurement model predicts the cost of significant impacts over a defined period of time – usually during the lifetime of the project, though for mining organisations, the mine rehabilitation period is included in their calculations. As suggested by a decision-maker at PH14, the CBA is quite complex:

> It's an extremely complex model, as complex as any financial institution will do. So, we are very thorough with that financial modelling.

Once the costs have been calculated, a common currency is applied and, several organisations, a discount rate is applied to provide an accurate estimate of the net present value of the project options. Unforeseen costs can also be added to the CBA measurement model, allowing decision-makers to compensate for any project uncertainty. For example, PH05 factored into its calculation the 'social license to operate' as well as the cost of 'social unrest'.

Aiming to integrate complex impacts, such as the environmental cost of mine rehabilitation or social development programmes, CBA offers organisations the ability to adopt a more inclusive approach towards their impact analysis. This includes more accurately factoring in the costs of their operations and impacts. Decision-makers at PH14 also expressed how the transferability and comparability of such analyses can be achieved. As CBA results are expressed in a common currency, CBA can be shared with stakeholders for better transparency in the calculation methods. As a respondent from PH14 reflects:

> All our costs are included. Our findings are often very close to each other.

Although CBA is a complex process which might require multiple stakeholder input, there was little evidence of substantive stakeholder engagement as part of their CBA process for organisations. It could be that the complexity of this tool prevented decision-makers from taking stakeholders' views into account. Engagement is limited to the sharing of results with stakeholders. Organisations willing to further engage with stakeholders at the impact analysis step tend to utilise more inclusive tools, such as risk assessment and materiality analysis. The next section details these processes.

Risk assessment and materiality analysis

Risk assessments were found to be conducted across a wide range of participating organisations, particularly those operating within the World Class category. When implementing a risk assessment to evaluate their impacts, organisations tended to assess and evaluate selected sustainability issues from the scoping step through a risk scoring system, including material issues identified through a materiality analysis. The key goal of a risk assessment is to refine broader sustainability issues into specific and measurable categories. This process has often been described as complex, but provides decision-makers with fundamental metrics that can be measured through scoring systems.

A variety of scoring systems have been established by international agencies (including, likelihood scales, consequences scales, level of risk scale, risk matrix and scale for risk evaluation). This study found that the two key methods used by participating MNEs were the level of risk scale (*e.g.*, negligible to very high) and consequence scales. For example, the head of operations for PH14 outlined its risk assessment approach, which was based on a consequence scale and linked with the business operations:

> [T]hose risks are evaluated from 1 to 10. We basically evaluate 10 different risks – 1 being there is no risk and 10 being we are at a very high risk. All of them are operations related. We say that the risk is high if it affects our operations.

Assigning the correct value to the risk can be complex, and decision-makers often complete this task through brainstorming sessions or focus groups. Additionally, a high level of technical knowledge is required to score environmental, social and economic impacts. Evidence indicates that organisations adopting these practices utilise, to some extent, stakeholder engagement when carrying out risk assessments. Insights shared by decision-makers from PH04 explain why it is important to engage stakeholders in risk assessment:

> Each engagement aims to build trust and confidence with the community. And by applying the proper measurements for the success of every initiative, [name removed] is able to build integrity into every program [risk assessment] and enable the community to sustain them over the long-term.

Figure 4.8 (adapted from PH04) provides further insights into the structure of such risk assessment matrices.

During the impact analysis step, it would appear that the key rationale for organisations engaging with stakeholders is to obtain stakeholder approval, and to build the organisation's credibility. This was found particularly in the case of mining developments, where projects can be contentious from a stakeholder

Risk analysis	Dimensions		Risk index (P x S)	Proposed mitigation
	Probability ▪ **5= Almost Certain** ▪ **4= Likely** ▪ **3= Possible** ▪ **2= Unlikely** ▪ **1= Rare**	**Severity** **1 to 10 Scale:** **1 Insignificant to** **10 Catastrophic**		
Risk A				
Risk B				
Risk C				

Figure 4.8 Example of a risk matrix.

perspective. During the impact analysis step, organisations tended to increase their engagement with stakeholders to gather further information about the analysis process and results. As mentioned previously, the results of risk assessments were also attained and communicated through a materiality analysis.

Summary

In summary, the evidence suggests that the impact analysis step involves a complex process which is largely anchored within the PEISS, providing organisations with the necessary methodological guidance to undertake this step. The guidelines provided by the EMB-DENR suggest that specific methodologies should be applied when analysing and forecasting environmental impacts. This study found that quantitative techniques are predominantly applied as a mechanism to comply with regulations. To correctly analyse and forecast environmental impacts, the PEISS mandates that organisations gather key metrics through baseline studies, providing environmental reference points to allow for further analysis of impacts.

Moving beyond the regulatory requirements and quantitative techniques, organisations operating with more comprehensive practices provided insights into how other key tools are used during this step. LCAs, cost-benefit analysis, risk assessments and materiality analysis were the predominant tools used by organisations that exceeded the regulatory requirements. These tools – particularly risk assessments and CBA – enabled a more holistic consideration of non-environmental issues. Additionally, it was highlighted that, due to the complexity of this step, stakeholders are often excluded.

Risk assessments and materiality analyses were found to be methods commonly used as they enabled more active and comprehensive engagement of stakeholders during the impact analysis step. The next section of this chapter explores the second step within the impact assessment stage – the alternative selection step.

Alternative selection step

This section presents the second step of the impact assessment stage, the development of alternatives to address issues previously identified. These alternatives may be strategies that either enhance or mitigate the specific impacts identified in the preceding step. Alternative selection is inherently linked with the broader sustainability objectives, goals and methods the organisation has implemented. The extent to which organisations engage with sustainability in general is critical in determining how well they develop and implement suitable strategies to address potential impacts.

The following sections explore the activities and practices of organisations within the sample which will reveal how they plan to address the impacts of their operations. The same structure will be used here as for previous steps, and so will begin by examining the practice classifications of organisations, followed by an in-depth analysis of the management practices within each category. Lastly, key tools and techniques commonly used by MNEs during this step of their sustainability assessment will be presented.

Practice classification

Turning first to the practice classification of organisations within the sample, Figure 4.9 below illustrates the category in which organisations were assigned according to their general practices during their sustainability assessment. There is consistency between steps with regard to how organisations have been classified; such that the same organisations were classified into the same categories for this step, as they were for previous steps. The World Class and International Standards categories continue to dominate, with 38% (n = 9/24) of organisations falling within each of these categories. A sizable percentage of organisations remain in the final category, Compliance Driven – representing 25% (n = 6/24) of the sample.

The following graph illustrates the number of organisations within the sample across each industry and classification category (Figure 4.10). Similar patterns of distribution to the previous step are evident, with utilities organisations continuing to dominate in the World Class category, while mining organisations continue to conduct practices consistent with the International Standards and Compliance Driven categories.

For organisations in the mining sector, there is a general trend for organisations to continue implementing a similar level of practices across steps and, to some extent, also reflects the common use of tools and techniques across steps. Only 25% (n = 2/8) of mining organisations were classified into the World Class category, while 38% (n = 3/8) of mining organisations were classified into the International Standards and Compliance Driven categories.

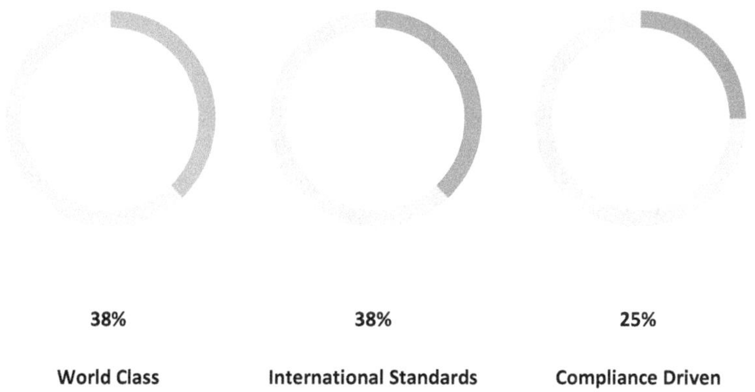

Figure 4.9 Practice classification – alternative selection.

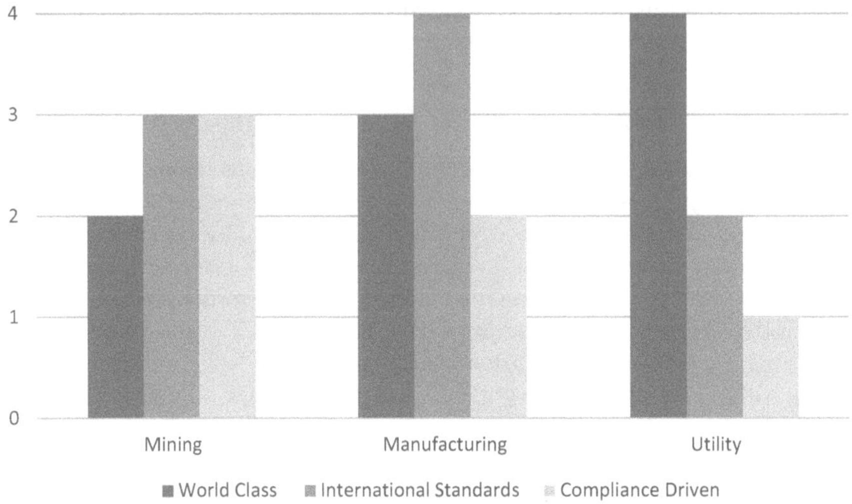

Figure 4.10 Practice classification per industry – alternative selection step.

For MNEs in the manufacturing section, approximately 33% (n = 3/9) were classified into the World Class category. The International Standards category clearly dominated the practices of these organisations, with 44% (n = 4/9) falling into this category. In the final category, only 22% (n = 2/9) of manufacturing organisations were classified as adopting Compliance Driven practices.

As mentioned above, the utilities sector continues to have the most organisations with practices that are classified as being World Class (57%, n = 4/7). Fewer utilities organisations were classified into the other two categories, with approximately 28% (n = 2/7) in the International Standards category and 14% (n = 1/7) in the Compliance Driven category. In the following section, the key management practices of organisations within these different classifications is presented.

Management practices

As noted above, this section will evaluate the general practices of organisations within each of the three categories, illustrating their key influences, frameworks and processes for the alternative selection step. Detailed examples are included for each category.

World class

Every organisation within the sample, including organisations within the World Class category, placed an emphasis on the financial aspects of their operations. This was also evident in the alternative selection step of their assessment. Here, organisations first considered alternatives that would improve their financial performance, before considering sustainability issues and exploring alternatives that would improve the impact of their operations. The two are not mutually exclusive, however, as some alternatives considered (such as improved technology being adopted in manufacturing) have an impact across multiple performance dimensions (including financial and environmental/social sustainability aspects).

In evaluating the practices of PH15 during the alternative selection step, they first considered their financial investment in the Philippines. This was evident from the corporate headquarters, which first evaluated the financial feasibility and the potential performance of its proposed operations against other neighbouring countries. This was aimed at determining where they should expand or begin operations. During interviews, respondents within the subsidiary of PH15 emphasised the importance of undertaking a detailed feasibility study to assist executive management in the home country to determine whether they should invest in the Philippines. This was focussed around the cost and competitiveness of the proposed investment as one respondent reflected:

> The first consideration in approving an investment is the Cost to Competitiveness. If [another country where the organisation has operations] makes the proposal, they are easily approved because their competitiveness is high. The Philippines is not good… However, there are other considerations such as complaints from stakeholders and the negative impact of causing unemployment. These issues have to be weighed… [but] the social issues must be balanced with the financial considerations.

Once the financial decision had been made on the value of the investment in the Philippines, a more detailed analysis was undertaken into the operations and planned activities. This included an analysis of the regulatory requirements of the Philippines government and any adaptations or alternatives needed for their operations. Those interviewed from the subsidiary operations reflected on this process, where there was a particular emphasis on the importance of the organisation adopting higher standards in their practices beyond those required by government regulations, as set by their headquarters:

> In addition to the compliance with Philippine government regulations, [subsidiary organisation in Philippines] complies with the [headquarter operation] global standards that address environmental concerns and other development issues… we have the [headquarter operation] global standards that are applied in each plant even if the local country does not require it. It is [the organisation's] responsibility as a global company.

Building from the initial investment decisions, including planning, design, incorporation of sustainability issues, alternative strategies implemented, through to broader sustainability strategies adopted, the process of going beyond compliance continues post-investment into the ongoing operations of the organisation. This is, in part, a reflection of the corporate culture of this organisation, but also reflects the commitments by the global headquarters to achieving certain higher standards within all of its operations. This includes a process of adapting and adjusting business activities to continuously address sustainability issues and impacts, across its global operations. As one participant described:

> Yes. [the subsidiary organisation's] business activities are aligned with global [headquarter] strategies. Before business activities are decided, a thorough study is first conducted, including potential problem analysis. This prevents the occurrence of issues with negative impact on the local community.

When considering the alternative selection practices specifically, adopting the requirements set by the corporate headquarters is also clearly evident. The organisation revealed that it undertakes particularly comprehensive social, economic and environmental analyses, through a product LCA. This process involves the organisation deconstructing different elements of the product life cycle, such as the consumption and usage patterns of the product by the consumer, and evaluates the different sustainability considerations within each element. By so doing, the organisation set global objectives for addressing the different impacts of its product through the phased introduction of mitigation and enhancement strategies.

Figure 4.11 below illustrates the intricate and comprehensive nature of the organisation's assessment processes. The foundation is focussed on the key

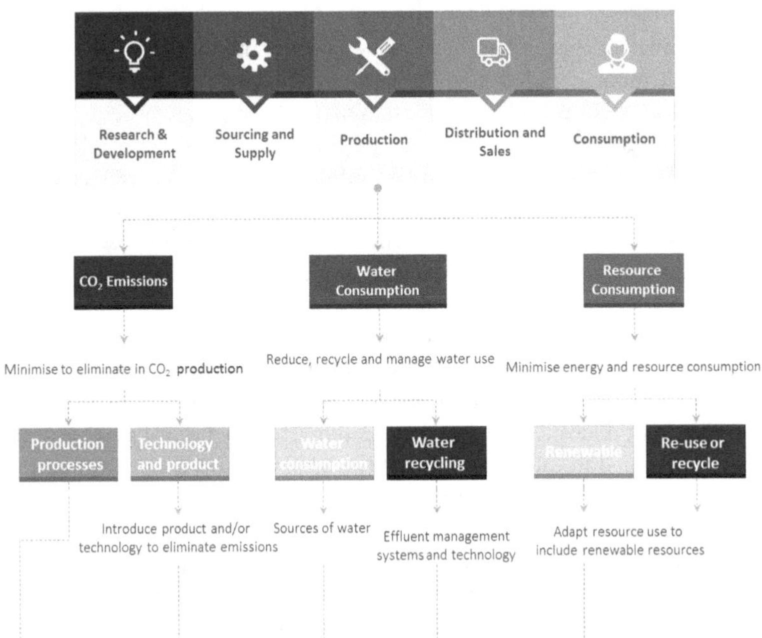

Figure 4.11 Product life cycle. Adapted from a participating organisation.

activities along the product life cycle, from research and design through to consumption and disposal of the organisation's product. For each component of the product life cycle, the organisation has identified the different sustainability issues, impacts and performance targets set through the global strategy. This component of the product life cycle is then deconstructed to address the particular sustainability issues the organisation is going to address.

One objective of PH15, for example, was to reduce (minimise) the CO_2 emissions generated by all of the organisation's production activities; it considered this through inputs and outputs, and supply and distribution. Its broad environmental performance target is to completely eliminate all CO_2 emissions within production. With this target in mind, the organisation evaluates a range of different manufacturing technologies that will enable it to reduce existing emission levels. This includes simplifying manufacturing processes which enables shortened production processes. It has also adopted all-renewable energy sources to power its factory, leveraging solar and wind power sources.

This process also clearly extends along the product life cycle. For example, in looking at downstream distribution activities, the organisation comprehensively evaluates how to mitigate and minimise emissions from its operations. This includes improving loading efficiency for trucking, fuel efficiency in the transportation fleet, evaluating efficient routes and distribution options. It also audits its suppliers and distributors, where these activities have been outsourced, to ensure that recommended changes to its operations are adopted.

What is clear from examining the organisation's operations is an ongoing cyclical evaluation of the various key issue and impact areas associated with its operations. From this, the organisation systematically evaluates methods for minimising or mitigating its environmental impact (makes alternative selections to reduce negative impacts). A similar approach is evident when examining key social and economic impacts, where the organisation charts its impacts and evaluates new alternatives to improve its performance.

International standards

When considering organisations in the International Standards category, their sustainability practices clearly demonstrate that they exceed the regulatory requirements set by the Philippines' government. There is also a tendency for these organisations to move towards more transparent reporting on the sustainability impacts of their operations, and the strategies they have implemented to address them. In a number of cases, organisations had already moved towards voluntary adoption of global sustainability platforms, such as the GRI standards. These organisations, however, often have a focus on detailing alternative strategies for the environmental dimension and have limited information detailing their holistic strategies for socio-economic considerations beyond regulatory requirements.

PH02, a mining organisation, is an excellent example of an organisation that was classified within the International Standards category, thus its practices generally exceed regulatory requirements. The organisation has operated in the

Philippines for a significant period of time and has incorporated the evolving set of regulatory requirements established for the mining sector. This includes the introduction of the requirement for community development programmes (as part of the SDMP), the ECC, EIS and EIA legislation.

The introduction of these different policy initiatives has resulted in the implementation of a series of changes, with the organisation focussing its analysis and alternative selection processes on social and environmental dimensions. This was particularly reflected in interviews with participants at the subsidiary level, as having an important impact on the engagement between the organisation and local communities. One participant described the introduction of the mining law in the Philippines:

> I think the Philippines Mining Law of 1995 is a blessing for the community. Before, social development of communities was company dependent and voluntary in nature. Until 2010, the Mining Law required only 1% of Operating cost to be spent on SDMP. In 2010, this was revised to 1.5% of Operating cost. So, that is a huge percentage and huge amount of money that will be spent for the benefit of the community. Also, thanks to the Law, the IPs are getting 1% of the gross sales yearly as their royalty.

The organisation was responsive to these different policy initiatives and adapted its practices to conform to the government's expectations. Following the introduction of the mining law in 1995, and the requirement to undertake more comprehensive community engagement programmes (through the SDMP), the organisation sought to undertake systematic processes for targeting the use of its funds to the community. This was not easy for the organisation, as it needed to learn and make adjustments to its operations, as articulated by one participant:

> The programs that we implemented are not focused on eliminating poverty. We are also guilty of that. The last 10 years, the company has been having 'dole-out' programs. So after reviewing all this, and based on the advice of Mines & Geosciences Bureau, we are focusing on [a different element of community] development.

The organisation also implemented social impact assessments to evaluate the impact and reach of its community engagement and CSR programmes. This practice now involves capturing data, so they can measure the efficacy of interventions and impacts from its activities. The organisation has also started to align its reporting with GRI requirements. Although this is still a 'work-in=progress', the result of this shift is particularly evident in capturing data around key sustainability issues and impacts.

However, when it comes to the alternative selection procedures, it appears that the organisation has maintained a sole focus on the environmental impact of its operations. Accordingly, it seeks ways of selecting and implementing mitigation strategies that reduce the negative environmental impact of its mining. These efforts are quite substantial and extends beyond the minimum requirements set by the government. For example, the organisation systematically assesses a broad set of key impacts, outlining management strategies that rely on both mitigation and minimisation approaches. As the operations have already been established for a significant amount of time, these strategies have been implemented already, which range from soil degradation, wastewater treatment, drainage, silt management, reforestation and management of flora and fauna.

However, there remain significant gaps in the information that the organisation provided around broader social and economic impact (despite the organisation conducting a social impact assessment). While it has a range of CSR and community development programmes in place to address regulatory requirements, it is not clear what strategies it has implemented to address other impacts created through its operations. Its reporting of social data is very limited and has a particular focus on internal information (such as health and safety, personnel employed) and social development programme spending. Overall, it was not evident from the interview data, nor from publicly reported information, what alternative selection strategies the organisation implements beyond its environmental focus and regulated community engagement.

Compliance driven

A review of the practices common with organisations in the Compliance Driven category revealed that the selection of alternative strategies or business activities was only considered if it was a regulatory requirement. These practices were consistent with what was required of MNEs during their initial investment process, where they had to acquire environmental compliance certification, implement a social development management programme (SDMP) or conduct a public hearing as part of the regulatory requirements.

PH24 is, once again, illustrates the practices of organisations that are compliance driven. The organisation experienced an extended process between the approval of the feasibility plan by the Board of Directors (in the home country) and the actual start of its operations in the Philippines. This was commented upon by one participant, who, during the interview, explained that the extended process was largely due to the extensive process of approvals required to meet the regulatory requirements in the Philippines:

> There were many requirements being asked of [the organisation] before it would be allowed to operate from DENR, from the provincial government and from the local government. We had to make sure that we are compliant with all Philippine and local laws.

A specialist department within the headquarters operations handled this process, including the evaluation of the feasibility of the proposed operations. This involved a very specific focus on the financial aspect of the operations, including evaluating the local market conditions. The specialist department also considered the regulatory requirements, including the requirement to attain an environmental compliance certification, as revealed in the following quote from a representative of the organisation

> The Overseas Investment Department in [home country] Headquarters develops the feasibility [economic, supply and demand and the ECC]. They submit this to the Overseas Investment Committee composed of members from different departments and the members look at all the technical aspects including financial and legal.

Despite participants suggesting that the organisation's operations were oriented towards implementing the 'best technology' solutions within the power plant to meet a 'world class' standard around emissions, it seemed more likely that a compliance driven approach dominated their consideration of alternative strategies. Beyond the implementation of existing technology utilised in its home country operations, the consideration of how to adapt its operations focussed solely on social issues and public hearings as part of the regulatory approval process. As one respondent reflected:

> The community was very much involved in the planning. We conducted public hearings about our plans. We created a MRT monitoring team that would ensure our compliance to laws and regulations. We developed a Corporate Social Responsibility (CSR) Program based on what the people requested and we went beyond compliance and integrated the community engagement into our business model.

Respondents revealed that the emphasis of the organisation in conducting public hearings was to achieve regulatory compliance. The CSR programmes, although at first appearing to indicate public engagement and participation in the organisation's investment, was linked to the regulatory requirement to undertake SDMP. This targeted the organisation's mandatory funding of community activities under the banner of being a CSR programme.

These requirements did not necessitate the further adaptation of its business activities, nor to engage in the active selection of alternatives to address impacts associated with its operations. Rather, this was based on providing positive benefits to the local community in line with the requirements stipulated by the government. The only additional consideration of adapting its operations was the local community's complaints about the fly ash from the power plant. In response, the organisation adapted its operational procedures, as explained by one participant:

> In one case, the fly ash was being blown away because of strong winds. We had to construct covers for the fly ash site so that it would remain stable before it is shipped. It cost us a lot but we did it because the health safety of the community is important to us. We have not received any complaint since.

The actions of the organisation during the alternative selection step appear to be largely driven by the government's regulatory requirements. Beyond this, there is only one instance, described above, where the organisation considered implementing any alternatives to address issues with its operations.

The presentation of findings now turns to the specific tools and techniques implemented by organisations across the sample.

Tools and techniques

This section explores the tools and techniques implemented by organisations when selecting alternative strategies in order to address and/or mitigate the impacts of its operations. The PEISS provides little guidance for organisations on the specific tools it could, or should, use and thus leaves the selection of mitigation strategies in the hands of the project proponent. However, other legislation encourages the use of four key techniques – prevent, reduce, repair or rehabilitate – for organisations to mitigate adverse impacts. These techniques are explored in further detail in the subsequent section.

Prevent, reduce, repair or rehabilitate

As mentioned earlier, the PEISS provides very little direction on which alternative selection strategies should be applied. From an analysis of official documents, no environmental impact thresholds to direct alternative selection strategies were evident. For example, thresholds around handling wastewater release limitations or CO_2 emissions were absent. Contrary to what was seen in the initiation and scoping steps, which rely heavily upon established lists and environmental thresholds, the implementation of mitigation solutions and alternatives is not guided by a prescribed set of tools. As seen in the structure below (Figure 4.12), representing the decision-making process of the PEISS, the EMD-DENR relies on the EIARC to assess the quality of the proposed EIS and consequently of the proposed mitigation solutions.

The legislation does not appear to provide any directions on appropriate alternative selection strategies or minimum mitigation solutions. In fact, the evidence suggests that environmental mitigation is always undertaken in relation to the values defined during baseline studies at the impact analysis step. The technical EIS handbook provided by the EMB-DENR[4] suggested that selecting appropriate alternatives should be left in the hands of the project proponent, as expressed in the handbook:

> This step [ECC Application] is wholly within the proponent's control… EMB-DENR personnel may clarify procedural and technical matters on the [EIS] process but is not allowed to take part in the [EIS] study.

Evidence suggests that within the PEISS, the EMB-DENR approves and validates the proposed impact analysis and alternative selection strategies or

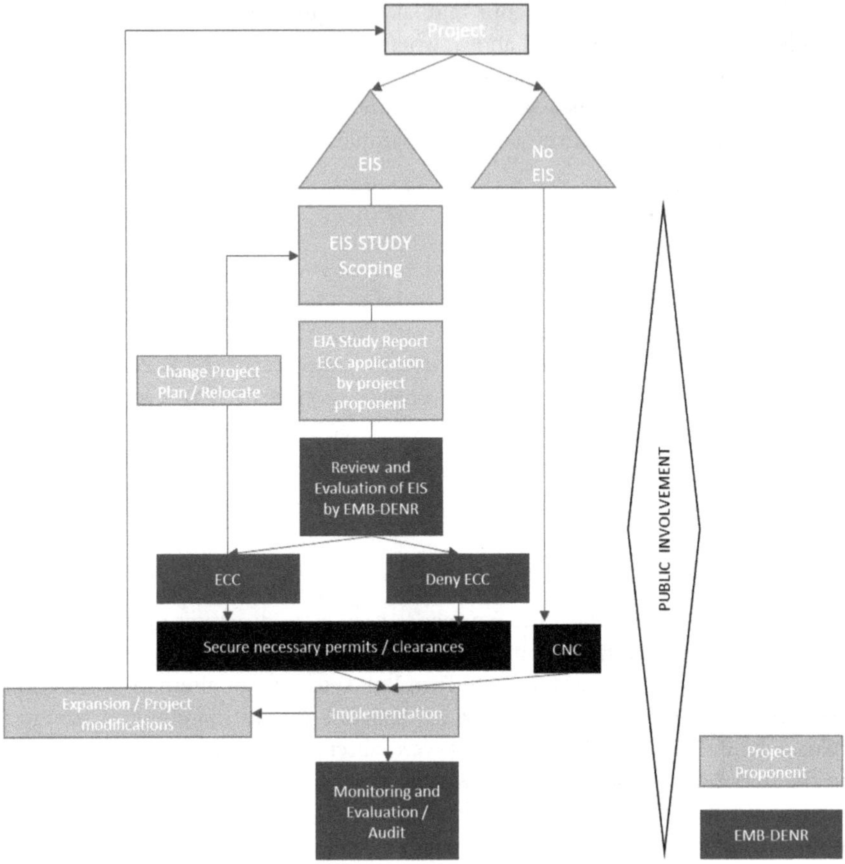

Figure 4.12 PEISS and ECC approval process.[3]

mitigation strategies. This approval is granted through the ECC. Proposed solutions are compared with the environmental baseline established during the impact analysis step. As mentioned previously, in projects where impacts threaten the ***capacity to sustain life or to continue functioning within baseline levels (DAO 2003), adequate mitigation strategies must be implemented.***

Further examination of mitigation strategies reveals four key methods are suggested by the EMB-DENR: Prevent, Reduce, Repair or Rehabilitate. No definition is provided in the current legislation, but interviews with organisations and key stakeholders revealed that these common strategies refer to the following concepts:

- Prevent: projects where significant impacts cannot be mitigated must be changed by design. For example, if the adverse effects of a mine are too important due to the location, the project's geographical position must be moved.

- Reduce: Best Available Technological (BAT) mitigation, one of the most common forms of mitigation, should be implemented where possible. As a key strategy, this concept is further developed in the next section.
- Repair: where significant impacts are unavoidable, compensation mechanisms can be implemented in order to repair the impact on the environmental baseline.
- Rehabilitate: for severe impacts, site rehabilitation might be the only applicable strategy. Site rehabilitation is often applied within the mining sector.

This study identified that the two key strategies implemented by organisations are 'reduce' and 'rehabilitate'. The project-related data collected in this study (interview transcriptions and publicly available documents) suggests that no projects conducted by any of the participating MNEs were subject to relocation. Further, there was no evidence of prevention by design or relocation. Similarly, repair strategies, such as CO_2 compensation schemes, did not emerge, nor were evident in any of the data sources.

The next section provides further insights into impact reduction and site rehabilitation; the two key methods employed by participating MNEs.

Best available technology – BAT

Those interviewed in this study revealed that the primary mitigation strategy implemented by organisations was a reduction of impacts through the implementation of the Best Available Technology (BAT). BAT, otherwise known as technological mitigation, is a non-formalised process whereby organisations implement the best available technology in the industry. Insights from decision-makers reveal that these mitigation techniques are applied whenever possible. While there are limitations in mitigation possibilities due to the nature and cost of the applied technology, such strategies have proven to be efficient in addressing environmental impacts.

Insights shared by decision-makers reveals that technological mitigation is most commonly used in environmental impact reduction. For example, CO_2 emission reduction is usually achieved by using efficient engines and better equipment. In some cases, the technological upgrade of machinery can be seen as one of the most effective mitigation solutions for environmental impacts. For example, when updating their production unit, decision-makers at PH14 considered noise reduction, as well as energy consumption and production output, from the implementation of BAT:

> Being sustainable and socially responsible, for us, is really embedded in what we are doing. The technology we use is the most environmentally-friendly technology.

Additionally, it was found that technological mitigation is often used to comply with national regulations. Examples of such activities were found in PH09, with insights from decision-makers showing that the organisation implemented specific technology to recycle wastewater which was produced as a result of its operational activities. The process was described by one participant:

> The technology that we installed… utilises bacteria to treat biological wastewater treatment. We do a monthly testing and it is part of the Self-Monitoring Report (SMR). We monitor the quality of the water based on the Clean Water Act. Before we discharge into the storm drain or municipal drain, we make sure that we meet the DENR standard, which is also part of the quarterly report that we submit to them. Actually, our drinking water is tested monthly.

However, organisations are often limited by the available technology (such as BAT) and can be faced with the prospect that technology may not produce the necessary impact reduction anyway. Additionally, a key disadvantage of BAT is that it is often only applicable in addressing environmental issues. While it is possible to address social issues, for example, addressing health and safety through noise reduction, the approach is rare in practice by participating MNEs. Further insights shared by operational managers at PH09 demonstrated technology use for noise reduction. This case, however, which involved PH09 implementing new noise abatement technology, was focussed on addressing local and surrounding community concerns, rather than employee issues:

> We also put barriers or containment actions to minimise the noise. There is a technology available in US which we use.

Beyond the use of BAT, particularly in cases where it cannot reach sufficient mitigation targets, further strategies are often implemented. This is particularly the recourse for organisations in the mining industry, due to the very nature (mineral extraction) of its operations and the likelihood of significant impacts on the local biosphere. In such cases, these organisations must rehabilitate the site after use and ensure that significant impacts are contained within the site. The next section explores how organisations consider rehabilitation strategies.

Project design and rehabilitation

Within the mining industry, site rehabilitation was found to be one of the key methods for addressing alternative selection and mitigation strategies. As defined by an operational manager at PH04, "*[m]ining means 'temporary land use'. It does alter the landscape*". During mining operations, few alternatives for protecting the land are available and thus landscapes are inevitably 'altered' or modified. This is perhaps why mining organisations focus on rehabilitation as an effective mitigation strategy, as it allows them to operate the mining site in the interim. This was aptly described by one participant:

> In general, people would like to maintain the original profile of the landscape, but because of the basic nature of mining - that is not possible. But you could always rehabilitate the area after mining, and that is what we are doing. There is progressive rehabilitation and planned rehabilitation after the area has been mined out. The top soil is reserved [retained] for rehabilitation.
>
> (PH04)

Further indications of rehabilitation plans were evident in the EIS of PH01 in their EMD-DENR submission reports. The organisation provided the EMB-DENR with a clear rehabilitation strategy, providing extensive ecology restoration plans as well as social rehabilitation. These are summarised in the following excerpt from a PH01 report:

- Mine Closure Plan during the project life to account for results from environmental monitoring and more detailed closure planning.
- Progressive rehabilitation of disturbed areas over the life of the Project, where possible.
- Decommissioning of the mine site including rehabilitation of the TSF and decommissioning of the mine pit and mine infrastructure areas at mine closure.
- Where necessary, site discharge water would continue to be treated to comply with adopted site discharge water quality standards in the closure phase.

(Excerpt from PH01's Project report)

Building beyond these regulation-driven approaches, organisations within the World Class category, in particular, often consider more complex tools when selecting alternative strategies to mitigate the impact of their projects. Two key methods emerged as being practiced by MNEs when selecting alternatives that also consider social and economic dimensions, including:

- Cost-benefit analysis
- Risk assessment

Cost-benefit analysis

Cost-benefit analysis (CBA) was found to be one of the main tools used when assessing the sustainability outcomes of projects and the value of implemented mitigation solutions (alternative selection). As mentioned in the previous section, CBA not only helps decision-makers to assess the significance and severity of specific impacts, but also provides a useful guide for selecting appropriate mitigation solutions.

At first, the CBA appears to be a simple process, which lists the mitigation solutions and their associated costs and benefits. When calculating the sums for each of the various options, decision-makers are able to determine the monetary value of the mitigation solutions. Figure 4.13, below, demonstrates an adapted (de-identified) example from a participating organisation.

However, this perceived simplicity is often coupled with the complexity involved in monetising and valuating the intangible impacts, which can lead to difficulties in the application of such methods. Moreover, the 'benefits' of a proposed solution are not necessarily quantifiable, and so monetising the benefit is similarly fraught with problems. Organisation PH14, which operates in the manufacturing sector, described their extensive use of CBA for operational activities, as well throughout their planning process. Decision-makers admitted that while they utilised CBA to inform their decisions, they shared their concern with regard to the complexity of such tools – specifically, the limitations of being able to consider a holistic view of all sustainability dimensions. One respondent reflected:

> I mean the problem I've seen with so many CBAs is they don't take into account everything. So, we [have] got to look at everything that's going to be included.

Given the challenges of using CBA, it was unsurprising that some organisations adopt alternative tools that provide a more holistic way of capturing both environmental and social dimensions. This is discussed next.

	Cost	**Benefit**	**Analysis result:**
Mitigation Solution **A**	*Monetary value*	*Monetary value*	Cost > Benefit
Mitigation Solution **B**	*Monetary value*	*Monetary value*	Benefit > Cost
Mitigation Solution **C**	*Monetary value*	*Monetary value*	Cost > Benefit
Mitigation Solution **D**	*Monetary value*	*Monetary value*	Cost > Benefit
Mitigation Solution **E**	*Monetary value*	*Monetary value*	Benefit > Cost
Total	*Monetary value*	*Monetary value*	Cost > Benefit

Figure 4.13 Cost-benefit analysis. Adapted from a participating organisation.

Risk assessment

The previous steps have shown that risk assessment was used by a range of organisations to select and assess the significance of impacts within their operations. Organisations tended to implement a consistent approach to using risk assessment methodology. Insights shared by key decision-makers within these organisations indicate the key advantage of a risk assessment is its non-monetary approach. No monetary value is needed or computed, as the entire process relies on the value judgement of decision-makers and key stakeholders.

The evidence suggests that this method is used across all industries and appears to be independent of the investment size. Further, it was found that risk assessments are prevalently used by organisations that have implemented specific sustainability guidelines (such as: GRI, IFC framework, World Bank). The key tool identified within this specific method is the *weighted* risk assessment. Like general risk assessments, they present the criteria for assigning weighted scores to each mitigation solution. The next section provides further insights into the use of this tool.

WEIGHTED RISK ASSESSMENT

This section presents further details of the mechanics of the weighted risk assessment and insights into how this tool was applied by participating organisations. Weighted risk assessments offer decision-makers further flexibility when selecting project alternatives and mitigation solutions. Various views and aspects of the decision-making process can be taken into consideration, such that values can be adjusted (weighted) to reflect the areas of contention within the project or key stakeholders. For example, if, during the scoping process, discussions around environmental impacts was contentious, a higher weighting could be applied in order to increase the focus on environmental issues during the final decisions and project activity selection.

Additionally, various mitigation solutions can be weighted according to a variety of factors. Evidence from analysing organisations practices suggests that the weighting can be done by scaling the mitigation solutions. For example, one organisation revealed that it distributed 100 points across five alternative mitigation solutions to rank their potential effectiveness. An average weight index was then calculated and applied to each mitigation solution. Table 4.1 provides a framework of how such weighted risk assessments were conducted.

This approach was evident across several organisations within the sample. For example, PH13 demonstrated the use of this approach consistently across the assessment process to inform its final decision-making.

> The criteria matrix there is an in depth score typically given to it, because as I mentioned, there are weightings that are usually provided and if the user is

Table 4.1 Weighted risk assessment

Proposed Mitigation Solutions for Risk 1	*Weight*	*Dimensions*		*Results*
	100 Points Distribution	*Probability (Not Probable/Highly Probable)*	*Severity (Low/ High)*	
Mitigation solution A	20	Probable	Low	
Mitigation solution B	30	Highly probable	High	Implemented mitigation solution
Mitigation solution C	10	Not probable	Medium	
Mitigation solution D	25	Probable	Medium	
Mitigation solution E	15	Not probable	Low	

> doing it correctly and using it correctly they should be adjusting the weightings from the context of the proposal. But there would be a score given to that [mitigation solution option] - and that score is going to weigh the cost of being there as well as some of the other softer factors.

The complexity of mitigation solution selection makes it difficult for decision-makers to integrate stakeholders into the process. The absence of stakeholder engagement can be seen as one of the weaknesses of a sustainability assessment. This study found that decision-makers are generally reluctant to engage with stakeholders for the following reasons:

- Complexity of the mitigation processes
- Stakeholder knowledge is not appropriate for the selection of mitigation solutions
- Stakeholders might contest and challenge the selected mitigation solutions, creating an impasse in activities and planning.

Notwithstanding this reluctance, some organisations were found to attempt to partially include stakeholders and use weighted risk assessments to capture their views. However, it should be noted that in these cases, even though stakeholders were consulted, the final decision of the mitigation solution remained with the organisations. As described by the community manager at PH05, stakeholder trust and understanding of social and environmental alternatives are critical:

> For environmental and community development, GF goes for world class standards. Filipino standards in some cases are not world class, and we would prefer to go for world class standards… Everybody needs to understand what we are doing and they need to trust the company.

Validating potential solutions through community engagement was reinforced through the views of the operational manager at PH03. When sharing insights into the recently implemented social programmes, he reflected:

> [Our aim is to] not just participate in their livelihood programs, but to connect with the local community on a very basic and human level; it is very important to build 'trust' and eventually roll out the right social projects that they 'really need' and not just what they wished for.

Extrapolating from these comments, the participatory role of stakeholders appears to be often limited to the validation and approval of the mitigation solutions. So, while it was important for participating organisations to build a strong link between the project and key stakeholders, their engagement was often limited to the communication of the project's impacts, as opposed to actively determining what solutions should be implemented. No evidence was found of active participation by stakeholders in the final decision-making processes of organisations within the sample; not even for those who adopted the most comprehensive practices.

In summarising the final step of the impact assessment stage, this study found that the PEISS provides the foundation of the mitigation strategies and alternative selection processes adopted by organisations within the sample. The EMB-DENR suggests that the mitigation strategies should be implemented across four key methods: prevent, reduce, repair and rehabilitate. However, insights shared by decision-makers suggested that the alternative selection step is focussed on reduction strategies and site rehabilitation (particularly in the context of mining operations).

This study found that key tools and techniques in selecting mitigation solutions are commonly utilised by MNEs in the Philippines. Specifically, organisations with more comprehensive practices generally applied the same tools as in the previous impact analysis step. Risk assessment and in-depth materiality analysis provided organisations with key metrics and information to make an informed decision. Interestingly, this study also identified that key stakeholders were often excluded from this step due to the complexity of evaluating the proposed mitigation solutions. However, some organisations, in an attempt at transparency, were found to invariably seek stakeholder approval and validation when selecting project alternatives.

Summary of stage two

The second stage of the sustainability assessment is structured around two key steps. First, organisations undertake an in-depth impact analysis for key sustainability issues previously identified during the scoping step. Our findings reveal that the PEISS provides the foundation of the impact analysis step. The documentation provided by the EMB-DENR suggests that when analysing environmental impacts, organisations mainly rely on quantitative techniques.

Quantitative techniques are usually centred on computational models assessing and predicting key biosphere and atmospheric indicators.

It was also found that organisations operating with more comprehensive practices use a range of tools and techniques to analyse the social and broader economic impact of projects. Risk assessments are particularly prevalent, enabling effective analysis of impacts across all sustainability dimensions, whilst also allowing for the inclusion of key stakeholders in the process.

Second, organisations must then select alternative mitigation strategies, and where appropriate, implement these solutions when the severity of the analysed impacts is deemed unacceptable. During this alternative selection step, the PEISS provides four key environmentally focussed mitigation strategies (prevent, reduce, repair, rehabilitate) which can be implemented by the project proponent. While the four strategies were suggested in the legislation (DAO 2003-30), this study identified that only impact reduction and site rehabilitation mitigation strategies are used in practice. Interviews with key decision-makers revealed that organisations operating with more comprehensive practices use tools such as CBA or weighted risk assessments to more thoroughly and systematically select the most favourable mitigation solution.

The next chapter describes the last stage of a sustainability assessment.

Notes

1 Information provided to project proponents available at: http://eia.emb.gov.ph/ecc-applications-and-issuance/requirements-for-securing-ecc/eis-screening-forms/.
2 Revised Procedural Manual for DAO 2003-30 available at: http://eia.emb.gov.ph/wp-content/uploads/2016/06/Revised-Procedural-Manual-DAO-03-30.pdf.
3 Adapted from the Revised Procedural manual for DA0 2003-30 page 14 available at: http://eia.emb.gov.ph/wp-content/uploads/2016/06/Revised-Procedural-Manual-DAO-03-30.pdf.
4 Adapted from the Revised Procedural manual for DA0 2003-30 page 19 available at: http://eia.emb.gov.ph/wp-content/uploads/2016/06/Revised-Procedural-Manual-DAO-03-30.pdf.

5 Impact monitoring and follow-up stage

Introduction

The final stage of the sustainability assessment, the impact monitoring and follow-up stage, enables organisations to monitor and evaluate their sustainability performance and implement changes in response to performance outcomes. This is, perhaps, the most critical of the stages, as it allows organisations to determine whether their targeted performance outcomes have been met, while also enabling iterative changes to ensure these outcomes are achieved. During this stage, organisations may implement alternatives to improve their performance either through mitigation efforts to address negative impacts or enhancement strategies to accelerate or improve positive impacts.

Within this stage, there are two key steps: (1) monitoring and evaluation and (2) feedback and follow-up, and the result for each will be presented below. Similar to previous sections, a description of typical MNE activities for each step will be provided, which will include organisational management practices, frameworks, policies and procedures, and the range of influences that direct their sustainability assessment structure. This will conclude the presentation of results for the 24 organisations that participated in this study (Figure 5.1).

Monitoring and evaluation step

The monitoring and evaluation step is oriented around establishing a monitoring system to enable the sustainability performance of the project to be evaluated. Monitoring and evaluation are inherently linked. Without an appropriate method to monitor the key sustainability issues and impacts, the organisation will be unable to determine (evaluate) its performance outcomes. These two activities thus provide a basis for organisations to determine whether corrective actions are required to address their performance outcomes.

The subsequent sections of this chapter will first focus on providing a high-level overview of the classifications of organisations at this step. Then, an in-depth description of the management practices across each of these classifications will be presented. This will include the key practices involved in each step, the context driving the decisions within this step and the general processes being

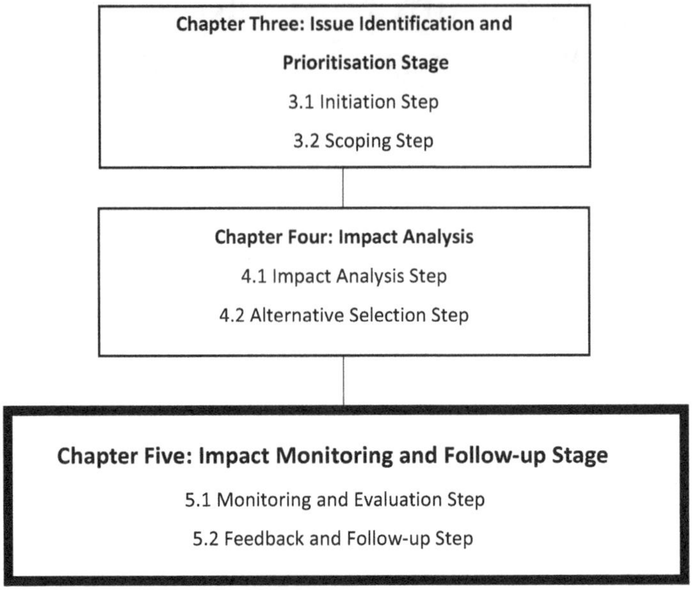

Figure 5.1 Data results chapter overview.

implemented by organisations. Lastly, key tools and techniques commonly used by organisations will be presented.

Practice classification

Figure 5.2 below illustrates how organisations were generally classifications into one of three categories. The categories that organisations were allocated to are consistent with how they were classified in previous steps. This includes 38% (n = 9/24) of organisations classified into the World Class category and 38% (n = 9/24) into the International Standards category. The remaining 25% (n = 6/24) of organisational sustainability activities were classified into the Compliance Driven category.

This reinforces earlier findings about the consistency of organisations in their practices across various stages and steps within the sustainability assessment process. This is, in part, attributable to the fact that organisations are using tools or techniques that naturally cover a series of steps within the assessment process. It is also an indication of the commitments that organisations have to particular practices, maintaining these across their entire sustainability practices.

This congruence across steps is particularly evident when observing organisational practices by industry (see Figure 5.3). The organisations per category and by industry maintain a similar standard of practices as was present in previous steps. The utilities sector continues to have the highest percentage of

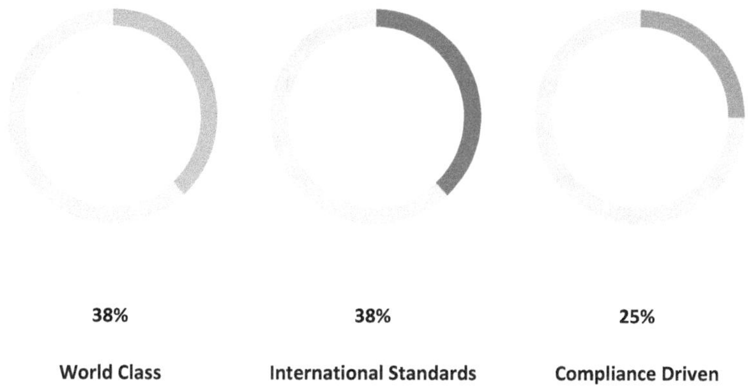

Figure 5.2 Practice classification – monitoring and evaluation step.

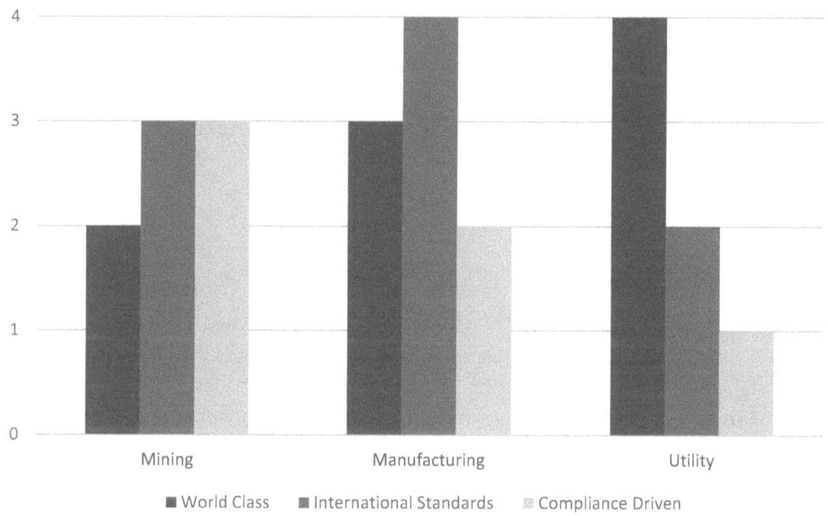

Figure 5.3 Practice classification per industry – monitoring and evaluation step.

organisations classified within the World Class category. Manufacturing continues to experience a higher percentage of organisations within the International Standards category and the mining sector is dominated by organisations within the International Standards and Compliance Driven categories.

It is evident that mining organisations are performing at a lower level of sustainability for the monitoring and evaluation step than other industries. Mining organisations that participated in this study represent the fewest number (n = 2/8) who adopted World Class sustainability standards (25%). International Standards and Compliance Driven classifications dominate the results, with approximately 38% (n = 3/8) of mining organisations classified into each category.

Organisations in the manufacturing sector perform slightly better, with 33% (n = 3/9) of organisations falling within the World Class category. The International Standards category dominates, with 44% (n = 4/9) of organisations going beyond minimum standards. Only 22% (n = 2/9) of manufacturing organisations were classified as being Compliance Driven.

The utility sector contains the largest percentage of organisations adopting World Class sustainability practices (57%, n = 4/7). A smaller percentage of organisations were classified into the other two categories: 28% (n = 2/7) of organisations were in the International Standards category, and 14% (n = 1/70 were in the Compliance Driven category.

The following sections will examine these results more closely, first focussing on the management practices being implemented across the three practice classifications.

Management practices

The following sections will begin with a discussion of the performance of organisations within each category, before proceeding to an in-depth examination of an exemplar case to articulate the specific activities undertaken by organisations within each category.

World class

Organisations classified within the World Class category commonly adopt comprehensive monitoring and evaluation practices to capture and evaluate their sustainability performance across multiple dimensions. Global sustainability platforms are a recurring influence in directing the practices of these organisations. Many of these global sustainability platforms, and particularly the GRI standards, direct organisations to present and report on information about their sustainability performance. These standards are prescriptive regarding the types of information that need to be presented and require organisations to report across the three key dimensions of sustainability.

The commitment of organisations to global sustainability platforms is particularly evident in the practices of PH12, a major manufacturing organisation. It utilises has a sustainability framework that is underpinned by the organisation's commitment to a range of key sustainability platforms, including the GRI, UNGC, CDP, the United Nations Business Alliance for Water and Climate Change, and a set of regional and international sector specific sustainability initiatives. The organisation has also begun to align all its sustainability objectives with the newly released Sustainable Development Goals released in 2016.

Matching this broad approach to sustainability commitments is a set of key ethics and values set by the headquarter operations, which then funnel down to operational policies and procedures. This enables the organisation to distil and codify its approach to sustainability into actionable practices. A range of policy documents are also available on the organisation's corporate website, and this was also emphasised in the interviews with the subsidiary representatives and regional headquarters. This approach has been adopted across the organisation's global operations, not just in the Philippines. As one respondent reflects:

> We have made our point in having one single Vision-Mission and one single set of values throughout the different countries that operate...

PH12's sustainability framework is clustered across three broad categories including people (within the organisation), communities (in which the organisation operates) and planet (which relates to environmental impacts). Under each category, the organisation has delineated a series of sub-categories covering key areas that it focusses upon across its operations, including training and development, community development, sustainable sourcing, water and energy use, waste and recycling.

Beyond its broad sustainability considerations, the organisation also undertakes a materiality analysis in the locations in which it operates. This allows for delineation and prioritisation of locally relevant sustainability issues. Sixteen broad issue areas were identified through its materiality analysis for the Philippines operation, including waste management, safety in the communities they operate within, health and safety, training and development, and energy and sustainable products, among others. Only a selection is presented in Figure 5.4 below to protect the anonymity of the organisation (these have also been slightly adjusted in terms of the terminology).

The broader issue categories within the sustainability framework, together with the materiality analysis and the reporting requirements to which the organisation has committed, are all linked to sets of indicators to determine their impact. This is monitored and evaluated on an annual basis (or, in some cases, a monthly basis for critical risk areas) and reported upon through the organisation's annual reporting mechanisms. As part of this process, the organisation has set clear targets that it wants to achieve within each of the key indicator areas, and aligns its performance (annually) to the performance target that has been set.

From examining their materiality analysis process, it is evident that PH12 largely relies on quantitative methods for monitoring and evaluation. It has a comprehensive set of indicators to cover different sustainability issues linked to the broad categories it has identified. Generally, this funnels down from the material issue, to the specific areas the organisation will monitor and evaluate, before looking at the specific data and the performance of the organisation.

This method of monitoring and evaluation is conducted longitudinally, building from a baseline data point the organisation established when it began the monitoring and evaluation process for the indicator areas. For example, as illustrated below (Figure 5.4), CO_2 emissions, are captured across the value chain (among other areas) to determine the relative performance of the organisation.

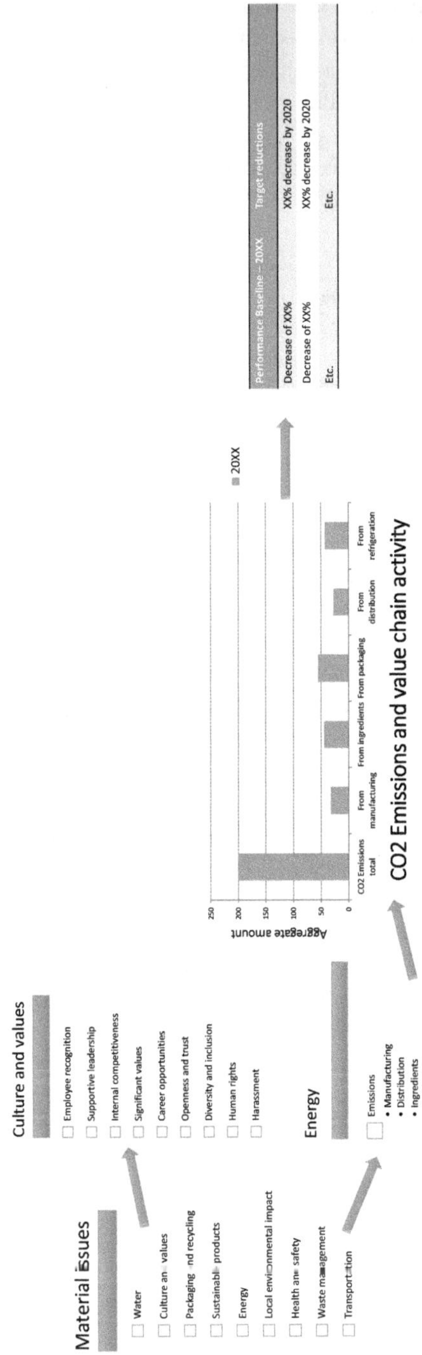

Figure 5.4 Example of monitoring and evaluation of material issues.

This is charted over an extended period of time, and performance improvements are compared against targets established by the organisation. This process is replicated across different material issues, and against the broad sustainability areas identified by the organisation.

International standards

Organisations within this category are clearly exceeding regulatory requirements, with a particular emphasis on implementing comprehensive monitoring and evaluation practices across the environmental and social dimensions of their operations. This is evident when examining the environmental performance of these organisations, with many starting to align their practices with different discipline-specific international standards, such as ISOs for environment-related issues. Social issues and impacts are also becoming increasingly evident in these organisations, although this appears to be less systematic and established than the environmental aspects of their operations.

PH09 is a component manufacturer and is a prime example of organisations going beyond the regulatory requirements within the Philippines. However, it is worth acknowledging some of the key monitoring and evaluation activities it performs for regulatory purposes, before proceeding to an overview of the practices that go above and beyond government requirements. The organisation provides reporting on its performance across environmental and labour issues to the Department of Environment and Natural Resources (DENR), Department of Labor and Employment (DoLE), Department of Health, Philippine National Police and Philippine Drug Enforcement Agency. The involvement of these departments is due not only to the common requirements for conducting an ECC and associated monitoring reports, but also to the composition of the materials utilised in the organisations' operations (including dangerous substances).

Environmental compliance relates to both the direct operations of the factory and how it affects local environmental conditions. The organisation reports on all of the environmental impacts that it has identified in the Environmental Impact Statement (EIS). This covers a range of environmental issues, as one respondent explained:

> In the environmental impact statement, it is already distinctive how we will handle the impacts of [our operations]. So the CMR, it's the Compliance Monitoring Report, we submit it semi-annually to the DENR. And aside from that, there's a separate Self-Monitoring Report [SMR] which is submitted quarterly to them. The CMR is basically compliance to the conditions stated in the ECC. The SMR [looks at the] amount of hazardous waste generated, the amount of hazardous waste treated, the duration of the operation of the generators, wastewater treatment facilities, [and the] air scrubbing system. We produce exhaust from our processes, so we have to clean the air before we throw it out into the environment. So all those reports that I mentioned, they are all notarised.

In addition, the organisation provides a range of safety- and health-related reporting that it conducts with the government. This includes specialist requirements due to the production and quality assurance processes it conducts for its product components. Beyond this, the organisation undertakes a range of other monitoring measures to identify any further issues that emerge from its operations and undertakes corrective actions where necessary. This includes public hearings and consultation processes that the organisation has implemented with the local communities surrounding its operations, as well as with its employees. Some of this is included in periodic monitoring and engagement processes; while other activities are part of a reactive approach to issues as they emerge. For example, when there were security issues with employees being targeted by local thieves, the organisation engaged with the local community, local authorities, officials and staff in addressing these issues. As one respondent reflected:

> Before, there was a security problem because there were many snatchers [thieves] in community [preying on the workers as they go to and from the company]. We convened a community forum that included the Philippine National Police [PNP] and barangay[1] LGU [Local Government Unit] and the community. We spearheaded this... So we were able to solve the problem by financing the additional security. We paid for the gasoline expenses of the PNP so that they can have more visibility in the area. We also gave financial support for additional barangay tanods [village police]... So we provided everything to solve all the problems.

Other issues emerged through this participatory engagement with the local community – for example, the noise generated by exhaust systems. Despite the noise level being within the limits set by the government, the organisation chose to reduce it further as it was a new community issue. It adjusted the layout of its building, incorporated new technology and put in containment areas which reduced the noise levels; thus the issue was mitigated and local communities were satisfied.

The organisation also has a set of international standards that it has adopted. These are mostly specific to environmental standards and product materials. It reports upon these standards from its headquarters. The standards require that the organisation regularly monitors and evaluates its performance across a range of different areas, including CO_2 emissions, waste management and energy utilisation. As one executive from PH09 commented:

> For the majors [i.e., serious issues], it is discussed in the management review which is done annually. If it is EHS-related [i.e., environment health and safety concerns], I discuss it with top management. I do a sort-of "state of the nation" presentation on EHS annually.

However, it was found that some of PH09's processes appear to be more *ad hoc* in their evaluation than others, such as the implementation of its recycling programme to minimise waste from its operations. The MNE evaluates the overall cost savings produced by implementing a recycling process, by on-selling waste as a regular function of the volume of its operation. This was described in detail by one manager:

> On our own, we do recycling. We sell it. Actually, our trash earned [amount withdrawn to de-identify] million last year. The money goes back to operations. When the hauler comes in, we have an agreed price. So we have to know how many kilos of trash we have on a monthly basis. For the past several years, our volume of trash is kind a flat. If there is an increase, it's not significant. The volume of waste is flat. The waste materials include cartons, bubble wrap, styro and everything. So it's always tied with volume.

These examples provide evidence that the organisation is going beyond what is required for regulatory compliance. It engages with the local community both through active, periodic processes and responds to their feedback. International standards are driving some of these practices, but management is also initiating some as well while it monitors different issues, evaluates the organisation's performance and makes any necessary adjustments to its operations.

Compliance Driven

Organisations within the Compliance Driven category consistently link their monitoring and evaluation practices and activities back to government requirements. This is particularly the case for the environmental compliance certification required across sectors and the social development management plans required within mining operations. Organisations within this category consistently expressed an emphasis on meeting their 'compliance' requirements, and this is highlighted in the interviews where participants explained these regulatory requirements. This included the process they undertake; the time period of monitoring, evaluation and reporting; engagement with communities; and scope/boundaries of their activities.

PH04 is a suitable example of an organisation that demonstrates a focus on only meeting the regulatory compliance requirements of the government. Throughout the interviews, key senior executives in the subsidiary operations repeatedly emphasised that their focus is on meeting the requirements of the government. There was a dearth of information available on the subsidiary operations. No website had been established for the subsidiary operations and no other information or documentation was available on its operations within the Philippines. It is thus assumed that the information provided by those interviews is complete and accurate.

Looking beyond the subsidiary, the corporate headquarters' reporting of activities identified only a small component of its subsidiary operations in the Philippines. This related to a recently implemented technology; no further information was provided by headquarters. It is clear that the scope of reporting was limited to focussing on the corporate headquarters, despite the organisation adopting the GRI standards.

It was apparent in the interviews with senior executives that the subsidiary operations are focussed only on government compliance requirements. At the start of the interview, one respondent detailed his/her focus on examining sustainability-related issues:

> Of course [we are] in compliance to the existing statutory regulations as prescribed by the law for companies like us. After 1995, we have to have a plan and a budget which is 1.5% of operating cost [for the SDMP] - from voluntary to mandatory. Earlier SDMP was based on our operating cost but now it is based on the direct milling and mining cost. There is a fixed guideline for the mining companies on how to have a positive impact on the communities of operation, by DENR through MGB. There is a minimum amount that has to be spent for the development of the community.

Organisational respondents stated that the thresholds for undertaking these activities are very specific in the SDMP guidelines. This includes not only the proportion of money invested in these programmes but also directing this money towards the requirements specified by the government. As one respondent said:

> We are strictly following the SDMP guidelines in our third SDMP where 75% [is] for community development, 15% for IEC [information and education campaigns] and 10% for mining-related studies.

Although this is prescriptive in terms of how funds are allocated, the organisation also follows the consultation requirements embedded within the laws. This requires regular monitoring and engagement with local communities to aid in the development of specific plans for the allocation of funds to different activities. These activities are also reported to the government, including the monitoring the organisation undertakes on the expenditures for different activities. This was captured by the comments of one respondent:

> With regards to our community development projects, we go into consultation activities with the community. We conduct monthly or quarterly meetings with the barangay officials, specifically barangay captains, to learn about the needs or immediate concerns of the barangays. These needs are assessed and if approved they are implemented. We conduct monthly monitoring and submit quarterly reports to DENR [and] MGB [Mines and Geosciences Bureau].

From an examination of the organisation's monitoring processes, it is evident that all activities are directed towards a compliance approach and that this determines the extent to which the organisation monitors sustainability-related issues within its operations. This ranges from the use of an MMT, through to the reporting cycle that it undertakes on the results of its monitoring. One respondent captured this succinctly:

> [the organisation's monitoring is] mandated by law to constitute a Multi-party Monitoring Team comprising 2 to 3 people. One person from the company and one from the impact barangay is the minimum requirement by law. The financial and physical aspects are to be monitored by the MMT on a monthly basis and this is collated quarterly and submitted to the DENR. Based on this report, the MGB constitutes a team to ratify the findings.

The organisation refers back to the scope of the impact as identified earlier in its environmental impact statement to determine where it needs to undertake its monitoring activities. Once the organisation has completed its monitoring activities, it then reports back to the government on the results. The government, through a Mining Environment Protection and Enhancement Officer (MEPEO), then participates in the evaluation of the results. Then, actions in response to this evaluation are funnelled back to the local representatives (of the government), who are in charge of the different impact areas that the organisation operates within. This was described by one participant:

> We group them, and normally the barangay captain will present issues to the Head of Mine at the site. There are problems related to infrastructure, health, education [and] livelihood which are discussed and presented to our MEPEO officer. Post evaluation, they are incorporated in the Plan. The solutions are presented to the impact barangays for consent and the feedback is incorporated.

It is therefore apparent that the organisation seeks only to meet the monitoring and evaluation requirements of the government. This includes across the environmental and social dimensions linked with their compliance requirements. Beyond this, there is no evidence to suggest that the organisation undertakes any more systematic evaluation, other than financial reporting to the corporate headquarters on its annual performance.

The next section will examine the tools and techniques commonly adopted by organisations in the monitoring and evaluation step.

Techniques and tools

Earlier chapters outlined the approval processes within the EMB-DENR, as well as the selection of project alternatives and mitigation solutions. Evidence suggests that organisations are, at the very least, implementing environmental monitoring in accordance with the requirements prescribed under the PEISS. The next section explains how organisations undertake the monitoring and evaluation step, and the techniques they utilise to evaluate the effectiveness of their mitigation strategies. This will initially focus on the influence of government regulations, including the role of the MMTs, and will describe the use of both qualitative and quantitative techniques. Following this, the manner in which organisations in the World Class category implement sustainability-reporting tools to more comprehensively monitor and evaluate the impact of their activities will be presented.

Multipartite monitoring teams

The PEISS provides organisations with additional guidance for the monitoring and evaluation of sustainability issues linked to the proponent's operations. Organisations that operate through the approval processes of an ECC are required to implement monitoring measures and must constitute an MMT. Under the PEISS, MMTs are composed of various key stakeholders as well as experts. Their goal is to assess the effectiveness of implemented mitigation strategies as well as ensuring overall compliance with the submitted ECC. MMTs directly report to the EMB-DENR and should raise any non-compliance issues. Insights provided by decision-makers at PH14 suggest that monitoring through MMT is a straightforward, yet thorough, process:

> [The MMT] go through all the provisions of the ECC. [We check] every provision [to see whether] we are compliant.
>
> (PH14)

Looking further into the monitoring process under the PEISS, results show that the MMTs mainly rely on a mixed-method approach, gathering both quantitative and qualitative data. Those interviewed revealed that decision-makers typically use round-table discussions to capture greater insights on monitored impacts. As explained in the earlier chapters, the ECC focusses solely on environmental impacts, comparing indicator "scores" with previously undertaken baseline studies. The next section details the quantitative and qualitative tools used to undertake the monitoring process.

QUANTITATIVE TECHNIQUES LINKED WITH REGULATION

Quantitative techniques were found to be a key tool in the monitoring and evaluation process; they are proposed by the MMTs and performed by the project proponent. Interestingly, it was apparent that MNEs' reporting frequency varies greatly. This was influenced by the nature of the project, as well as the indicators being monitored. For example, monitoring of air quality or atmospheric contaminants was often implemented through continuous data collection (*e.g.*, sensors), whereas noise pollution was assessed on a yearly basis. The importance of the MMT was described by one respondent:

> DENR is also required to explain what the MMT is supposed to be. It is in the law. It is a requirement of the DENR. And today every ECC has a built in clause that you are to have an MMT. It's part of the ECC. Even before the plant operates, so during the construction phase, we should already organise the MMT.
>
> (PH14)

All organisations in the sample demonstrated that they had some sort of monitoring system that was linked to mandatory requirements for their activities and the ECC approval of their operations. A range of quantitative monitoring systems were evident across the organisations. These systems provided information to the organisation across a range of environmental indicators directly related to key project-induced impacts.

Organisations tended to rely on quantitative measurement techniques to monitor environmental indicators, particularly when linked with regulatory requirements. Project proponents often defined the measurement ranges in the baseline study, which were established at the impact analysis step. To ensure the consistency and measurability of impacts throughout the project lifetime, the same measurement techniques were applied. As with the baseline studies, it is evident that the monitoring activity is industry-specific. For example, in the monitoring activities of PH14, operating a large manufacturing facility, environmental indicators were focussed on the monitoring of air quality and water releases, as revealed by one participant:

> The Department of Environment and Natural Resources (DENR) conducts quarterly monitoring of our ambient air, stack emissions, water effluents. Also, there are regular meetings of the Pollution Control Officer with the community in each plant.
>
> (PH14)

These measurements reflect the impacts associated with its operations, with a particular focus on waterways and water supply. It was clear that for the manufacturing and mining industries, there was a significant focus on the regulation of water usage through aquifers and water-level measurements. This was oriented around water usage as the primary impact and, therefore, directed the focus of the monitoring activities. It was also evident that specific measurements were undertaken by such organisations in areas such as discharges and turbidity levels.

The measurement of biosphere indicators as part of monitoring processes was found in the rehabilitation phase of only one mining project. The project proponent had the responsibility to ensure that rehabilitation was undertaken according to the EIS and ECC guidelines. The rehabilitation was ongoing and, so far, successful according to government evaluation. With the help of local communities, the organisation undertook a species survey to determine the flora and fauna present during its operations. This survey provided valuable information about the progress and effectiveness of the rehabilitation process in terms of reinstating biodiversity. During this process, key species (defined as reference species in the baseline study) were tracked and counted, providing a quantitative measurement of their presence in the rehabilitation site. As explained by the decision-maker responsible for site rehabilitation:

> In just three years, the 'mine-out' area has been [re]forested and the species are being tracked. This is bio-diverse. We keep track of every bird and insect that goes into the area.
>
> (PH02)

It was also found that organisations across all industries conducted atmospheric measurements. The primary focus and influencing factor behind these monitoring matrices was greenhouse gases (*i.e.*, CO_2, methane and NO_X). Automated monitoring systems were found where atmospheric releases were the primary environmental concerns for organisations. In addition, in some specific cases, the EMB-DENR implemented air-quality measurement systems (*i.e.*, particles per million and dust releases).

> The Department of Environment and Natural Resources (EMB-DENR) conducts quarterly monitoring of our ambient air, stack emissions, water effluents.
>
> (PH14)

Quantitative techniques appear to be a key basis for conducting, monitoring and evaluating environmental impacts. However, when looking at broader sustainability issues and impacts, and how organisations monitor the impacts of implemented projects, it appears that organisations often prefer qualitative techniques.

QUALITATIVE TECHNIQUES LINKED WITH REGULATION

While quantitative techniques provide an understanding of the change induced by organisational activities, qualitative techniques provide an understanding of how broader sustainability issues are taken into account through monitoring and evaluation activities. As discussed in earlier sections, the main goal of MMTs is to assess environmental impacts, but in some projects where an SMDP is required, MMTs can also play a role in monitoring the social impact of a project. However, analysis of organisational practices suggest that the monitoring of social impacts is largely undertaken through internally driven processes. Organisations often take the lead on monitoring activities, as well as associated reporting on social issues/impact performance. This is reflected in the insights shared by a decision-maker from PH14:

> The report to be submitted is done through MMT… It's done by the company in consultation with the community. You can say that the community validates and monitors the [report].

The same processes were found to be practiced across other industries when monitoring and reporting of social issues and impacts. The community manager at PH03, for example, provided similar comments reinforcing the self-monitoring process undertaken by the organisation:

> Monitoring is done by the project team which is supervised by the Project manager. All the project reports are compiled and sent to the corporate. We review it and consolidate it so that it can be presented to MGB in an appropriate manner.
>
> (PH03)

While no formal processes were found in the monitoring of social issues and impacts through MMTs, the local communities and key stakeholders were often engaged as part of the internal monitoring process. During this step, informal discussion groups were one of the primary vehicles with which decision-makers engaged with stakeholders. During these discussions, key stakeholders were given the opportunity to provide additional insights into how social issues were being managed and to highlight areas for improvement. When reflecting on the process of finalising the monitoring report, a decision-maker provided further insights into the mechanics of such informal group discussions:

> The writing of the report is done together by the entire group. We flash the data on the screen and the members can ask questions and raise comments. (PH14)

Operational managers are often a key link in this informal process, with specific stakeholders engaged on an *ad hoc* basis:

> With regards to our community development projects, we go into consultation activities with the community. We conduct monthly or quarterly meetings with the barangay officials, specifically barangay captains, to learn about the needs or immediate concerns of the barangays. These needs are assessed, and if [mitigation strategies are] approved they are implemented. (PH04)

Interestingly, while monitoring reports are submitted to the government, organisations applying more comprehensive practices often have well-defined reporting guidelines in which to communicate their monitoring and evaluation results to key stakeholders. The next section analyses the two key monitoring frameworks used by organisations within the sample.

Sustainability reporting

Sustainability reporting is a key aspect of the monitoring and evaluation step. Organisations operating with more comprehensive practices often use reporting tools to engage with stakeholders, as well as to improve their current practices and assessment processes. The next section describes the two key tools linked with sustainability reporting: risk assessment and GRI reporting standards.

RISK ASSESSMENT – KEY PERFORMANCE INDICATORS

As identified in previous chapters, some organisations conduct risk assessments throughout the entire lifetime of projects. Those interviewed from the organisations that implemented this tool provided interesting insights into its use at the monitoring and evaluation step. Underpinning the use of risk assessments at this step is the use of Key Performance Indicators (KPIs). As reflected in the comments from key decision-makers, the reporting of environmental, social and economic impacts is done through KPIs. Usually, these indicators are similar to measurement points selected at the scoping step. For example, one decision-maker made the following comment:

> We set ourselves KPIs on an annualised basis and those key performance indicators are set up in accordance with the three main strategic pillars of our business.
>
> (PH05)

Organisations emphasised that the implementation of KPIs in risk assessments is often complex and requires additional organisational resources. As highlighted by a decision-maker for PH05, KPIs often tie together all organisational levels, from higher management and the strategic goals to the operational level:

> There's often a big challenge in translating a lot of those strategic key performance indicators down to something that a supervisor can impact on a low level.
>
> (PH05)

KPIs can be quantitative or qualitative (*i.e.*, risk scales) and provide a comprehensive overview of how the organisation is performing according to its identified sustainability issues. Through this comprehensive approach, organisations are able to correctly identify areas for improvement and implement the necessary changes required to address sustainability performance shortfalls. Additional insights from a decision-maker at PH05 suggest that the reporting frequency of this tool is annual:

> [KPIs] are assessed on an annualised basis and… we derive a lot of information out of monitoring those key performance indicators because it can tell us a lot about the business and how we're actually tracking against what we set out to achieve.
>
> (PH05)

Furthermore, there was evidence of organisations pro-actively monitoring social impacts. This was conducted through risk matrices, where organisations captured key social risks through metrics such as employability of the local workforce, workplace diversity, value-chain integration or education level of the workforce. Decision-makers revealed that such social metrics were integrated within KPIs and that this integration allowed organisations to better monitor and evaluate the social impact of their projects.

KPIs implemented through risk assessments can be classified as an internal tool aiming to provide a comprehensive monitoring and evaluation framework to assess impacts across environmental, social and economic dimensions. Despite the broader utility of risk assessments in capturing information across sustainability dimensions, there was little evidence that comprehensive stakeholder engagement was undertaken as part of this process. The process was undertaken internally, and the results of the KPI analysis were only shared with selected stakeholders at the completion of the assessment.

GRI REPORTING STANDARDS

The Global Reporting Initiative (GRI) offers a structured framework to assess and report on a wide range of sustainability issues and impacts. While the GRI reporting guidelines require the reporting of a broad range of economic, environmental and social issues/impacts, they also enable the refinement and focus of reporting around those issues that are most 'material' for key stakeholders. Material issues identified at the scoping step, through the materiality analysis, are reported on in this step, to augment the more comprehensive indicators within the GRI framework. This allows mitigation strategies to be contextualised, so they meet with stakeholder expectations. It is likely that the use of the GRI framework and guidelines also provides further credibility to the organisation's overall monitoring, evaluation and reporting process. The reporting mechanisms were described by a decision-maker within PH05:

> We also started pursuing assurance over our annual report and then also started reporting in accordance with the GRI and then also started providing limited assurance over many of the indicators that we were reporting inside the annual report.
>
> (PH05)

Sustainability reporting through the GRI framework ensures that sustainability issues and mitigation efforts are measured continually across the lifetime of the project. In analysing the organisational practices of MNE's participating in this study, it is clear that this is the case. GRI reporting standards are embedded in the annual reporting requirements for organisations who choose to adopt it. A respondent from PH05 reflected on this when discussing the monitoring and evaluation mechanisms they implement throughout their operations:

> Now within our annual reporting process we've got numerous indicators that we're constantly monitoring and measuring in terms of the GRI and some more specific measurements that we've got in place and when we go through the annual reporting process.
>
> (PH05)

While the monitoring and evaluation process is often perceived as an internal process with stakeholders partially engaged, the use of GRI reporting standards directs decision-makers to be more inclusive of stakeholders' views and concerns, while also capturing a broader range of key sustainability issues and impacts. Through the weighting system provided by the materiality analysis, stakeholders are able to contribute to the refinement and prioritisation of issues included within the monitoring and evaluation process. Utilising this tool allows organisations and their key stakeholders to provide direction to the focus of monitoring and evaluation activities and to optimise current operational activities by focussing the organisation on particular issues or impacts of concern.

Summary

It is evident that the national regulatory framework provides a solid foundation for the monitoring and evaluation of environmental issues and impacts. Clear monitoring and evaluation processes were identified across all organisations through the implementation of MMTs and required measurement indicators specified by the government and linked with industry or operation. The monitoring teams also provided organisations with a formal process to evaluate the environmental impact of their projects, drawing on both internal and external participants.

There was also some indication that MMTs provided guidance on the monitoring and evaluation of social factors when implementing SDMPs. A range of projects that required the implementation of SDMPs highlighted that MMTs allowed some limited engagement with external stakeholders, including those through the use of qualitative methods such as focus group discussions, and that this provided some structure to the monitoring process.

Organisations operating within the World Class and International Practices categories demonstrated more advanced monitoring and evaluation tools. These tools were adapted from international guidelines such as the GRI reporting standards and risk assessments. Both tools require a cyclical approach to the assessment of sustainability issues and impacts across organisational activities; however, it was the GRI reporting standards that empowered greater stakeholder engagement. This was particularly true of earlier processes associated with the materiality analysis and the scoping step, which funnelled through to the monitoring and evaluation processes where these material issues were reported upon.

Feedback and follow-up step

As the final step of a sustainability assessment, the feedback and follow-up step provides a mechanism for organisations to address the outcomes of their monitoring and evaluation activities. To re-cap from the explanation provided in Chapter 2, this is an iterative step, enabling organisations to not only to introduce new alternative selection strategies, but also to address or adjust existing mitigation or enhancement strategies based on the outcomes of monitoring and evaluation. At its broadest level, this step enables organisations to ensure that they are able to achieve their sustainability outcomes, objectives or goals, which provide overarching direction on what the organisation wants to achieve from its sustainability assessment.

The following sections adopt a similar structure to previous steps, beginning first with the broad classification of organisational practices across World Class, International Standards or Compliance Driven categories. This is delineated into the results for different sectors within the sample, showing the distribution of organisations across these categories. The presentation of results then focusses on management practices or MNE's which involves establishing the key characteristics, influencing factors and practices of organisations within this step. The key tools and techniques implemented by organisations are then presented.

Practice classification

While previous steps have shown a consistency across the organisational practices and classifications, this step presents a key departure point for the classifications. For this final step, dramatic reduction is evident in the number of organisations falling into the World Class and International Standards categories. Within the World Class category, the percentage of organisations decreased from the 38% in the monitoring and evaluation step to 29% at this step. This shift becomes more stark when looking at the changes in the organisations within the International Standards category; whereas the previous step had 38% of organisations in this category, in the feedback and follow-up step this fell to 17%.

In contrast, the number of organisations within the Compliance Driven category has doubled, rising from 25% of organisations in the previous step to approximately 54% in this step. This result indicates that more than half the organisations in the sample adopt sustainability practices that only meet the regulatory requirements of the government. Part of this shift is a result of the fact that this step is still an under-explored and under-developed area of practice within the sustainability practices of organisations. The proportion of organisations in each category is illustrated in Figure 5.5.

Figure 5.6 below displays the distribution of the organisations across these different categories based on their industry. It is evident that both the mining and manufacturing sectors have seen a dramatic increase in the number of organisations classified as Compliance Driven. While the shift has also been significant in the utility sector, almost half (43%, n = 3/7) of the organisations remain in the World Class category. This reinforces the general conclusion that those

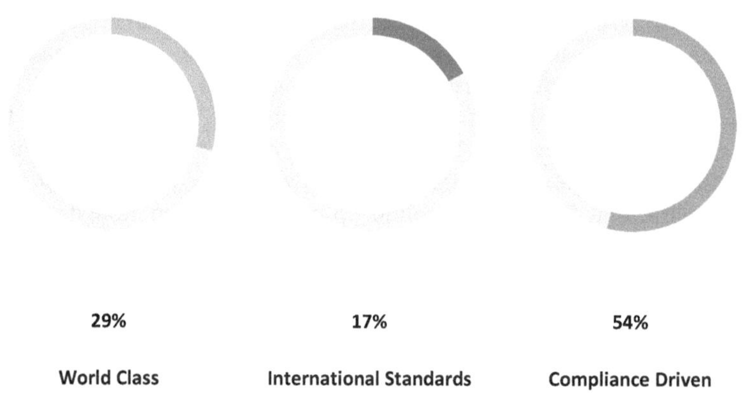

Figure 5.5 Practice classification – feedback and follow-up step.

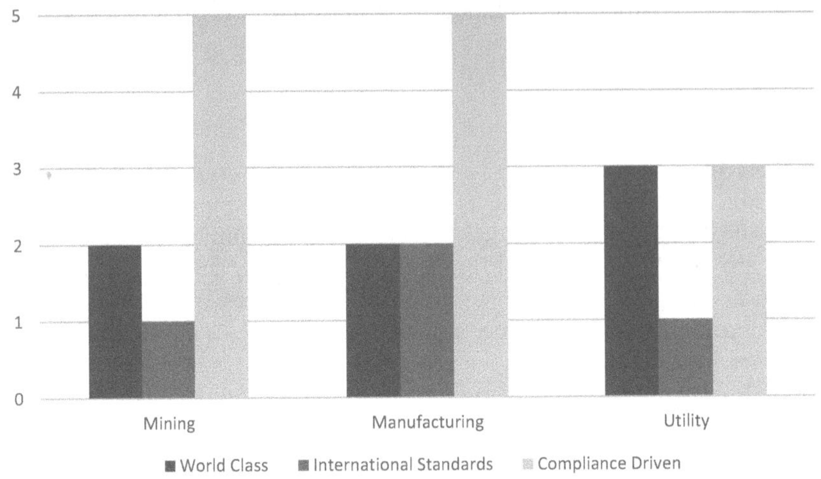

Figure 5.6 Practice classification per industry – feedback and follow-up step.

organisations in the utility industry outperform organisations in the other two categories throughout the entire sustainability assessment framework.

In examining these results more closely, the mining sector has most noticeably seen a shift in organisations previously classified into the International Standards category. While the previous steps had approximately 38% (n = 3/8) of organisations in this category, this has decreased to approximately 13% (n = 1/8). The World Class category has retained approximately 25% (n = 2/8) of organisations, while the Compliance Driven category has seen a substantial increase from 38% (n = 3/8) of organisations to approximately 63% (n = 5/8) for this step. This could partly be explained by the fact that much of the assessment activity is skewed towards the beginning of mining operations, with rigorous processes put in place to determine and manage any potential impacts. However, the main reason for this shift is that the practice of iteratively changing operations in response to performance outcomes is not evident in the data analysed from these organisations.

A similar shift is evident in the manufacturing sector, although this has occurred across both organisations classified within the World Class and International Standards categories. In terms of the World Class category, this has decreased from 33% (n = 3/9) of organisations within the previous step, to 22% (n = 2/9) within the feedback and follow-up step. This is even more dramatic for the decrease in International Standards, which was previously 44% (n = 4/9) of organisations but decreased to 22% (n = 2/9) of organisations at this step. The reductions in these two steps are matched by the dramatic increase in the number of organisations in the Compliance Driven category, with approximately 56% (n = 5/9) of manufacturing organisations classified within this category.

As mentioned, utilities organisations have performed somewhat better than those from the other two industries. Nevertheless, a similar shift is apparent, with fewer organisations in both the World Class and International Standards categories. The World Class category now accounts for approximately 43% (n = 3/7) of the organisations, while the International Standards category represents approximately 14% (n = 1/7). These decreases are matched by the increase in the number of utilities organisations adopting a Compliance Driven perspective, from 14% in the previous step to approximately 43% (n = 3/7) in this step.

This dramatic shift for organisations in all industries highlights the importance of examining this step in more depth, not just in this study but also in future studies. The next section will examine the management practices of different organisations classified under each of the three key categories.

Management practices

This section further details the results of examining the feedback and follow-up practices of organisations within the sample. Presentation of results will start with a broad overview of the general practices of organisations within each of the three categories, before moving to a detailed analysis of exemplar cases for each category. These cases provide an in-depth basis for understanding the practices, key influencing factors and general approaches to feedback and follow-ups being implemented by organisations.

World class

The importance of a clear sustainability framework and operational process is clearly evident in the practices of organisations within the World Class category during the feedback and follow-up step. Organisations in the World Class category had well-established sustainability practices that were embedded into frameworks that organised their activities systematically. This invariably included the organisation's broad commitment to global sustainability platforms, through to regulatory compliance and specific policies and practices to direct their sustainability efforts. However, it should be noted that while it was evident that all of the organisations classified at this level had processes in place to respond to their performance outcomes from monitoring and evaluation practices, it was sometimes difficult to link this specifically to the operational changes put in place. This is, perhaps, a reflection of international practices focussing on reporting performance outcomes, rather than performance management systems to improve or address performance outcomes.

Notwithstanding this limitation, PH19 is an interesting example to illustrate the types of practices evident in organisations in this category. PH19 is a complex joint venture arrangement in the Philippines, which is heavily influenced by the corporate headquarter operations of the two joint venture partners, as well as the consolidated corporate operations managing their project in the Philippines. At the headquarter level, when examining the joint venture partners, it is clear that both organisations have a comprehensive approach to engaging with sustainability. Not only do both organisations have broad sustainability values and objectives established for their operations, but they also have sustainability frameworks and policies to direct these activities.

Underpinning this, both organisations have commitments to different global sustainability platforms, such as the GRI standards, the UNGC, the IFC social and environmental standards, and a host of ISOs for operational procedures across social, health, safety and environmental issues. Both organisations appear to also be cognisant of the Sustainable Development Goals (SDGs) recently introduced by the United Nations and are linking these into their operational activities.

However, at the corporate level within the Philippines, the managing organisation for PH19 has adopted a comprehensive multi-level approach to engaging with sustainability. This builds on a set of key principles and objectives to direct the network of strategic business units in the Philippines, including the way that the organisation engages with stakeholders, embedding social responsibility as a core part of its business practices. The organisation also considers the long-term impact of its operations and embeds the values of responsibility, innovation, integrity and teamwork within its business activities. This is well-aligned with a set of objectives that guide consideration of inclusive growth, commercial sustainability, selecting and retaining the right people, and addressing environmental impacts holistically. These values and objectives arose during an interview with a respondent from the subsidiary, who emphasised:

> We at [the subsidiary organisation] put a strong emphasis on community issues and in new constructions. For us, significant issues are community-related, the mental and social footprint we have on them and on the business, the art of developing power plants. There is a time frame for financial and economic issues, but the more important issues are social, legal and environmental. We shift from our focus on engineering to more the developmental aspects of the community. We build communities with local support and by protecting rights of Indigenous people who have hosted us.
>
> (PH19)

These broad principles and objectives were operationalised through a triple bottom line approach, which directed how the organisation plans and engages with its sustainability activities. This funnelled down into a sustainability framework for directing business activities and a corporate social responsibility programme that engages more broadly with surrounding communities. The organisation emphasises the importance of the triple bottom line approach to operationalising its sustainability approach, as it allows the development of measurable objectives that are linked to clear targets and regular monitoring activities to establish the organisation's sustainability performance.

Linked with its strategic approach and operational activities, the corporate operations in the Philippines also had an explicit commitment to the GRI standards. This guided the implementation of its sustainability activities through (1) a set of actionable areas it had to address and (2) the reporting requirements to provide accountability for its operations. This is embedded and organised under the triple bottom line approach and the sustainability framework, which directs how the organisation links different GRI indicator areas, under people, planet and profit, as broad overarching categories.

Guiding its sustainability activities are both the broad commitments embedded within the GRI standards on areas that must be addressed, and the importance of the materiality analysis in determining those issues that are most important to the organisation's stakeholders. Looking first at the standard areas to be addressed, the organisation developed a range of performance indicators that were consistently applied and measured across all of its operations. This was attached to the material issues that were previously determined by undertaking a materiality analysis (Figure 5.7).

What is evident from the example adapted from PH19 is that the organisation funnels down from the broad sustainability framework, organised under the triple bottom line approach, through to linking with the GRI content and material issues. This then provides a platform for the measurable areas that it focusses on for its indicators, and the monitoring and evaluation activities. Building from this multi-layered approach, the organisation then examines and determines its performance in the key sustainability areas across its operations (Figure 5.8).

The organisation had a set of broader objectives across the 'planet' aspect of its operations, but perhaps the key one was to become carbon neutral in all of the organisation's operations. This is linked with one of its key material issues about the production and management of GHG emissions. The organisation utilised a series of follow-up activities to address its performance. While this is somewhat difficult to connect through its different reporting activities, it was organised to show the general flow of activities and links between the organisation's efforts and performance in different environmental issues.

From exploring the organisation's practices, it appears that it is attempting to either minimise or completely mitigate negative impacts, or enhance positive impacts, of its project. For example, it was evident in the 'people' aspect of its

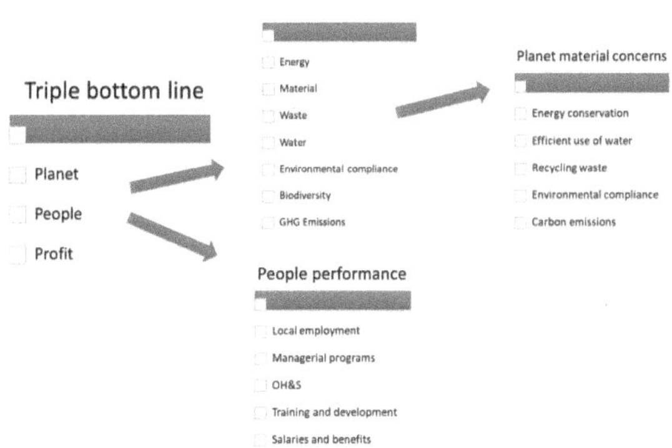

Figure 5.7 Material issues during feedback and follow-up.

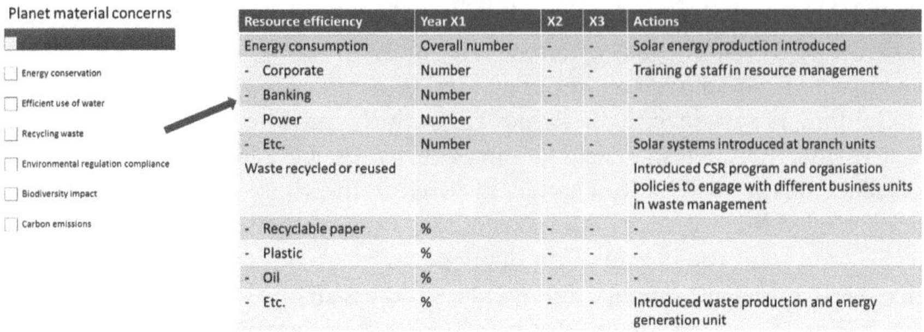

Resource efficiency	Year X1	X2	X3	Actions
Energy consumption	Overall number	-	-	Solar energy production introduced
- Corporate	Number	-	-	Training of staff in resource management
- Banking	Number	-	-	-
- Power	Number	-	-	-
- Etc.	Number	-	-	Solar systems introduced at branch units
Waste recycled or reused				Introduced CSR program and organisation policies to engage with different business units in waste management
- Recyclable paper	%	-	-	-
- Plastic	%	-	-	-
- Oil	%	-	-	-
- Etc.	%	-	-	Introduced waste production and energy generation unit

Figure 5.8 Example of the required actions under materiality analysis.

operations that there was a key focus on enhancement strategies to engage with, and develop, staff who were drawn from local communities. The organisation has a series of strategies in place to improve its performance in developing staff and local communities, through both its sustainability framework and its CSR programmes.

International standards

Within the International Standards category, PH14 is a good example of an organisation that clearly goes beyond regulatory requirements, although the detail driving the feedback and follow-up processes is lacking. This is consistent with the other three organisations also in this category, which all had gaps in their reporting approach and a lack of transparency of all their monitoring and evaluation processes (which underpin the feedback and follow-up step).

Nevertheless, before turning to the actual practices that exceed compliance, it is worth contextualising the measures taken due to government approval or evaluation process requirements. Most of the activities to meet compliance have been undertaken before the operations actually began, so in some ways, the activities reported here simply reflect those undertaken during alternative selection.

For example, the organisation was required to undertake the necessary environmental compliance certification. This required an inspection of the plants and that they had considered the environmental issues that needed to be addressed. The certification requirements directed the organisation to follow-up on the current performance of the plant it was acquiring to ensure that the smoke emissions, water use and other pertinent issues were up to the DENR standards. This is reflected in the comments of a respondent:

> In terms of formal regulatory process, the company complied with the laws related to environment. It complied with DENR standards on smoke emission, water effluents, and others.
>
> (PH14)

This also required the organisation to engage with the local community through public hearings to determine whether there were any other issues that it should consider. A key issue identified was how it used water in its operations. The organisation responded to this feedback and evaluated alternatives as part of its planning. It conducted a cost-benefit analysis to identify the most cost-effective and environmentally sustainable method of dealing with water use. One respondent shared the following:

> The issue of water was raised by the LGU and the community during the public hearing that was done prior to the approval of the [location removed] plant. The Company conducted a cost-benefit analysis. Even though the water treatment involved a huge amount of investment, the Company was able to justify it because they looked at it from a long-term perspective. Also, they subscribe to the idea that some returns-on-investment cannot be quantified but should be viewed from a qualitative perspective such as building [a good] relationship with the community and the LGU.
>
> (PH14)

Beyond the initial public hearings and changes made to its operations, the organisation was required to create a multipartite team to continue its engagement with local communities after the approval process and maintain ongoing monitoring of community concerns about its operations. As a result of this, the organisation followed government directions and established a pollution control officer to examine pollution related issues. One respondent reflects on this:

> In every [factory], there is a Pollution Control Officer [PCO] to monitor pollution concerns. After an investment is done, we create a multipartite team (composed of people from Headquarters and from the plants) to talk to the community and regularly discuss social concerns – whether at the barangay level, people in the community or in the province. The PCO is a de facto member of the team. There is a monthly meeting or quarterly meeting depending on the urgency of the matter themselves. After the investment is done, there is a multipartite group.
>
> (PH14)

PH14 is also regularly evaluated by the DENR, which evaluates a range of environmental issues to ensure that the organisation is meeting the standards required. This adds to the existing monitoring and evaluation the organisation must undertake to ensure it conforms to regulatory requirements. Hence, a two-fold approach is used, which requires both regular interaction and feedback from the community on organisational performance and identification of any issues, matched by a technical approach with the government auditing its practices.

The organisation has also implemented procedures that go beyond this regulatory perspective. Some of this may be due to the fact that it is committed to a range of ISOs (ISO9001; ISO14001; ISO18001) and industry standards. From the interviews, it seems that the organisation also has a specific focus on continuous improvement in its business processes, especially with the environmental and social impacts of its operations.

For example, the organisation originally set an objective of maximising the sources of renewable energy to power its operations. While the organisation did not require this as part of its investment approval, management had progressively increased the amount being used within its operations. This adoption of more renewable energy sources has meant that "*[m]ore than 90% of [organisation's] power needs are from renewable energy sources, reducing its carbon footprint*" (respondent from PH14).

Another example is PH14's progressive monitoring of community movements and population growth in the local area. While the organisation was originally located away from local communities, regular monitoring, and then feedback and follow-up revealed that the area surrounding the factory was increasingly populated by local residents. This gave rise to concerns about the noise and air pollution generated by the factory. The organisation received this feedback and followed-up by adjusting its activities, introducing advanced European technology to reduce the noise and air pollution it created.

There is a range of other examples of how PH14 has slowly adapted and improved the technological processes within its factory to improve the impact of its operations. This includes installation of an internal water plant to recycle 100% of the water used during its operations; changes to its water-holding processes, so no water is extracted from local water sources; and new technology to reduce the energy use of its production processes, among others. While the organisation does not present individual data to detail the overall effect of these initiatives on its environmental footprint, they do undertake a cost-benefit analysis to demonstrate the value of implementing changes.

Compliance Driven

The Compliance Driven approach appears to dominate the practices of organisations across all sectors for the feedback and follow-up step. This is despite the fact that organisations within this category had previously been categorised in either the International Standards or World Class categories. One of the dominant reasons for the increase in the number of organisations classified within this category is the lack of evidence demonstrating substantive activities towards responding to outcomes from the monitoring and evaluation step.

This category includes organisations that have adopted a series of global sustainability platforms and different international and industry standards. Perhaps the best example illustrating a shortfall in the practices, and lack of transparency in reporting, of this step is PH22, a utility company. This organisation had, for previous steps, adopted World Class practices, with a range of mechanisms in place to address sustainability issues both prior to the initiation of its operations and subsequent to it being established and operational. Indeed, the organisation had collaborated with the World Bank and IFC in undertaking a comprehensive social and environmental impact assessment process, and has a range of sustainability policies in place.

Despite this, and substantiated through the interviews and secondary data, the organisation did not articulate an ongoing process of addressing its sustainability performance outcomes through iterative actions to improve or reduce impacts associated with its operations. Instead, it applied the consistent approach of meeting the requirements of the investment approval, including monitoring and evaluation of its environmental impacts through the DENR and ECC. It also adopted, prescriptively, the requirement for social contributions through a community CSR-based programme.

Beyond this, it was evident that the majority of actions to alter or change its operations were instigated at beginning of the investment process, before becoming operational. The only identifiable changes to its operations post-implementation were to issues around data security and calculation mechanisms for measuring impacts. The interview data did not reveal any further changes that had been implemented, or that the governmental processes had led to any changes in the organisation's operations and methods for addressing sustainability outcomes.

Tools and techniques

This section presents the different tools and techniques used by organisations when undertaking the feedback and follow-up step. First, the current regulatory framework is described, providing an understanding of the legislative requirements and current processes implemented by organisations as a result. Insights from organisations currently operating under an ECC are explored, providing further information on informal discussion rounds with MMTs.

This study identified a range of activities by organisations operating within the World Class category that involve using specific tools to engage with stakeholders when conducting feedback and follow-up activities. The next section begins by providing an overview of the tools and techniques applied by organisations that follow regulation. As for the monitoring and evaluation step, organisations use specific guidelines to accurately report the impacts of their activities.

Regulatory basis

This study found that the PEISS provides little guidance on the feedback and follow-up processes that organisations should adopt. Documentation provided by the EMB-DENR does not mention any well-established guidelines. As depicted by the PEISS diagram (Figure 5.9), when the ECC is denied or suspended, an organisation must undertake the necessary action to comply with the initial ECC.

Examining the MNE project and monitoring reports revealed that, at the time of the interviews, all organisations were operating under an approved ECC and had specific requirements to meet as entailed through this certification. In the case of non-compliance with the ECC, the EMB-DENR has the authority to impose monetary sanctions. However, there was no evidence of the application of any fines to the organisations that were part of the sample. It is thus assumed that all organisations met minimum regulatory requirements.

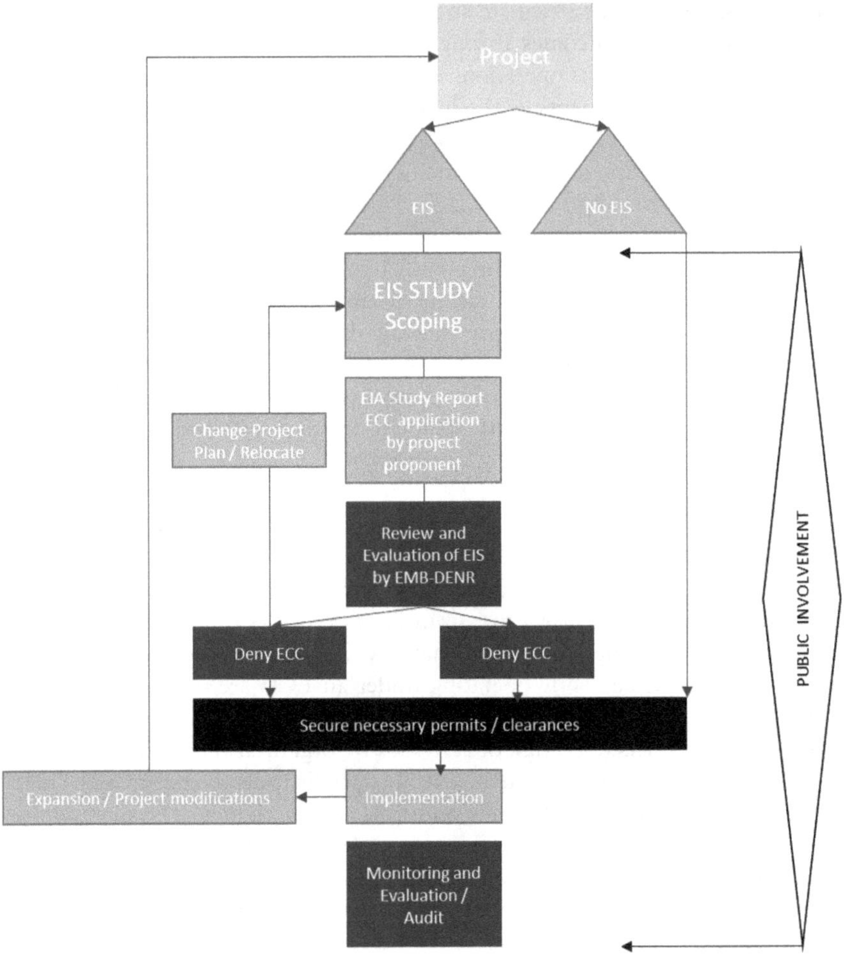

Figure 5.9 The current PEISS (DAO 2003-30).

In terms of compliance, several organisations were identified that had infringed the initial ECC requirements due to unforeseen impacts. The process for addressing these impacts appears to be based on *ad hoc* decisions. For example, both operational managers and key decision-makers at PH24 revealed that the organisation solved these impacts through the implementation of immediate changes that addressed the impacts:

> In one case, the fly ash was being blown away because of strong winds. We had to construct covers for the fly ash site so that it would remain stable before it is shipped. It cost us a lot, but we did it because the health and safety of the community is important to us. We have not received any complaint since.
>
> (PH24)

Additionally, while the design of the plant might not have taken into account the environmental and social impact of fly ash (a by-product of the combustion of coal), the initial MMT had raised this issue. As a result, the EMB-DENR required changes to the initial plant design and the provision of effective mitigation solutions to reduce the impact of fly ash on the local population. A straightforward solution was chosen, through the confinement of this waste material. It is somewhat surprising, however, that the disposal of the fly ash was not taken into consideration within the initial project design and ECC. The organisation undertook a similar action to comply with the demands of the EMB-DENR, as one respondent revealed:

> We also had to think how to dispose of the fly ash in a cost efficient manner. Similar to the fly ash incident, we had to address it even if it was not part of the original design of the plant.
>
> (PH24)

Analysis of the secondary data revealed that the organisation disposed of the fly ash through a partner organisation, approved by the EMB-DENR, which specialised in the disposal of toxic industrial waste products. Beyond this type of *ad hoc* implementation of environmental mitigation solutions, it appears that the PEISS does not provide guidance for methods to be applied to address performance outcomes that do not address original targets (particularly in terms of social issues).

In some cases, through the implementation of SDMP, issues raised by the local community were addressed. However, it appears that these organisations were using a learning and adaptation process to build on the requirements of the SDMP, improving the methods that they were already implementing and using the funds. No information gathered from the interviews indicated that organisations were relying on government directions or requirements for this step. One respondent from PH08 explained:

> As the Monitoring Team for the SDMPs, we are not satisfied with the first two SDMPs. Now with SDMP3 we have a great role to play and want to involve the community. Our learnings from the first 2 SDMPs has been that there should be better involvement of the people in planning and implementation.
>
> (PH08)

Additional insights shared by decision-makers across various organisations underlined the informal and unstructured nature of activities undertaken during this step. No reports were required, and the feedback and follow-up actions were left to the judgement of organisations. This was evident across the interviews of operational managers at the subsidiary level for PH10 and PH13:

> There isn't a formal reporting process [involving the submission of reports]; it's more of an oral presentation and oral feedback from them. No formal mode of assessment.
>
> (PH10)

> In an informal basis, we talk to them and we get feedback.
>
> (PH13)

Throughout this last step of the assessment process, particularly for those organisations adopting a Compliance Driven approach, stakeholders were poorly engaged, implementation of further mitigation strategies was done on an *ad hoc* basis (largely in response to unforeseen incidences), and response decisions were decided internally. As mentioned earlier in this chapter, organisations operating with more comprehensive practices exceeded the regulatory requirements and implemented some more advanced feedback and follow-up processes. Occurrences of these tools and techniques are explored in the next section.

Voluntary feedback and follow-up tools

For those organisations utilising more advanced or comprehensive practices, this study identified two key tools commonly adopted during this stage to inform the adjustment and changes in organisational practices: materiality analysis and reporting guidelines. These tools were used to conduct project follow-ups as well as to capture stakeholder feedback on proposed and intended changes to existing operational activities. Site rehabilitation processes also appeared to be linked to some active feedback and follow-up activities by organisations within the sample. The next section provides further insights into these two tools and the site rehabilitation process applied in the last step of the assessment process.

MATERIALITY ANALYSIS AND REPORTING GUIDELINES

Linked to the requirement to report on sustainability performance, it was evident that organisations adopting global sustainability platforms were much more likely to apply different mitigation or enhancement strategies to address any gaps in performance outcomes. This was particularly the case with the GRI reporting standards, which require organisations to document their performance across a range of sustainability dimensions and indicators.

Linked to the GRI reporting standards, the materiality analysis was a key tool in the feedback and follow-up step to aid the development and implementation of changes to project activities. The cyclical nature of a materiality analysis approach provides a key advantage during this step. As commented upon by an operational manager at PH05:

> It's a never ending cycle. That's why stakeholder engagement is so important. You can be blind to potential risks and to potential opportunities in the absence of actually engaging with people - but I think that's where a lot of companies have gone wrong.
>
> (PH05)

Evidence from organisations within the sample suggests that while stakeholder engagement is limited across Compliance Driven organisations, those organisations operating with more advanced practices engaged much more extensively with stakeholders and relied upon their unique knowledge to inform the organisation's activities at this step. This included the identification of key issues but also feedback on performance and the implementation of new strategies to address performance outcomes.

SITE REHABILITATION

Organisations operating with more comprehensive practices also pro-actively mitigated unforeseen environmental and social issues. This was particularly evident in organisations where site rehabilitation was implemented. During this lengthy and complex mitigation process, unforeseen environmental impacts are likely to arise. Strong feedback and follow-up tools are therefore needed to ensure that such processes are undertaken properly.

Interviews with decision-makers from PH04 provided further insights into how organisations undertake site rehabilitations. One of the key challenges faced by the organisation was unexpected environmental impacts due to acidification and contamination of topsoil. This specific issue was not part of the initial ECC, but it was part of the broader environmental management plan to conserve the topsoil layer for further site rehabilitation.

After project implementation, it appeared that this layer of soil had been damaged through excessive acidification. Noticing the degradation in soil quality through quantitative measurements (pH levels), the organisation reacted by applying soil conditioners such as limestone and dolomite. This old, but effective, technique is widespread across the mining industry. By so doing, the organisation was able to rehabilitate the site, as revealed by one respondent:

> However, limestone is needed in the soil to neutralize the soil and make it less acidic. Both limestone and dolomite are soil conditioners. So these minerals are used to treat basicity (neutralize the soil) or make it less acidic. So we have to preserve the soil to rehabilitate the top soil.
>
> (PH04)

No stakeholders were involved in this process, but through the careful monitoring of environmental indicators, the organisation was able to implement rapid and effective mitigation solutions.

Summary

For the feedback and follow-up step, little guidance of organisational activities is provided by the PEISS. Insights shared by decision-makers suggest that, while MMTs were involved, no formal processes were evident and that by and large, organisations are left to their own discretion on what to do during this step. Compliance driven organisations were found to generally provide feedback to

MMTs through informal group discussions. Additionally, when organisations identified a need for further mitigation, it was found that they implemented such strategies on an *ad hoc* basis, with little involvement of key stakeholders.

For organisations that chose to operate with superior practices, the findings suggest that the implementation of materiality analyses and reporting guidelines supported their feedback and follow-up processes. The materiality analysis, which was identified across a majority of steps during the sustainability assessment, strengthened the participatory dimensions of the process, being more inclusive of stakeholders. Furthermore, organisations operating at superior practice levels suggested that the GRI guidelines helped identify and direct their performance strategies.

Chapter summary

This chapter examined the organisational practices linked with the impact monitoring and follow-up stage of a sustainability assessment. The analysis of primary and secondary data collected during this study suggests that this stage is mainly driven by the voluntary practices of organisations. Limited guidance was evident from the national regulatory framework across these two steps.

Those interviewed from the compliance driven organisations, together with documentary data gathered, revealed that, despite the guidance received by MMTs on the monitoring and evaluation of environmental impacts, little was provided for the analysis of social impacts. Nevertheless, projects that required social development programmes (SMDPs) under the current legislation displayed slightly more stringent monitoring and evaluation processes. Additionally, no formal processes were identified when examining the PEISS within the context of the feedback and follow-up step.

Organisations adopting practices that are more comprehensive consistently implemented monitoring and evaluation systems that were adapted from international guidelines (particularly from the GRI standards). With a better understanding of project-related impacts, organisations were able to select the most appropriate mitigation solution when required. Additionally, the study also found that these organisations also implemented tools such as weighted risk assessments to include stakeholder knowledge in this last stage of the sustainability assessment. Building on stakeholder knowledge appeared to be key for such organisations and the overall sustainability impacts of the project.

The next Chapter synthesises the key findings and develops an adapted sustainability assessment framework based on the results of this study.

Note

1 A barangay is the smallest administrative division in the Philippines.

6 Conclusion

Introduction

This chapter draws upon the findings of this study to re-cast the sustainability assessment process. The newly proposed conceptual framework provides organisations with a road map for best practice towards sustainable development. The chapter then presents the practical implications of these findings, the significance of the research and key limitations. The findings also spark areas warranting further research, each of which is discussed.

Developing a new conceptual framework

This exploratory investigation into sustainability assessments aimed to provide insights into the project level activities of foreign MNEs operating in the Philippines. It focussed on both the broader management processes and the key tools and techniques utilised by organisations when adopting sustainability assessments for their business activities. We suggest that the new conceptual framework may be a useful guide for MNEs operating in other countries too.

Building from the conceptualised framework presented in Chapter 2, which was derived from reviewing current knowledge, a revised framework is presented here. It integrates and summarises the key findings of this study and embraces the identified activities that occur throughout the management processes involved in sustainability assessments. It incorporates the key tools and techniques that are commonly adopted in practice. The overall flow of the sustainability assessment is retained, demonstrating the value and utility of such a process in providing an organising theory for examining the sustainability practices of the private sector (see Figure 6.1).

Using this revised framework, each stage and step is explored below, highlighting the key insights provided by this empirical study. Through this process the general influence of regulation and voluntary practices is illuminated, along with the key tools and techniques that have been identified from this study as reflecting 'best practice'.

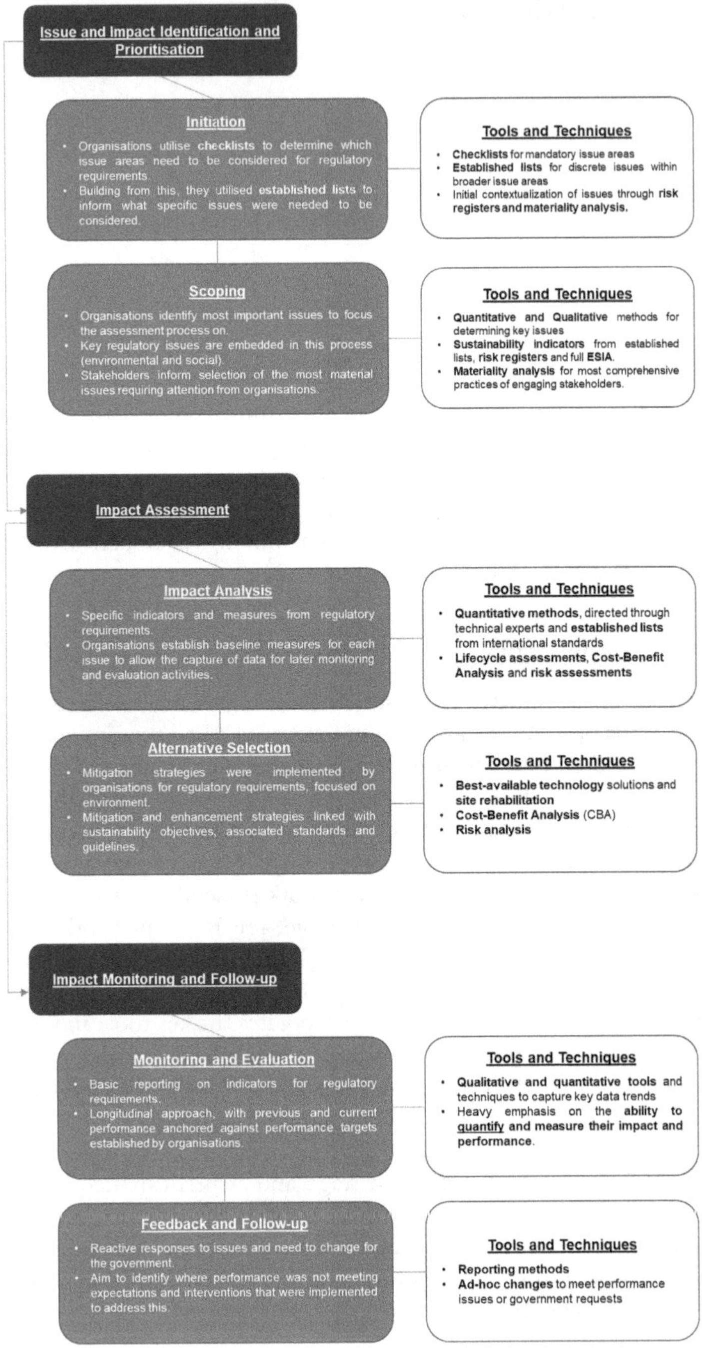

Figure 6.1 Sustainability assessments of MNEs in the Philippines.

Issue and impact identification and prioritisation stage

When examining the sustainability framework against data on leading practices implemented by these organisations, it appears that initiation and scoping practices are inherently connected. Therefore, it is proposed that these two steps are integrated into a common procedure whereby the identification of key issues occurs in parallel with the prioritisation of these issues.

Sustainability standards, and particularly the Global Reporting Initiative (GRI), form a key basis for many organisations when determining their sustainability objectives and practices for their international operations. The current practice of following global, best practice, standards, as identified in this study, suggests that issue identification and prioritisation should be first formed from these standards which essentially form a key set of issue areas in which organisations can concentrate (similar to a checklist or matrix-style approach). Second, unique aspects of the project, including the context, should be generated next, involving key stakeholders in the project.

Initiation step

Mandatory regulatory requirements formed the key basis of the initial sustainability domains considered by organisations. This oriented organisations towards addressing both environmental and social considerations specific to their industry, in line with a limited and prescribed basis for what is included within their sustainability assessment. While this did not represent the full array of activities that are undertaken by organisations exceeding local requirements, it provided an important foundation for organisations to build upon when implementing sustainability assessments.

When considering how the local regulatory context informed the specific tools and techniques utilised by organisations at this step, the Philippines Environmental Impact Statement System (PEISS), Environmental Compliance Certificate (ECC), the Environmental Impact Statement (EIS), Social Development Management Plan (SDMP) and Free and Prior Informed Consent (FPIC) procedures all guided MNE activities. Specifically, organisations used checklists to determine the need to undertake further analysis for regulatory requirements and then used established lists to inform their decisions on specific issues that needed to be considered. While this was rather limited, particularly in terms of social issues, that was practiced by all organisations within the sample.

Importantly, the corporate commitment of organisations to international standards and global sustainability platforms also formed a critical basis for more comprehensive activities within the initiation step. It was found that these commitments funnel down to specific corporate policies, procedures and strategies that direct how they go about identifying the key sustainability issues considered within their operations. This included the selection of tools utilised to guide a more comprehensive analysis of sustainability issues that should be considered within the initiation step.

From examining the practices of these organisations further, it was observed that checklists were often formed using both qualitative and quantitative techniques that drew upon both expert and stakeholder input. These checklists formed an initial basis for a more comprehensive examination of the three sustainability dimensions, extending beyond the regulatory requirements. However, it was the international commitment to global sustainability platforms that was most influential in driving organisations towards a holistic consideration of sustainability issues using established lists. These established lists were derived from a variety of global sustainability platforms, including the GRI standards, the UNGC, the IFC environmental and social standards and the CDP.

To refine and contextualise the broad range of sustainability issues derived from these international commitments, organisations commonly used risk registers and materiality analysis techniques. Both of these techniques are evident across both steps of the issue impact identification stage, involving analysis of the issues that are most critical for inclusion within the entire sustainability assessment process.

Although the local regulatory context provides a fundamental and important basis for initiating activities within a sustainability assessment, it is the voluntary practices implemented by organisations that play a critical role in driving a comprehensive approach to identifying important sustainability issues. This is typically directed from the corporate policies, procedures and strategies of headquarter operations.

Scoping step

During scoping, the second sustainability assessment step, decision-makers selection the most important sustainability issues that will be incorporated throughout the assessment process. Similar to the initiation step, this study found that the key sustainability issues were partly informed by the respective industries in which the organisations were operating.

The PEISS provided clear guidance on the identification and selection of environmental issues that were pertinent across all three industries. It is worth noting that the mining industry had more stringent and mandatory environmental compliance requirements applicable to the scoping step. Moreover, they had regulatory requirements regarding social issues, whereas organisations in the other sectors did not. The Philippines' regulations require organisations operating in the mining sector to obtain approval from local communities and Indigenous inhabitants through the FPIC process. This involves organisations directly engaging with key stakeholders and selecting key social issues which must be considered and addressed in the later stages of their sustainability assessment.

For organisations choosing to go beyond compliance, two other tools were pervasively used: GRI standards and materiality analysis, which together, helped drive their more comprehensive practices. When undertaking these practices, organisations engaged directly with stakeholders (internal and external), identifying and classifying key sustainability issues linked to their operations. This enabled decision-makers to incorporate the sustainability issues relevant to the project and local context whilst also incorporating additional issues that were important to the organisation's broader operational areas and international commitments.

The GRI standards provided a strong framework to engage with internal and external stakeholders and when supplemented with a materiality analysis, the collected information could be translated into key sustainability categories to direct the specific actions of MNEs throughout the project. From these sustainability categories, organisations identified a range of associated sustainability areas that they would consider and, attached to this, determined the different indicators that would be integrated into their assessment processes. These indicators often translate directly into operational standards and measurement practices later in the sustainability assessment and the project itself.

Organisations operating beyond the regulatory requirements of the Philippines' government also engaged with three other key tools at this step, including:

- Sustainability indicators (often linked to international standards and guidelines)
- Risk registers
- Environmental and Social Impact Assessments (ESIAs)

Risk registers were often used in conjunction with other tools and techniques and relied on matrices to organise and prioritise the issues that had to be considered. Perhaps the most comprehensive tool (or management process) was the ESIA, which integrates a range of different qualitative and quantitative methods for collecting and prioritising issues to be considered, which emphasised the requirement for stakeholder engagement.

Impact assessment stage

The impact assessment stage comprises two aligned steps: impact analysis and alternative selection. While these steps are inherently linked, it is important to note that practices normally pursuant to the alternative selection step – were evident across the entire sustainability assessment process. For example, as the projects rolled out, organisations invariably had to re-consider the impacts it was making, and determine new ways of addressing them. As such, alternatives had to be re-generated and selected each time this occurred. Notwithstanding this occurrence, this step should remain within the second stage to highlight the central and critical role it plays in sustainability assessments.

While the regulatory requirements in the preceding stage were influential in determining how organisations commenced each of the steps, this is less apparent in the case of impact analysis. For this step, there was limited guidance from regulations on organisational practices. Hence, organisations invariably turned to the sustainability commitments that had been already made under various international standards and global sustainability guidelines and platforms.

Likewise, regulation had a more limited role in directing the practices of organisations during the alterative selection step. When there was regulation, it largely focussed on environmental or CSR type activities. When organisations engaged in more comprehensive practices, they did so voluntarily.

Impact analysis step

While regulation continues to form a starting point for the types of activities undertaken by organisations, in the Philippines context, there appears to be little regulatory guidance given on how organisations should undertake this step. A range of very specific indicators and measures were evident for the environmental aspect, and some guidelines for determining the social issues to be addressed and how to contribute towards doing so. The need to establish a baseline was also highlighted, although the lack of specificity in the guidelines meant this was not particularly influential in organisational practices. The ability to extrapolate any management practices or processes from the regulation on impact analysis was not possible as it was not clearly stated.

For organisations operating at the most comprehensive level (deemed World Class) the common practice was to use multiple international standards and global sustainability platforms. These organisations drew not only on platforms like the GRI to direct how they measure impact, but also on a host of international standards (ISOs), CDP, IFC social and environmental standards and the UNGC. The result of implementing such practices was the translation of broader sustainability issues identified in the initiation step, into those that were considered most material or 'risk'-related for organisations, and then into mitigation or enhancement strategies.

Organisations then established baseline measures for each issue to allow the capture of data for later monitoring and evaluation. The types of indicators and measures utilised by organisations were often prescribed and directed by the commitments these organisations had made to international standards and global sustainability platforms. This arguably leads to a more robust basis for determining the impact of their activities and, with reporting requirements, creates a more transparent process for establishing the baseline measures.

The types of issues, and their potential impact and measurements invariably informed the types of tools and techniques that organisations adopted when conducting the impact analysis step. The majority of organisations used quantitative methods which provided an objective measure of impacts and mitigation effects, and were well aligned with the requirements of reporting commitments at the corporate headquarters level. The quantitative methods were often directed by technical experts, both within and outside the organisation, to establish and direct how impact was measured. Other tools were also used by some organisations including: lifecycle assessments, CBA and risk assessments. Lifecycle assessments were perhaps the second most comprehensive tool adopted as it allowed organisations to chart their environmental impacts across the entire lifecycle of their activities, including post-project completion.

Alternative selection step

The regulatory requirements influenced decisions during the alternative selection step, and reinforced an ongoing starting point from which organisations begin their sustainability activities. This involved the adoption of a largely environmental focus, although social issues were partially considered, particularly from a CSR-style approach. While four types of mitigation strategies were identified in the regulation, the implementation of other techniques, including best-available technologies and site rehabilitation, were the predominant methods employed to address negative impacts.

Organisations adopting voluntary practices were significantly influenced on what tools to use due to their commitments to international standards and global sustainability platforms which guides 'best-practice' activities. These commitments were translated into sustainability objectives linked to the different areas within the preceding steps, and directed the focus of alternative selection for organisations. Both enhancement and mitigation strategies were implemented by organisations, although the process by which the organisation chose these strategies was not clear. This could be indicative of either an ad hoc approach in responding to areas of concern, or limitations in the information revealed by organisations.

Organisations following the regulatory requirements were largely informed through by two key types of tools – reduction and rehabilitation. Reduction-based approaches were particularly important for the implementation of best-available technology solutions in the manufacturing sector. Rehabilitation was more common in the mining sector and its site rehabilitation strategies to address environmental impacts.

Organisations exceeding the regulatory requirements tended to utilise CBA or risk analysis. CBA was particularly prevalent and extended beyond simply looking at the different types of issues that the organisations should focus upon. Rather, it extended to looking at key issues linked to the broader sustainability objectives of the organisations, which then focussed on key issue areas. It was then useful in helping decision-makers consider different types of alternatives to address areas of stakeholder concern. Similarly, organisations using risk analysis extended the basic list of the issues that were most important into evaluating different types of strategies to address each issue and sometimes embedded a cost-benefit aspect to the evaluation of each risk.

The factors that influence organisations, and the practices they adopt, reflects the importance of the commitments that these MNEs make to different international standards or global sustainability platforms. However, more research is needed to more fully investigate the underlying decision-making that leads to different types of alternative selection strategies. Although this was not the specific focus of this research, the significance of which strategies are chosen, and then implemented, by organisations to address their impacts is critical in leading to better outcomes from the entire process and is, therefore, a research area worthy of further investigation.

Impact monitoring and follow-up stage

The final stage, impact monitoring and follow-up, is composed of two key steps: (1) Monitoring and evaluation, and (2) feedback and follow-up. These two steps bring together an evaluative function to determine the sustainability performance of the organisation. During this stage, organisations also respond to their monitoring of impacts and thus may undertake changes to their activities as a result of their impact monitoring and evaluation. An emphasis on voluntary activities dominated this stage, particularly with the final step – feedback and follow-up – where the commitment to international standards and global sustainability platforms directed the ongoing evaluation and implementation of changes in sustainability practices. However, it should be noted that these standards were either bereft, or very light, of content to guide practice during the feedback and follow-up steps which lead to some organisations adopting ad hoc strategies to mitigate unexpected impacts, or to adjust strategies that were not working as effectively as planned (*e.g.*, changing how to deal with fly-ash when the first method was not successful).

Monitoring and evaluation step

From a regulatory perspective, organisational practices appear to closely align with the requirements of the PEISS system. This included the involvement of the multipartite monitoring team (MMT), which is technically required to monitor and evaluate environmental and social impacts of projects. However, there was very little evidence of organisations engaging with the MMTs, other than ensuring that compliance requirements were met.

Organisations adopting more comprehensive practices were found to generally collect data regarding their impacts on a fairly regular basis. This includes organisations classified in either the International Standards or World Class categories, with the former tending to focus on a narrowly prescribed set of indicators. Organisations operating with World Class practices appear to adopt much more systematic and holistic monitoring and evaluation practices across the three dimensions of sustainability.

Embedded within these processes is a longitudinal approach, with previous and current performance levels compared against performance targets established by the organisation. This is particularly associated with the reporting requirements linked to the GRI standards. It is evident that there are multiple and overlapping commitments to different standards, which these organisations seek to align and integrate into a consistent and clear platform for monitoring and evaluating their sustainability performance.

From examining the organisational practices of participating MNEs, it is clear that, overall, their commitments to international standards and global sustainability platforms are a key influence driving broader sustainability practices. This includes the initial steps and continues through to the monitoring and evaluation step. Early practices, such as determining the most material or 'risky' issues, were repeated within the activities at this step, showing a clear sequencing and holistic process. As a final point to note, practices for monitoring and evaluation were largely presented through annual reports. However, insights from these organisations also suggests that their activities are much more agile and responsive to changes needed to better manage impacts. This allowed organisations to progressively address sustainability performance issues as required, rather than waiting for annual performance outcomes to determine if current mitigation or enhancement strategies are appropriate or need adjusting.

Organisations commonly use specific qualitative and quantitative tools and techniques to capture key data trends, with a heavy emphasis on the ability to quantify and measure the impact and performance of their projects. From a regulatory perspective, this tends to be linked to very specific and scientific methods of capturing, largely environmental, measures of impact. Financial data was also used in line with regulatory requirements on mandated contributions to local communities, particularly within the mining sector, which required them to focus on the level of socio-economic impact as part of the SDMP.

The use of KPIs was also evident across the majority of organisations – but particularly those operating beyond compliance. This was often informed by a range of international commitments to voluntary guidelines and standards. Again, GRI standards played a key role, guiding a range of key sustainability indicators and measurement bases that could be used across the three dimensions of sustainability. As noted in the general practices, this was often conducted from a longitudinal perspective and reliant on quantitative measures of impact. A range of further international standards and global sustainability platforms further guided the use of tools and practices to monitor and evaluate impact, which subsequently influenced how organisations addressed any impact shortfalls.

In summary, it is clear that commitments made by the headquarter organisation to international standards and global sustainability platforms are key in informing the monitoring and evaluation activities. This is particularly evident in the reporting requirements embedded within these global standards, which sometimes required the involvement of external auditors to evaluate and check the validity of what organisations were reporting. This voluntary adoption of different sustainability standards and guidelines is influential in driving more comprehensive and transparent practices around monitoring and evaluation.

Feedback and follow-up step

The final step of the sustainability assessment framework, feedback and follow-up, is not well understood and an area where further development of best practice insights is clearly needed. The underlying idea behind this step is to constantly improve the sustainability goals and outcomes of the project, transfer the project experience to upcoming projects, and share new insights across the industries and with stakeholders. This step has not been extensively studied by the extant literature due to a lack of data available from organisations to analyse. This study found a similar situation, though some inroads, and thus insights to current practice, has been gained.

Initial insights from the analysis of organisational practices shows that regulation provides very little or no guidelines for the practices that should be adopted by organisations during this step. Activities that were conducted were mostly reactive and in response to changes required by the government. For example, community-based stakeholders or the organisation itself may identify a new and unexpected impact which requires the organisation to respond thereafter. This may have only become apparent during regular monitoring, and required feedback to those stakeholders.

Furthermore, there were limited sources of evidence available into situations where organisations were required to implement changes due to regulation on a cyclical basis. Hence, any changes to operational activities after commencement of the project that were instigated by a regulatory requirement were not evident from those interviewed nor documents assessed. The only evidence confirming that organisations engage in this final step of their sustainability assessments was from organisations choosing to operate beyond compliance and minimum standards. In these situations, organisations internally determined the initiatives they would conduct in response to outcomes from the analysis from the previous step.

The light touch within regulatory guidelines for this last step further highlights the importance of the voluntary standards and guidelines in the practices of these organisations. However, beyond these general practices associated with both compliance and voluntary approaches, it was not clear what tools or techniques were commonly utilised, or for some, whether any were used at all. Rather, it appears that organisational responses to different performance outcomes reside within a set of management decisions that may funnel back to the alternative selection step, and further consideration of appropriate mitigation strategies.

Practical implications from the study

This section provides an overview of the practical insights and implications drawn from this study which involved an empirical investigation of the sustainability assessment process of 24 MNEs operating in the Philippines. It investigated how organisations at the project level identified and assessed key sustainability factors and issues. It provided evidence that empirically tested the conceptual framework presented in Chapter 2 which was generated from synthesising previous findings and conceptions. It allowed for a refinement of this process such that the sustainability assessment framework is now updated, informed by scholarly research and organisational practices.

This study found that decision-makers applied a similar process to their sustainability assessments, mostly adopting the broadly conceptualised management practices and processes. While the earlier conceptual framework was largely presented as a linear process, it was also noted that in practice it can be cyclical and iterative. Organisations in this study reinforced this practice, with sustainability practices not occurring in distinct phases of ex-ante, ongoing and ex-post but rather appearing as iterative and ongoing processes. Distinctions between different points in time, evident in the literature's emphasis on distinctions between the phases of projects and related activities, do not accurately reflect the contemporary state of organisational practices in the Philippines by leading MNEs.

Instead, these organisations' practices are heavily influenced by the commitments that the headquarter operations have made to international standards and global sustainability platforms. These not only funnel down into corporate practices, policies and procedures, but also direct the types of activities and methods adopted by the subsidiary organisations when addressing sustainability within their operations and local contexts. What this suggests is that contemporary practice is driven by voluntary practices, informed by global standards and guidelines, driving these organisations to go beyond the regulatory requirements of the countries in which they operate. Organisations appear to be shifting towards a greater consideration of sustainability, linked to global agendas and an acknowledgement of its impact on their operations, irrespective of the limitations that may be present in the regulations of other countries. While some regulations are (understandably) more prolific based on industry (*e.g.*, mining) it appears that there is much more that organisations often do to go beyond these requirements across sectors.

Regulation, nevertheless, plays a role guiding organisational practices, although to a more limited extent. It underpins a compliance mindset by organisations in ensuring their ongoing operations continue without threat of repercussions for a breach of mandated standards. While this notion was somewhat addressed across the theorised sustainability assessment, it was largely limited to environmental issues (across sectors) and some smaller consideration of social issues (particularly in the mining sector). As was evident in the descriptive analysis of organisational classifications across key steps, a significant proportion went beyond the minimum requirements necessary to fulfil a compliance approach.

Beyond the broader management process and flow of steps and stages within the sustainability assessment, this study also shows a disjuncture between a significant number of the theorised tools and techniques that can be utilised to support sustainability assessments and practices. Here, it was again commitments to various international standards and global sustainability platforms that had the more significant impact on the identified tools and techniques. This includes, at the initial stage, utilising checklists and established lists, with the inclusion of materiality and risk analysis, to identify the most significant or material issues for organisations to consider.

Organisations often framed their tool and technique selection around the requirements of the international standards to which they had already committed. GRI was particularly prevalent, as it encouraged the use of established lists and materiality analysis which then informed many of the subsequent steps. This included the use of technical and scientific measures to capture many multi-dimensional issues in impact analysis, and monitoring and evaluation. Further research is needed on the processes by which organisations go about the alternative selection and feedback and follow-up steps. The tools and techniques utilised within these steps to inform how organisations address sustainability issues and adjust their operations remain an area that needs further investigation to reveal decision criteria and decision-making processes.

Limitations

Although this study has empirically contributed to the understanding of current organisational practices and in elucidating a more accurate sustainability assessment framework, there are some limitations of the research that need to be cited. Four key limitations refer to discussed: (1) location, (2) sample size, (3) industry and (4) cross-sectional study. Hence, the results of this research should be considered in light of these limitations.

Although this study was conducted with organisations in the Philippines which provided a rich context for the study of MNE practices within a developing country, it also limits the generalisability of the findings. This is particularly the case when considering the role of regulations, which in this case were shown to have a limited impact on organisational practices. While this yielded interesting insights, such as the fact that MNEs often refer to voluntary guidelines and standards when presented with a country context where the sustainability guidelines have not yet extended to consider foreign multinationals, it may obfuscate the influence well-established national or regional regulations may have on practices. This could be evident, for example, when looking at the emerging sustainability regulations and initiatives in Europe, which may drive business practices more than voluntary initiatives.

Another key limitation around the generalisability of the findings relates to the sample size. While the number of participating organisations (24) provided a strong base for an exploratory study, particularly in identifying the key activities within the sustainability assessment process, a larger sample may have aided the generalisability of the findings. This could have included other key industries/sectors within the Philippines, or an extension of the sample size to account for a greater variety of organisations (size/ownership, *etc.*). Thus, the sample size must be considered a key limiting factor when generalising the results of this study. However, the limitation of industries included in this study, to three, meant that some density of organisations in each industry was possible. Thus, the results are likely to accurately reflect organisational practices in these industries.

As noted above, and again linked with the sample size, the narrow coverage of industries was a key limitation. These industries were selected due to their likely impact, the significance of investment and the fact that they are a major focus of the registered businesses with the Philippines Board of Investments. A broader coverage of industries/sectors may have identified more meaningful patterns that could be extrapolated across all business sectors, improving the overall generalisability of the framework that has been developed.

A final limitation of this study is that it adopted a cross-sectional approach. By so doing, it provided a snap-shot of the current sustainability assessment practices, constrained to a limited timeframe that was linked to a contracted research project. However, as illustrated in the extant literature, assessment frameworks evolve across project lifetimes and can be adapted across different points in time. While this study has gathered insights from organisations at different points in their planning or operational activities, there would be significant value in investigating organisational practices from a longitudinal perspective to determine the full impact of time and project life cycle on sustainability activities.

Future research directions

In light of the findings and the current state of the existing research, this study broadly calls for further empirical investigation at the project level for sustainability assessments. It is clear from examining the existing literature that there is a limited amount of research that provides an empirical examination at the project level, and with private sector organisations and their corresponding perspectives. A predominant amount of the research to date is confined to theoretical or conceptual discussion. This has resulted in a significant shortfall in empirically validated frameworks and insights into practices implemented by organisations. Accordingly, we call for others to validate the conceptual framework developed here.

More specific areas in need of further investigation include: (1) expanding the industry/sector and country focus, (2) broadening the sample to account for different-sized organisations or different ownership structures, (3) undertaking longitudinal research on sustainability practices, (4) adopting a more specific focus on tools and techniques, and (5) focussing more specifically on decision-making criteria for alternative selection and feedback and follow-up steps.

Due to constraints on time and budget, this study applied a narrow industry focus within one country. However, expanding the country context may reveal more insights into the role of regulation, particularly if future research efforts also included the organisational practices of projects in developed countries that have more sophisticated sustainability regulations. Likewise, as noted above, the restriction to three key industries focussed the implications of this study and limits the overall generalisability of the revised framework for sustainability assessments. Further studies are thus needed that broaden both the industry and country context, which will enable a more generalisable framework to be developed.

This study also focussed on foreign MNEs that had made quite significant investments. Future research would benefit from examining the extent of influence of international and global standards and guidelines for domestically based organisations. The findings of such studies will help shed a light on the overall influence of these standards and guidelines in directing and informing the sustainability practices of organisations within developing countries. Differences may also exist in how publicly listed and private organisations operate, particularly with the increasing scrutiny given to publicly listed companies and increasing requirements for them to be listed on the stock exchange. Similarly, future research could reveal how SMEs are also driving change in addressing sustainability issues, including how the constraints of size and resources influence their practices, which would produce significant insights since small-to-medium-sized enterprises (SMEs) form the vast majority of businesses within most sectors.

While this study adopted a cross-sectional approach due to the limitations in time and resources, longitudinal studies would be recommended in the future. Such studies may uncover important differences in the types of practices adopted, reveal important learning processes, and show whether there are in fact meaningful differences dependent on the lifecycle of the project. This type of research would be extremely valuable, given that it may assist in a reduction in the variety of perspectives proposed by theoretical research within the extant literature. If commonality can be found across different stages within project implementation, this may better allow the development of practice through an aggregate and generalisable framework. At present, the scope of proposed activities, processes, perspectives and frameworks within the literature, and the significant gaps in testing these, obscures the value of research within the field to guide or inform business practice.

A final valuable area for future research is in the tools and techniques being adopted to assist in implementation of sustainability assessments and sustainability practices in general. The literature review and framework demonstrates a variety of potential tools and techniques, which, at the same time, have not been shown in practice. This study showed the types of tools and techniques being utilised by MNEs in the Philippines, and further research would be valuable to investigate why these are chosen over others, and explore the decision-making processes behind those choices. This may better empower the private sector to choose appropriate tools, and also open up pathways for designing more effective tools and techniques that fit the requirements of the private sector.

Concluding statement

It is hoped that this research has contributed to a nascent process of understanding and framing private sector practices in addressing sustainability and contributing towards sustainable development. This work was conducted from the perspective of a sustainability assessment, integrating a focus on tools and techniques commonly used across industries, in order to address a paucity of empirical research in the area. This study has demonstrated the overall utility and value of the sustainability assessment in providing an organising theory for how the private sector can better address sustainability and sustainable development. It is hoped this study will open multiple avenues of future research to further explore and document these practices, and play a supportive role for the decision-making processes of the private sector in better engaging with sustainability through their business activities.

References

Aaker, DA, Kumar, V, Day, GS, Lawley, M & Stewart, D 2007, *Marketing Research*, 2nd Pacific Rim Edition, John Wiley & Sons, Australia.

Adams, C 2017, Integrated Report 2017, ICAS, viewed 15 October 2018, http://integratedreporting.org/wp-content/uploads/2018/01/SDGs-and-the-integrated-report_summary_.pdf.

Arodudu, O, Helming, K, Wiggering, H & Voinov, A 2017, 'Towards a more holistic sustainability assessment framework for agro-bioenergy systems — A review', *Environmental Impact Assessment Review*, vol. 62, pp. 61–75.

Arushanyan, Y, Ekener, E & Moberg, Å 2017, 'Sustainability assessment framework for scenarios – SAFS', *Environmental Impact Assessment Review*, vol. 63, pp. 23–34.

Bill 300, 2019, *The Amendments to Philippines Investment Law 2019*, viewed 12 February 2020, www.stalawfirm.com/en/news/view/philippines-foreign-investment-law-2019.html.

Binder, CR, Feola, G & Steinberger, JK 2010, 'Considering the normative, systemic and procedural dimensions in indicator-based sustainability assessments in agriculture', *Environmental Impact Assessment Review*, vol. 30, no. 2, pp. 71–81.

Bond, AJ & Morrison-Saunders, A 2011, 'Re-evaluating sustainability assessment: Aligning the vision and the practice', *Environmental Impact Assessment Review*, vol. 31, no. 1, pp. 1–7.

Bond, AJ, Morrison-Saunders, A & Howitt, R 2013, *Sustainability assessment: Pluralism, practice and progress*, 1st edn, Routledge - Taylor and Francis, Abingdon.

Bond, AJ, Morrison-Saunders, A & Pope, J 2012, 'Sustainability assessment: The state of the art', *Impact Assessment and Project Appraisal*, vol. 30, no. 1, pp. 53–62.

Borgert, T, Donovan, JD, Topple, C & Masli, EK 2018a, 'Initiating sustainability assessments: Insights from practice on a procedural perspective', *Environmental Impact Assessment Review*, vol. 72, pp. 99–107.

Borgert, T, Donovan, JD, Topple, C & Masli, EK 2018b, 'Determining what is important for sustainability: Scoping process of sustainability assessments', *Impact Assessment and Project Appraisal*, vol. 37, pp. 33–47.

Bravante, MA & Holden, WN 2009, 'Going through the motions: The environmental impact assessment of nonferrous metals mining projects in the Philippines', *The Pacific Review*, vol. 22, no. 4, pp. 523–547.

Brown, RB 2006, *Doing your dissertation in business and management: The reality of research and writing*, Sage Publications, Oxford.

Bryman, A & Bell, E 2015, *Business research methods*, Oxford University Press, New York.

Cadeddu, S, Donovan, JD & Masli, EK 2013, 'Foreign direct investment and economic development: An exploratory study of the internalisation strategy of a technology-intensive multinational', *Journal of International Business and Economy*, vol. 14, pp. 1–30.

Canter, L & Ross, B 2014, 'A basic need for integration – bringing focus to the scoping process', *Impact Assessment and Project Appraisal*, vol. 32, no. 1, pp. 21–22.

Coteur, I, Marchand, F, Debruyne, L, Dalemans, F & Lauwers, L 2016, 'A framework for guiding sustainability assessment and on-farm strategic decision making', *Environmental Impact Assessment Review*, vol. 60, pp. 16–23.

Dalal-Clayton, B & Sadler, B 2004, *Strategic environmental assessment: An international review*, International Institute for Environment and Development, London.

De Ridder, W, Turnpenny, J, Nilsson, M & Von Raggamby, A 2007, 'A framework for tool selection and use in integrated assessment for sustainable development', *Journal of Environmental Assessment Policy and Management*, vol. 9, no. 04, pp. 423–441.

Devuyst, D 1999, 'Sustainability assessment: The application of a methodological framework', *Journal of Environmental Assessment Policy and Management*, vol. 1, no. 4, pp. 459–487.

Dizdaroglu, D 2015, 'Developing micro-level urban ecosystem indicators for sustainability assessment', *Environmental Impact Assessment Review*, vol. 54, pp. 119–124.

Donovan, JD, Topple, C, Masli, EK & Vanichseni, T 2017, *Corporate sustainability assessments: Sustainability practices of multinational enterprises in Thailand*, Routledge, London.

Duinker, PN & Beanlands, GE 1986, 'The significance of environmental impacts: An exploration of the concept', *Environmental Management*, vol. 10, no. 1, pp. 1–10.

Duncan, R & Hay, P 2007, 'A question of balance in integrated impact assessment: Negotiating away the environmental interest in Australia's basslink project', *Journal of Environmental Assessment Policy and Management*, vol. 9, no. 03, pp. 273–297.

Eales, R, Smith, S, Twigger-Ross, C, Sheate, W, Özdemiroglu, E, Fry, C, Tomlinson, P & Foan, C 2005, 'Emerging approaches to integrated appraisal in the UK', *Impact Assessment and Project Appraisal*, vol. 23, no. 2, pp. 113–123.

Escamilla, EZ, Habert, G & Wohlmuth, E 2016, 'When CO_2 counts: Sustainability assessment of industrialized bamboo as an alternative for social housing programs in the Philippines', *Building and Environment*, Vol. 103, pp. 44–53.

Ezzy, D 2002, *Qualitative analysis: Practice and innovation*, Routledge, London.

Fielding, NG, Lee, NFRM & Lee, RM 1998, *Computer analysis and qualitative research*, Sage, London.

Gibson, B, Hassan, S & Tansey, J 2013, *Sustainability assessment: Criteria and processes*, Routledge, London.

Glasson, J 2005, 'Better monitoring for better impact management: The local socio-economic impacts of constructing Sizewell B nuclear power station', *Impact Assessment and Project Appraisal*, vol. 23, no. 3, pp. 215–226.

Green, P 2002, *Slices of life: Qualitative research snapshots*, Melbourne, RMIT University Press, pp. 3–17.

Guba, EG & Lincoln, YS 1989, *Fourth generation evaluation*, Sage, London.

Guba, EG & Lincoln, YS 1994, 'Competing paradigms in qualitative research', in NK Denzin & YS Lincoln (eds), *Handbook of qualitative research*, Sage, Thousand Oaks, CA, pp. 105–117.

Guest, G, Bunce, A & Johnson, L 2006, 'How many interviews are enough? An experiment with data saturation and variability', *Field Methods*, vol. 18, no. 1, pp. 59–82.

Guest, G, MacQueen KM & Namey, EE 2012, *Applied thematic analysis*, Sage, Thousand Oaks, CA.

Hacking, T 2019, 'The SDGs and the sustainability assessment of private-sector projects: Theoretical conceptualisation and comparison with current practice using the case study of the Asian Development Bank', *Impact Assessment and Project Appraisal*, vol. 37, no. 1, pp. 2–16.

Hacking, T & Guthrie, P 2008, 'A framework for clarifying the meaning of Triple Bottom-Line, Integrated, and Sustainability Assessment', *Environmental Impact Assessment Review*, vol. 28, no. 2–3, pp. 73–89.

Huberman, M & Miles, MB 2002, *The qualitative researcher's companion*, Sage, London.

IFC 2012, 'Performance Standards on Environmental and Social Sustainability Effective January 1, 2012', viewed 12 February 2020, www.ifc.org/wps/wcm/connect/c02c2e86-e6cd-4b55-95a2-b3395d204279/IFC_Performance_Standards.pdf?MOD=AJPERES&CVID=kTjHBzk.

Ike, M, Donovan, J, Topple, C & Masli, EK 2019, 'The process of selecting and prioritising corporate sustainability issues: Insights for achieving the Sustainable Development Goals', *Journal of Cleaner Production*, vol. 236, pp. 1–13.

Ingelson, A, Holden, W & Bravante, M 2009, 'Philippine environmental impact assessment, mining and genuine development', *Law, Environmental and Development Journal*, vol. 5, p. 1.

Kosack, S & Tobin, J 2006, 'Funding self-sustaining development: The role of Aid, FDI and Government in Economic Success', *International Organization*, vol. 60, no. 1, pp. 205–243.

Labuschagne, C, Brent, AC & Van Erck, RP 2005, 'Assessing the sustainability performances of industries', *Journal of Cleaner Production*, vol. 13, no. 4, pp. 373–385.

Lee, N 2006, 'Bridging the gap between theory and practice in integrated assessment', *Environmental Impact Assessment Review*, vol. 26, no. 1, pp. 57–78.

Li, H, Dong, K, Sun, R, Yu, J & Xu, J 2017, 'Sustainability assessment of refining enterprises using a DEA-based model', *Sustainability*, vol. 9, no. 4, pp. 620–635.

Lion, H, Donovan, JD & Bedggood, RE 2013, 'Environmental impact assessments from a business perspective: Extending knowledge and guiding business practice', *Journal of Business Ethics*, vol. 117, no. 4, pp. 789–805.

Lion, H, Topple, C & Donovan, JD 2017, 'The corporate sustainability assessment', in JD Donovan, C Topple, EK Masli & T Vanichseni (eds), *Corporate sustainability assessments: Sustainability practices of multinational enterprises in Thailand*, p. 40.

Locher, H 2001, *Summary Report* Basslink Integrated Impact Assessment Statement: Potential Effects of Changes to Hydro Power Generation, Hydro Tasmania, viewed 22 July 2018, www.hydro.com.au/docs/default-source/environment-page/gordon-river-monitoring-reports/summary-report.pdf.

Marshall, R, Arts, J & Morrison-Saunders, A 2005, 'International principles for best practice EIA follow-up', *Impact Assessment and Project Appraisal*, vol. 23, no. 3, pp. 175–181.

Milner, SJ, Bailey, C, Deans, J & Pettigrew, D 2005, 'Integrated impact assessment in the UK—use, efficacy and future development', *Environmental Impact Assessment Review*, vol. 25, no. 1, pp. 47–61.

Mishra, PK & Saxena, R 2009, 'Integrated impact assessment model for explaining differential impact of watershed development projects', *Impact Assessment and Project Appraisal*, vol. 27, no. 3, pp. 175–184.

Moldavska, A & Welo, T 2018, 'Testing and verification of a new corporate sustainability assessment method for manufacturing: A multiple case research study', *Sustainability*, vol. 10, no. 11, pp. 1–40.

Morgan, RK 2012, 'Environmental impact assessment: The state of the art', *Impact Assessment and Project Appraisal*, vol. 30, no. 1, pp. 5–14.

Morrison-Saunders, A & Arts, J 2004, 'Lessons for EIA follow-up', in A Morrison-Saunders & J Arts (eds), *Assessing impact: Handbook of EIA and SEA follow-up*, Earthscan, London, pp. 286–314.

Morrison-Saunders, A & Fischer, TB 2006, 'What is wrong with EIA and SEA anyway? A sceptic's perspective on sustainability assessment', *Journal of Environmental Assessment Policy & Management*, vol. 8, no. 1, pp. 19–39.

Morrison-Saunders, A & Pope, J 2013, 'Conceptualising and managing trade-offs in sustainability assessment', *Environmental Impact Assessment Review*, vol. 38, pp. 54–63.

Morrison-Saunders, A, Pope, J, Gunn, JAE, Bond, A & Retief, F 2014a, Strengthening impact assessment: A call for integration and focus. *Impact Assess Project Appraisal*, vol. 32, no. 1, pp. 2–8.

Morrison-Saunders, A, Pope, J, Bond, A & Retief, F 2014b, 'Towards sustainability assessment follow-up', *Environmental Impact Assessment Review*, vol. 45, pp. 38–45.

Myllyviita, T, Antikainen, R & Leskinen, P 2017, Sustainability assessment tools – their comprehensiveness and utilisation in company-level sustainability assessments in Finland, *International Journal of Sustainable Development & World Ecology*, vol. 24, no. 3, pp. 236–247.

Ness, B, Urbel-Piirsalu, E, Anderberg, S & Olsson, L 2007, 'Categorising tools for sustainability assessment', *Ecological Economics*, vol. 60, no. 3, pp. 498–508.

Orenstein, M, Fossgard-Moser, T, Hindmarch, T, Dowse, S, Kuschminder, J, McCloskey, P & Mugo, RK 2010, 'Case study of an integrated assessment: Shell's North Field Test in Alberta, Canada', *Impact Assessment and Project Appraisal*, vol. 28, no. 2, pp. 147–157.

Patton, MQ 2002, 'Two decades of developments in qualitative inquiry: A personal, experiential perspective', *Qualitative Social Work*, vol. 1, no. 3, pp. 261–283.

Pope, J, Annandale, D & Morrison-Saunders, A 2004, 'Conceptualising sustainability assessment', *Environmental Impact Assessment Review*, vol. 24, no. 6, pp. 595–616.

Pope, J, Bond, A, Hugé, J & Morrison-Saunders, A 2017, 'Reconceptualising sustainability assessment', *Environmental Impact Assessment Review*, vol. 62, pp. 205–215.

Pope, J, Bond, A, Morrison-Saunders, A & Retief, F 2013, 'Advancing the theory and practice of impact assessment: Setting the research agenda', *Environmental Impact Assessment Review*, vol. 41, pp. 1–9.

Pope, J & Klass, D 2010, 'Decision quality for sustainability assessment', IAIA10 transitioning to the green economy, *Conference Proceedings of the 30th Annual Conference of the International Association for Impact Assessment: Transitioning to the Green Economy*, Held Geneva, Switzerland.

Pope, J, Morrison-Saunders, A & Annandale, D 2005, 'Applying sustainability assessment models', *Impact Assessment and Project Appraisal*, vol. 23, no. 4, pp. 293–302.

Ranis, G, Stewart, F & Ramirez, A 2000, 'Economic growth and human development', *World Development*, vol. 28, no. 2, pp. 197–219.

Robson, C 2002, *The analysis of qualitative data: Real world research: A resource for social scientists and practitioner researchers*, Blackwell, Malden, MA.

Rotmans, J & Asselt, M 1996, 'Integrated assessment: A growing child on its way to maturity', *Climatic Change*, vol. 34, no. 3–4, pp. 327–336.

Sachs, JD 2005, *Investing in development: A practical plan to achieve the Millennium Development Goals*, Earthscan, London.

Sadler, B 1996, *Environmental Assessment in a Changing World. Evaluating Practice to Improve Performance-final Report*, Canadian Environmental Assessment Agency, Quebec.

Sala, S, Ciuffo, B & Nijkamp, P 2015, 'A systemic framework for sustainability assessment', *Ecological Economics*, vol. 119, pp. 314–325.

Saunders, MN, Lewis, P & Thornhill, A 2015, *Research methods for business students*, Pearson, London.

Schneider, A & Meins, E 2012, 'Two dimensions of corporate sustainability assessment: Towards a comprehensive framework', *Business Strategy and the Environment*, vol. 21, no. 4, pp. 211–222.

Schöggl, JP, Fritz MMC & Baumgartner, RJ 2016, 'Sustainability assessment in automotive and electronics supply chains-A set of indicators defined in a multi-stakeholder approach', *Sustainability*, vol. 8, no. 11, pp. 1–20.

Shields, DJ, Blengini, GA & Šolar, SV 2011, 'Integrating life cycle assessment and other tools for ex ante integrated sustainability assessment in the minerals industry', *American Journal of Applied Sciences*, vol. 8, no. 11, pp. 1214–1227.

Shields DJ & Šolar, SV 2004, *Sustainable mineral resource management and indicators: Case study Sloveni*, Geological Survey of Slovenia, Ljubljana.

Shields, JF & Shelleman, JM 2017 'A method to launch sustainability reporting in SMEs: The B Corp Impact Assessment framework', *Journal of Strategic Innovation & Sustainability*, vol. 12, no. 2, pp. 10–19.

Sinkovics, R & Alfoldi, EA 2012, 'Facilitating the interaction between theory and data in qualitative research using CAQDAS', in G Symon & C Cassel (eds), *Qualitative organizational research: Core methods and current challenges*, Sage, London, pp. 109–131.

Sinkovics, RR, Penz, E & Ghauri, PN 2008, 'Enhancing the trustworthiness of qualitative research in international business', *Management International Review*, vol. 48, no. 6, pp. 689–714.

Sippe, R 1990, 'Power and accountability: The contribution of environmental impact assessment to sustainable development in Western Australia', *Science, Assessment and Sustainability Conference*, Vancouver, Canada, p. 7.

Strauss, A & Corbin, JM 1990, *Basics of qualitative research: Grounded theory procedures and techniques*. Sage, Thousand Oaks, CA.

Strauss, AL 1987, *Qualitative analysis for social scientists*. Cambridge University Press, Cambridge.

Tajima, R & Fischer, TB 2013, 'Should different impact assessment instruments be integrated? Evidence from English spatial planning', *Environmental Impact Assessment Review*, vol. 41, pp. 29–37.

Therivel, R 2004, *Strategic environmental assessment in action*, Earthscan, London.

Therivel, R & Fischer, T 2012, 'Sustainability appraisals in England', *UVP Report*, vol. 26, no.1, pp. 16–21.

Topple, C, Donovan, JD, Masli, EK & Borgert, T 2017, 'Corporate sustainability assessments: MNE engagement with sustainable development and the SDGs', *Transnational Corporation*, vol. 24, no. 3, pp. 61–72.

United Nations (UN) 2012, *Resilient people, resilient planet: A future worth choosing*, United Nations Secretary-General's High-level Panel on Global Sustainability, New York and Geneva.

United Nations Development Programme (UNDP) 2015, *World Leaders Adopt Sustainable Development Goals*, viewed 3 April 2018, www.undp.org/content/undp/en/

home/presscenter/pressreleases/2015/09/24/undp-welcomes-adoption-of-sustainable-development-goals-by-world-leaders.html.

Van Asselt Marjolein, BA & Rijkens-Klomp, N 2002, 'A look in the mirror: Reflection on participation in integrated assessment from a methodological perspective', *Global Environmental Change*, vol. 12, no. 3, pp. 167–184.

Wessels, JA 2013, 'Factors that influence the independence of EIA follow-up verifiers: A developing country perspective', *Impact Assessment and Project Appraisal*, vol. 31, no. 3, pp. 169–179.

Yin, RK 2003, *Case study research: Design and methods*, Sage, Thousand Oaks, CA.

Zikmund, WG, Ward, S, Lowe, B, Winzar, H & Babbin, BJ 2011, *Marketing research*, 2nd Asia-Pacific Edition, Cengage Learning, Australia.

Index

Note: **Bold** page numbers refer to tables and *Italic* page numbers refer to figures